THE MATRIX
OF POLICY IN
THE PHILIPPINES

THE MATRIX OF POLICY
IN THE PHILIPPINES

HARVEY A. AVERCH, JOHN E. KOEHLER,
AND FRANK H. DENTON

100562

PRINCETON UNIVERSITY PRESS
PRINCETON, NEW JERSEY
1971

L.C. Card: 70-154989
ISBN: 0-691-07541-7

This book has been composed in linotype Granjon
Printed in the United States of America
by Princeton University Press

To Barbara, Jane, and Joan

Preface

THIS BOOK has two objectives: (1) to analyze several related social problems of concern to Philippine policymakers and those who deal with them; (2) to address the problems systematically with empirical methods. Thus the book is not a "balanced" comprehensive treatment of the state of the nation. We seek to test no general a priori theories about political and economic development. Even if a persuasive political and economic theory about LDCs could be found, the Philippines would be deviant.

The things that often concern academic scholars about the country—for example, the working out of kinship ties or *utang na loob* —are not our concerns. The criterion we use is that the problem must be perceived as important or vexing to policymakers and one where new information or new perception—either specific or contextual—might make a difference in the conduct of policy. Nevertheless, the rigorous quantitative analysis of politics, economics, crime, and dissidence does enrich our understanding of the country as a whole. Furthermore, domestic and foreign perceptions of the Philippines and its problems often have their roots in poor and distorted information. Often the proclamations of general crisis that dominate politics and the press in Manila rest on evidence that is inherently shaky or improperly analyzed. Getting information straight, or at least straightened out, should open up new options and lend greater precision to policy debate within the Philippines and perceptions outside it. This does not mean that new options will necessarily be taken up. That process depends upon the public demand for new options and the willingness of the government to try them. In a sense this book is about the determinants of current demand for options and their supply.

The data used in the book carry us to summer 1969—before the reelection of President Marcos and the subsequent student riots early in 1970. Why Marcos won can easily be inferred from Chapters 4 and 5. Why the students rioted is a subject on which we have no systematic evidence. Nevertheless, the notion that the Philippine government might topple as a result of student riots seems to us to be mistaken. We would give very good odds against such an event.

Our research on the Philippines was sponsored by the Agency for International Development (AID) as part of a contract with

The Rand Corporation calling for two interdisciplinary country studies. The countries selected were Colombia and the Philippines.[1] The aim of the studies was to provide substantive analysis of the two countries and, by this experience, to devise improved methods of analysis for use by AID. Additional research on the extent and nature of insurgency in the Philippines was sponsored by the Advanced Research Projects Agency (ARPA) of the Department of Defense. ARPA also funded the large-scale data processing efforts required for the preparation and writing of the final manuscript. We are grateful for their support.

In the course of this research we spent more than a year in the Philippines—March 1968 to June 1969. We were based in Manila and had offices in the AID Mission. Because the Philippines is geographically and ethnically so heterogeneous, we made a special effort to travel about the country—from Aparri to Jolo, as the Filipinos would put it. We tried to check our data against our own firsthand perceptions.

Our field research could not have been carried out without the help of many Americans and Filipinos—too numerous to be listed here. But thanks are particularly due to Rafael Salas, formerly Executive Secretary of the Philippine Cabinet, for his encouragement and insight. At crucial points in the research, large bodies of data were made available by Tito Mijares, Director of the Bureau of the Census; by Mercedes Concepcion of the Population Institute, University of the Philippines; and by General Vicente Raval, formerly Chief, Philippine Constabulary. We gratefully acknowledge, in addition, the support and encouragement received from the AID Mission, especially from Wesley Haraldson, then AID director for the Philippines, and Ernest Neal, then deputy AID director.

Large-scale quantitative research in economics and the social sciences cannot be carried out without the support of many people at the home base. The computational pipeline was 7,000 miles long. Invaluable assistance was provided by the staff of Rand's Computer Sciences Department, particularly Harold Casali and Dean Hatch, and Marina Mann and David Weinschrott of Rand's Economics Department.

We wish to thank our Rand colleagues Paul Hammond, Alvin Harman, Marvin Lavin, Robert Slighton, and Charles Wolf, Jr.

[1] See Richard R. Nelson, T. Paul Schultz, and Robert L. Slighton, *Structural Change in a Developing Economy*, Princeton University Press, 1971.

for their vigorous criticism at various stages in the life of the manuscript. Thanks are also due to Richard R. Nelson of Yale University for the many contributions he made to the manuscript. Many of their suggestions are incorporated in this book. The conclusions and interpretations, however, as well as any errors, remain our responsibility.

Helen B. Turin, our editor, ruthlessly excised awkwardness: at every stage in preparing an essentially quantitative manuscript she forced us to consider the clear presentation of argument and evidence. The reader owes her thanks.

Our secretaries, Jean Martin, Ruby Morita, Johanna Staehling, and Linda Taft mastered our handwriting and produced draft after draft with admirable speed and care.

HARVEY A. AVERCH
JOHN E. KOEHLER
FRANK H. DENTON

Santa Monica
September 1970

Contents

List of Figures

List of Tables

THE MATRIX OF POLICY IN
THE PHILIPPINES

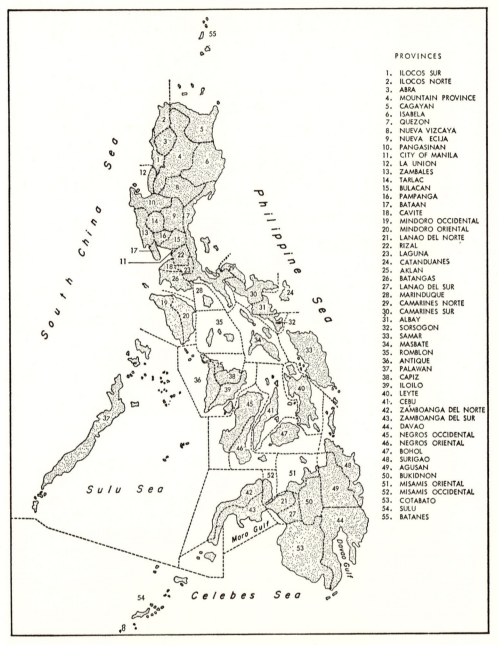

Republic of the Philippines, 1960

Introduction

THIS BOOK began with a misperception. Our research was originally intended to illuminate some of the links among the serious problems supposedly besetting the Philippines: crime, insurgency, political instability, and poor economic performance. However, when we began to examine the alleged problems and to search for the links, it became apparent that the problems themselves were exaggerated, or imaginary, or different in important ways from the manner in which they had been generally understood.

The misperception with which we began was widely shared. The view commonly upheld in the U.S. and Philippine press, the U.S. Congress, and even in scholarly work was predominantly negative.[1] Even within the State Department, AID, and the Philippine government it was difficult to find a dissenting opinion. Individuals did disagree on particular points, and there was some difference between snap judgments and more thoughtful assessments, but it is fair to say that in all of these places the collective opinion held that the performance of the Philippines had been disappointing and that the future looked unpromising at best.

Forced to redefine the social and economic problems of the Philippines, we were led to a reconsideration of the ways in which policymakers—particularly U.S. policymakers—go about understanding events in other countries. Our book is not a proper study of the general process of perception in foreign affairs or of U.S. government intelligence and information. However, we have analyzed the deficiencies of the information with which Philippine policymakers must work, and we know that these deficiencies remain as the information is transmitted through U.S. reporting systems.

Whether the pathology of organizational intelligence that ap-

[1] See E. O. Reischauer in Kermit Gordon, ed., *Agenda for the Nation*, Brookings Institution, Washington, D.C., 1968, p. 432. See also John Mecklin, "The Philippines: An Ailing and Resentful Ally," *Fortune* 80 (July 1969), 19. For a typical view of the American press, see *The New York Times*, January 17, 1969, "Philippines Facing a Time of Austerity." This article finds causal relations among economic disorder, alleged oligarchic rule, and violence and corruption.

plies to the Philippines applies elsewhere is an open question. Studies that address the actual content and accuracy of information gathered by State, AID, the CIA, or the press are apparently scarce. So any generalization of our observations must rest on a line of reasoning more common to anthropology than to any of the other social sciences: this is the way it was in one exotic locale; we know of no reason why this place should be unique; it would be worth while to investigate whether or not the problems are general.

The Kind of Information Produced

Every year U.S. agencies in the Philippines produce an enormous quantity of reports and analysis.[2] From what we saw, much of this reporting and analysis is very good. However, none of the analysis employs any quantitative tools, and much of the information is taken unexamined from Philippine sources. These two characteristics of the typical reporting style account for the failure of intelligence we have been discussing.

That the foreign service does not use any of the quantitative tools of modern behavioral science is a commonplace observation. In fact, the tradition and culture of the foreign service have been characterized as positively hostile to such methods, favoring the ideal of the expert so deeply immersed in a situation as to become a part of it and able to analyze problems almost intuitively.[3]

Much useful reporting and analysis can be performed without reference to any of the tools of statistical inference and without any rigorous definition and testing of formal models, verbal or mathematical. But failure to apply quantitative methods at some point carries several hazards. One arises from the difficulty of aggregating intuitive perceptions. For example, an observer who saw numerous armed guards in Manila, read about insurgent incidents in Pampanga province, and talked with pessimistic local politicians would conclude that the country was in bad shape. Another observer who

[2] See John P. Leacacos, *Fires in the In-Basket*, World Publishing Co., New York, 1968, pp. 469-477 for illustrative figures on the magnitude of the State Department's annual communications traffic worldwide.

[3] Grant G. Hilliker, "Man and the Fact Machine in Foreign Affairs," *Foreign Service Journal* (forthcoming). This style of analysis has been characterized as "literary." See also Kenneth Boulding, "The Learning and Reality-Testing Process in the International System" in John C. Farrell and Asa P. Smith, eds., *Image and Reality in World Politics*, Columbia University Press, New York, 1968.

4

spent his time in a peaceful provincial city and talked with local Jaycee boosters would conclude the contrary. Without some quantitative test, there is no way to decide which observer saw the "true" Philippines. Furthermore, statistical techniques are mandatory for any analysis that hopes to capture the diversity of the Philippines. How else could we find answers to questions such as "Are parts of the country being left far behind the rapidly developing areas?" and "Are the dissidents found in Pampanga likely to enjoy success elsewhere?"

Ultimately, nonquantitative interpretation of events in a country must rest on nonreproducible intuition. This may be highly accurate; a skilled and perceptive observer will be able to answer some questions quite well. The problem is to distinguish the skilled and perceptive from the blind and ignorant. If at some point arguments rest on a statement such as "I can't explain exactly why, but I'm sure that's the way it is," then an outsider is left powerless to check the statement without spending years in becoming immersed himself. In short, intuitive analysis carries with it no mechanism for the self-correction of error.[4]

Self-correction is made even more unlikely by lack of independent sources of data. Much of the information reported through U.S. channels originates in the reporting agencies of the Philippine government. This is, of course, most characteristic of economic and social information; U.S. agencies have no capability to generate an independent estimate of GNP or unemployment or school enrollments without reference to official Philippine statistics. Political reporting may contain a large dose of independent observation, but here again at least a part of what is reported is likely to be the view of prominent Filipinos rather than independently gathered information.

[4] It can be argued that the reporting systems have a pessimistic bias. The worst risk the analyst runs is to make some firm prediction that is shown to be false while the original prediction is still remembered. The astute analyst can avoid such embarrassment with little more than the judicious selection of qualifications. He is likely to know, as well, that although those at the top of the system are most unhappy when surprised by some unpredicted and unpleasant event, they may soon forget a hedged but unfulfilled prediction of disaster. This asymmetry builds into the reporting system a propensity to predict worst cases. In the Philippines, there has always been a rolling prediction of revolution. Every reprieve is explained as evidence that the elite bowed at the last moment or that the boundless good will and subservience of the Philippine peasantry again prevailed.

Reliance on host-country sources for information implies that the views of government officials and the Manila elite will be reported quite accurately. For many purposes, that is precisely what policy-makers want to know. But the corollary of this proposition is that if the government and the elite are mistaken in their judgments of conditions in the rest of the country, their mistakes will be shared.[5]

How to Improve Reporting Systems

Our image of how reporting systems could be improved is inevitably colored by the experience of producing this book. To keep the record straight, we must confess that the method described here and elaborated in subsequent chapters just grew; it was not carefully plotted in advance. In retrospect, it appears to have been a good way to proceed. The style of quantitative investigation we promote here is not in any sense a substitute for the detailed reporting at the operational level that is now conducted. It does, however, offer ways to construct context more systematically than has been done before and to check periodically on the image of a country.

The prescription we offer has three directives: be quantitative, get inside the information systems, use multiple tests and new measures. The commitment to quantitative analysis is the fundamental feature. This commitment carries with it a focus on behavior that is relatively well measured or measurable. Thus in our discussions of elections we focus on voting behavior rather than on the alleged conspiracies of the Filipino elite. (The elite, as we have already noted, is quite well looked after by the present reporting systems.) The use of quantitative tools introduces a self-correction mechanism, because it is easier for a critic to detect error in the analysis. Models have to be made explicit, and test procedures are widely known. Anyone with the same data can check to see if the results are true or whether an alternative formulation of a model is superior.

[5] A senior foreign service officer once made much the same point to one of the authors in the following fashion:

All during the '60's the Iranians complained bitterly that their country was going to the dogs, nothing got done, the bureaucracy was hopeless, the cattle died for lack of government veterinarians and so on. Their pessimistic view of the country was reflected in the tone of cables flowing from our Teheran embassy to Washington. All the time, of course, Iran was moving from strength to strength. In the same period the Pakistanis were buoyantly confident about their country's economic and political prospects. Their confidence colored our reporting on the country and seduced us into presenting perhaps too optimistic a view to Washington.

Since information typically comes from the host country's reporting systems, it is important to get inside the system, to understand precisely where data come from, what they mean, and how they are gathered. In the Philippines, different government agencies often report contradictory data about what are ostensibly the same phenomena. Sometimes there are real errors, as we shall see in the data on crime. More generally, however, different agencies are really reporting on different things but giving them the same name. For example, alternative estimates of employment in manufacturing are produced from the economic census and the population census. The latter is three times as large as the former. The reason for the discrepancy becomes clear when we understand how the data are being gathered. The day-to-day reporting procedures of U.S. government agencies really assume that data that bear the same name in two countries measure the same characteristic, so that a sensible comparison can be made between, for example, values of some variable in Thailand and in the Philippines. Obviously, without the capability to analyze rigorously just how the numbers are being generated in both countries, the comparison is likely to be misleading.

Finally, given the uncertainties inherent in analysis, it is important to try to use different data and methods—preferably totally independent—to test for the existence of the same phenomena. In our analysis of politics, for example, we use reported vote and various province-level data to uncover some of the factors important in Philippine elections. This approach suffers from defects related to problems of aggregation and the types of data that are available at this level. The basic hypotheses are then checked by survey data. Survey data suffer inherent problems of response bias, control of field work, and reliability of coding. Their problems, however, are different from those of the aggregate data. If both sets of data support the same general image of the world, we can have higher confidence in it.[6]

The Plan of the Book

The line of argument is continuous from Chapter 3 to Chapter 7. We are concerned with the prospects for political modernization, economic progress, and social stability in the Philippines. Chap-

---

[6] On this point see Eugene J. Webb et al., *Unobtrusive Measures: Nonreactive Research in the Social Sciences*, Rand McNally, Chicago, 1966, especially Chapter 1.

7

ter 3 considers the opinions of the public, politicians, and bureaucrats toward the performance of the political system and toward each other. All three groups have realistic expectations of each other, and their needs interlock so closely that the odds are against any sharp change.

Having established the context of attitudes within which political action occurs, we proceed to an analysis of Philippine elections in Chapter 4. Election outcomes, we found, are determined more by ethnic solidarity, local political control, and the delivery of pork barrel than by any issues arising out of poverty, unemployment, or tenancy. Our search for a group that is responding to programmatic appeals goes unrewarded, with the single exception of the rapidly growing but only slightly atypical modern labor force.

In Chapter 5 we look at the relations between politics and the economy. Despite the political motivation of much of government economic policy, the economy has turned in a respectable performance over the last two decades, better than usually thought. The demands of politics, however, have built a pattern of lurching, uneven growth into the economy. And although it has done reasonably well, political constraints may keep it from ever achieving a spectacular rate of growth.

Chapter 6 considers the problem of crime. The perception of "mounting crime" is an error, based on changes in reporting procedures and simple arithmetic mistakes. Nonetheless, the level of violence in Philippine society is generally high, yet it varies markedly across the country. Some violence is related to politics; some appears to be determined by the same ethnic factors we found to be important in the analysis of voting; some appears to come from urbanization. There is no evidence that Philippine crime should be considered to flow from general social deterioration.

Yet, if the society appears to be as stable as this analysis suggests, how do we explain the persistence of dissidence in Central Luzon? Chapter 7 looks for the determinants of dissident success and tries to weigh the relative importance of social protest and simple terror. Here as in other fields, the principal obstacles to government success appear to be the requirements of politics.

Before we begin the analysis, we need a better understanding of the structure of the country and its recent historical evolution. Chapter 2 describes the overall structure of the Philippine social system, the context in which perceptions and attitudes are formed.

The country is a patchwork of ethnic, political, religious, and economic groups.[7] What then do we mean when we talk about the Philippine nation? It is customary to begin the analysis of a country's social and economic structure with a historical and geographical overview. We shall not follow this procedure, since the basic descriptive work is available elsewhere.[8] Instead, we shall attempt to summarize quantitatively the pattern of constants and variables over the last thirty years.

[7] Philippine ethnic cleavages do not erupt into violence, although awareness of these cleavages is pervasive. They definitely affect the politics of the country.

[8] For the most recent geography of the Philippines see F. L. Wernstedt and J. E. Spencer, *The Philippine Island World: A Physical, Cultural and Regional Geography*, University of California Press, Berkeley, 1967.

Philippine Geography and Society: Factor Analysis

Introduction

THE PHILIPPINES stretches more than 800 miles from Aparri in the north on the flood plain of the Cagayan river to Jolo in the south. Contained within the country is a range of geography, climate, culture, and economic structure as broad as we can find anywhere. Christianity and Islam are the two major religions; there are 11 major languages and over 70 minor languages;[1] and styles of living range from the Ifugao of Central Luzon who occasionally revive the headhunting customs of their ancestors to Manilans as at home in Paris and Washington as in Makati. Figure 1 shows the locations of the major language groups.

Since the country is diverse in so many dimensions, we use factor analysis—a data-description technique—to summarize the relations among social, political, economic, and cultural characteristics in different parts of the country. We know that each area has a few fundamental characteristics (ethnic composition, economic structure, and so on). The large number of attributes for which we can obtain measures are all highly correlated with these few fundamental characteristics. For example, if we know that urbanization, high incomes, and the proportion of the labor force in manufacturing all go together, then we can speak of a composite of these indicators, which we may want to call "development." Our interest is to provide a compact portrait of the country using these composite indicators as a context for later analysis.

Factor Analysis

VOCABULARY

The substantive idea behind factor analysis is that different phenomena may be part of the same underlying cluster or pattern.[2]

---

[1] See Wernstedt and Spencer, *The Philippine Island World*.

[2] See H. H. Harman, *Modern Factor Analysis*, 2nd ed., University of Chicago Press, Chicago, 1968; P. Horst, *Factor Analysis of Data Matrices*, Holt, Rinehart and Winston, New York, 1965. For applications see I. Adelman and C. T. Morris, *Society, Politics and Economic Development*, The Johns Hopkins Press, Baltimore,

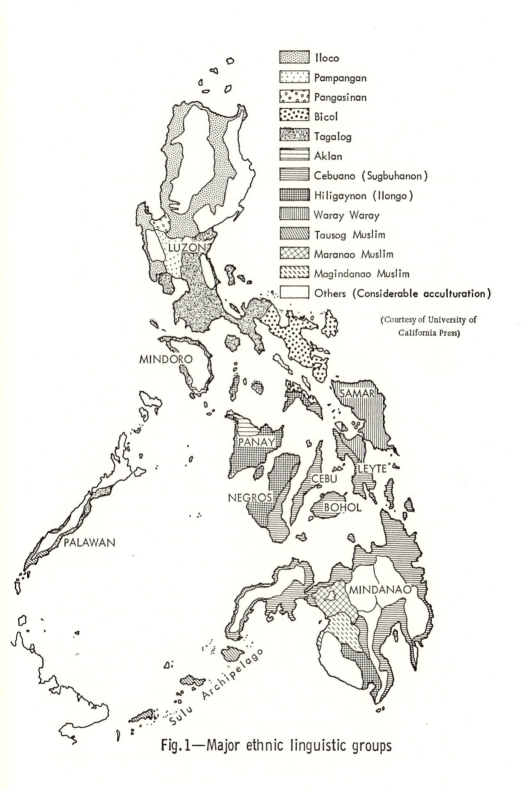

Iloco

Pampangan

Pangasinan

Bicol

Tagalog

Aklan

Cebuano (Sugbuhanon)

Hiligaynon (Ilongo)

Waray Waray

Tausog Muslim

Maranao Muslim

Magindanao Muslim

Others (Considerable acculturation)

(Courtesy of University of
California Press)

LUZON

MINDORO

SAMAR

PANAY

LEYTE

CEBU

NEGROS

BOHOL

PALAWAN

MINDANAO

Sulu Archipelago

Fig. 1—Major ethnic linguistic groups

For example, by economic development we mean not just increases in GNP per capita, but a set of political and social changes we believe are related: urbanization, education, communication, emergence of a modern labor force—the list could be extended indefinitely. Without some formal device for reducing the number of variables at hand, we cannot readily describe or grasp the nature of complicated processes. Factor analysis is one such formal device. It is a systematic way of reducing the dimensions of a problem and of revealing clusters of associated variables.

The technical vocabulary of factor analysis is unfamiliar but not difficult. With a few definitions the results of a factor analysis can be read quickly by laymen and policymakers. Results are usually displayed in table form with such labels as factors, loadings, and communalities. A *factor* means an *underlying pattern* or *association* among a set of variables. A *factor loading* means essentially the *correlation* between a variable and a factor. For example, urbanization might load (correlate) $+.9$ on a "development" factor, suggesting that urbanization and development are associated. A *communality* means the sum of the squares of the factor loadings. This sum shows the total contribution of the factors operating together in explaining the (standardized) variance of a given variable. It is analogous to the multiple correlation coefficient in regression analysis.

A *factor score* is the ranking or rating of cases or observations on all the variables entering a pattern or factor. Factor scores have a standard normal distribution, so 80 percent of the scores will lie in the interval $[-1.28, 1.28]$. If high GNP per capita, urbanization, communication, and education were part of a general development factor, then the United States would score high with, say, a score of 2, Japan might be in the middle with a score of 0, and Nepal might be near the bottom with a score of -2. The factor scores permit us to make rankings of geographic units such as provinces, states, or nations, using all the available information in a systematic way. Scores can be plotted on maps rather than presented as lists.

Because we wished to analyze historical change in the geographic distribution of economic and political activity and of dissidence, we selected provincial data for three different census years—1938, 1948, and 1960.[3] Sometimes important variables were measured

---

1967; and E. Soja, *The Geography of Modernization*, Syracuse University Press, Syracuse, 1968.

[3] The province is the smallest geographic unit for which most types of data are

only for other years. We added some post-1960 data, such as 1965 voting patterns, to see their relation to the evolving economic and political structure. The three years taken together give us some idea of change and constancy in the Philippine social system.[4]

A SUMMARY OF SPATIAL PATTERNS

We had expected to find that economic and social change would be closely related, so that a small number of factors would explain variation across provinces. However, the variables we defined to represent various aspects of the social system load on separate factors indicating statistical independence on a geographic or spatial basis.[5] There do not appear to be strong interconnections between economics and crime or crime and politics or politics and the provincial economies. In general we can state the following:

✦ The location and organization of development, dissidence, agriculture, and population did not change greatly from 1938 to 1960. The relative characteristics of a province in the 1960s were much what they were in 1938.[6]

✦ Growth in population and commercial establishments has *not* been centered in the most developed part of the country. With the

---

available. Thus provinces as units give us the maximum amount of fine-grained detail. Moreover, Philippine provinces are often homogeneous with respect to ethnic and language groups. In a country where ethnic heritage is important, provinces are a desirable unit on a priori grounds. But for some purposes provinces are too large. For example, in the factor analysis below, Camarines Norte is labeled "Modern" when most of it is not. It appears as a modern province because of highly concentrated mining activity before the war.

[4] Actually the Philippine government operates with very little current information. In economics the last full set of data are for 1961. The economic census of 1967 remains unreported at this writing. It is characteristic of the Philippines and perhaps other LDCs that they operate with "old" information. Furthermore, reporting is biased toward the presentation of highly aggregated data. See Chapter 5 for a fuller discussion. Appendix B describes the data and sources for the factor analysis. Included are data representing spatial trends with respect to politics, economics, crime, and dissidence. Sometimes we could define only a single variable to represent provincial variation. For example, from a variety of sources, we compiled a provincial "dissidence index." To represent the economic development of provinces, we included a number of separate items, since no single one can characterize the development of a province. Included are variables on urbanization, the size of the modern labor force, and the number of commercial establishments.

[5] This does not preclude the existence of some complex links between the sets of variables that are not captured by a simple linear test.

[6] But see Chapter 5 for a discussion of changing regional patterns since 1960.

exception of Rizal province, which contains the suburbs of Manila, the high growth areas have been the "frontiers." The frontier has moved from Northern Mindanao in the prewar era to Southern Mindanao since 1948.

✦ Politics is not strongly related to economic development. To a limited extent the more developed areas do vote differently from the rest of the country. However, ethnic components appear to override this difference.

✦ The distribution of dissidence has been relatively constant over time. Dissidence occurs on the fringes of the most developed provinces and in the areas of high tenancy and sugar cultivation. Pampanga historically has served as the major site for such dissidence, but explanations of this phenomenon differ.[7]

✦ Crimes against property are very much centered in the developed sector. Crimes against persons seem to be ethnic specific.

✦ The agricultural structure of the country remains diverse. No single area of the country appears to have shown consistent agricultural prosperity or growth. Rather, Philippine crop prices have fluctuated as international prices of agricultural commodities changed (often in response to U.S. commercial policies).

A COMPOSITE FACTOR ANALYSIS—1938-1960

Table 1 shows the factor structure for a combined set of data, 1938 and 1960.[8] The names assigned to the factors are: modern, growth, tenancy/sugar, coconut, Cebuano politics, Ilocano politics. This factor structure suggests that there are not strong interconnections between politics and the provincial economies, since the political variables load on separate factors and seem related primarily to ethnic blocs. However, the robbery rate does appear to be related to the provincial economies.

The modern sector is characterized by a "modern" labor force—that is, a high fraction of the labor force in noncraft manufacturing, transportation, power generation, or white collar work. It is also characterized by urbanization, radios, crimes against property, and so on. But unemployment has only a moderate association with this developed sector (loading of —.47). Figure 2 shows the plot of the province scores on the modern factor.[9] The modern sector runs

[7] See Chapter 7.

[8] There are 55 variables observed across 49 provinces.

[9] A high score on "modern" factor summarizes these characteristics of relative development.

14

TABLE 1

COMPOSITE FACTOR ANALYSIS, 1938-1960
(55 variables)

Variable[a]	Modern	Growth	Tenancy/ Sugar	Coconut	Cebuano Politics	Ilocano Politics	Communality R²
Modern labor force, 1938	—.67						.68
Modern labor force, 1960	—.83						.74
Percent of labor force in transportation, 1938	—.53						.64
Percent of labor force in transportation, 1960	—.86						.66
Percent population with radios, 1960	—.73						.63
Percent population urban, 1960	—.69						.54
Robbery rate, 1960	—.77						.74
Population growth rate, 1960		.81					.65
Population growth rate, 1938		.61					.72
Out-migration, 1960		—.77					.80
In-migration, 1960		.79					.76
Relative migration, 1960		.75					.85
Public works per capita		—.61					.37
Liberal mayors, 1963		—.51					.31
Percent tenancy, 1938			—.85				.88
Percent tenancy, 1960			—.81				.82
Percent sugar, 1938			—.60				.63
Percent sugar, 1960			—.59				.61
Dissidence index, 1938			—.68				.62
Percent workers in farming, 1938			.53				.73
Ratio of farmland to total land, 1938			—.64				.78
Ratio of farmland to total land, 1960			—.60				.76
Percent coconut, 1938				.80			.85
Percent coconut, 1960				.80			.86
Percent sugar, 1938				—.56			.63
Percent sugar, 1960				—.55			.61
Criminal cases per capita, 1934				.50			.46
Percent of vote for winner, 1957					—.71		.80
Percent Cebuano, 1960					—.90		.86
Vote dispersion, 1957					—.73		.63
Percent of vote for winner, 1961					.60		.69
Percent of vote for winner, 1961						.50	.69
Percent of vote for winner, 1965						.67	.50
Percent Ilocanos						.81	.84
Vote dispersion, 1957						.57	.63
Vote dispersion, 1965						.53	.41
General vote dispersion						.63	.66
Exposure typhoons						.62	.78
Irrigated land, 1938						.56	.67
Irrigated land, 1960						.57	.57

NOTE: Percentage of variance explained: 62; percentage explained by last factor: 5.

[a] The numbers in the columns are the factor loadings. Loadings below .5 excluded.

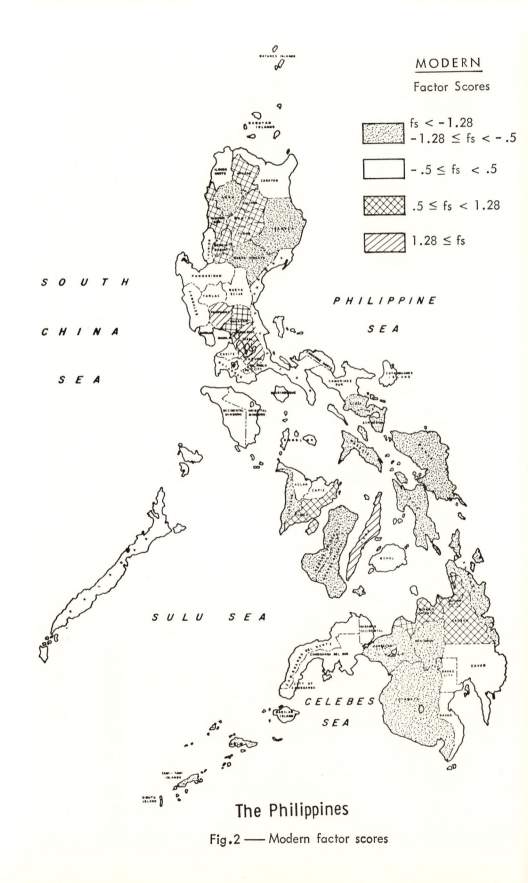

SOUTH

CHINA

SEA

PHILIPPINE

SEA

SULU SEA

CELEBES

SEA

The Philippines

Fig.2 —— Modern factor scores

from Zambales around Manila to Batangas. A semimodern enclave borders the Mindanao Sea and is served by the Philippines' second largest city, Cebu. Iloilo and Albay form secondary distribution centers, and some of the mining areas show up with a relatively high modern score. Northern Luzon and Southern Mindanao are the areas with the least modern activity along with Negros and Samar-Leyte.

The growth variables do not correlate with the factor distinguishing modern from traditional sectors. These load on another factor we have called the "growth" factor. Population growth rates load on this factor along with establishment growth rates and migration rates. The road density indexes and ratio of cultivated area to total land load on the growth factor, but negatively (—.47 and —.40 respectively). The growth factor tells us the most rapidly growing areas in the Philippines have been areas with a high percentage of uncultivated land and a low road density.[10] This is a frontier type of growth in contrast to the traditional model of an urbanizing, industrial sector drawing people from the farm.[11] The in-migration, high growth areas are the Cagayan valley in Northern Luzon, Quezon and Camarines Norte provinces, and Mindanao. Almost all of the Visayas and Ilocos have low relative growth or negative growth. Among the "developed provinces," only Rizal, Bataan, and Zambales are high growth areas. Figure 3 is a map of the factor scores on the growth factor.

Most of the agricultural variables load on two factors.[12] One factor we believe is related to coconut agriculture and processing, the other to tenancy and sugar. In addition to the percent of land planted to coconut, variables with high loadings include sugar negatively, crime in 1934, unemployment in 1938.

The depression hit the coconut industry very hard. The price of copra in 1938 was only 36 percent of what it had been in 1929. In contrast, sugar prices were supported during the depression be-

---

[10] Growth here does not mean the economist's growth in total provincial output per capita, although growth in farm output per capita loads on the growth factor.

[11] See John C. H. Fei and Gustav Ranis, *Development of the Labor Surplus Economy: Theory and Policy*, Richard D. Irwin, Homewood, 1964, for the fullest statement of this model.

[12] The agricultural sector is not completely represented by the variables we included. It is considerably more diverse than sugar and coconuts, although these are the two most important export crops.

17

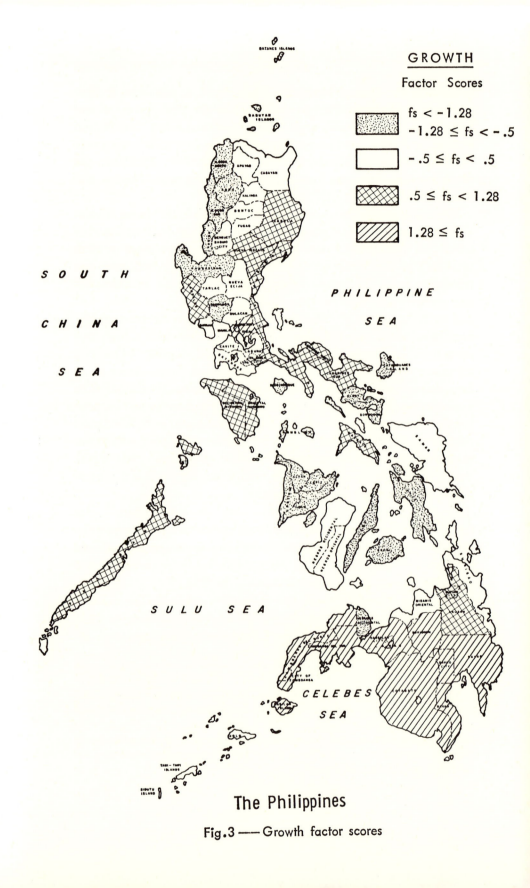

The Philippines

Fig.3 —— Growth factor scores

cause of U.S. quota procedures.[13] After the war the relative price of sugar, which was fixed in dollars under the quota system, was low. Thus, the relative value of the two major export crops changed sharply. This may have been reflected in general social conditions. In the 1930s some coconut areas experienced great unrest and, from the available data, had very high crime rates. After the war these areas were relatively stable and low in crime.

The sugar variables also load on the tenancy factor, as do the dissidence variables. The sugar areas prospered in 1938 but lost ground relative to other farm areas from 1938 to 1948. The growth of value of farm product from 1948 to 1960 was average in sugar areas. The devaluation in 1960 should have changed this as the relative price of sugar improved.

There appear to be two political factors, one relating to the Cebuanos and the other to the Ilocanos. These two groups are alleged to be the most politically cohesive groups in the Philippines, especially when their own candidates are running. For example, in 1957, the Cebuano candidate was elected President, and percent of vote for winner loads positively on the Cebuano factor; in 1960, the Cebuano candidate lost, and percent of vote for winner loads negatively. Similarly, the percent for winner in 1960 loads on the Ilocano factor, since Ilocanos voted heavily for Macapagal (whose wife is an Ilocano). In 1965 there was an Ilocano candidate, so percent winner in 1965 loads on the Ilocano factor. The vote dispersion indexes also load on the Ilocano factor, suggesting the deviant nature of the Ilocano voter.[14] Examining the factor scores on the two political factors, we find that Cebuano provinces score high on Cebuano politics: Bohol scores 2.48 and Cebu 2.86. Ilocano provinces score very high on Ilocano politics.[15] Ilocos Norte scores 2.45; Ilocos Sur, 1.84; La Union, 2.42.

1960 FACTOR ANALYSIS

For 1960 we carried out another factor analysis across the same 49 provinces as before. This time there were 35 variables. In addi-

[13] In 1929 a picul of sugar was worth 55 percent of the value of 100 kg. of copra. In 1938 the picul of sugar was worth 115 percent of the value of 100 kg. of copra. See George Hicks, *The Philippine Coconut Industry: Growth and Change, 1900-1965*; National Planning Association, Washington, D.C., June 1967, Appendix, p. 31.

[14] The other variables that load on this factor are the physical characteristics of the Ilocos—high exposure to typhoons and a large fraction of irrigated land.

[15] See Chapter 4.

19

tion to the previous variables we added some political and crime variables. We expected or hypothesized that there would be six factors, the four previous ones—modern sector, growth, coconut, sugar—and two additional ones—a politics-voting factor and a violence factor. We believed that political variables and crime variables would load on separate factors because of the regression analysis and the survey data reported in Chapters 4 and 7.

Table 2 shows the 1960 factor analysis. The factor scores suggest

TABLE 2

1960 PROVINCIAL FACTOR ANALYSIS

(35 variables)

Variable[a]	Mod-ern	Growth	Poli-tics	Vio-lence	Coco-nut	Sugar	Commu-nality R^2
Modern labor force, 1960	.81						.82
Percent with radios, 1960	.85						.83
Percent labor force in transportation, 1960	.77						.75
Establishments per thousand	.81						.83
Robbery rate, 1962	.75						.68
Percent urban	.81						.77
Percent farm workers	−.71						.76
Road density	.61						.74
Percent Tagalog	.55						.59
Population growth		−.93					.91
Growth of farm product		−.77					.69
Out-migration		+.70					.68
In-migration		−.82					.82
Growth of establishments		−.77					.87
Growth of manufacturing establishments		−.74					.73
Percent vote for winner, 1961			.77				.61
Percent Ilocano			.65				.79
Percent Cebuano			−.77				.73
Communications, 1961			−.61				.66
Irrigated land			.65				.64
Murder-homicide rate, 1962				−.61			.70
Percent Muslim, 1960				−.54			.37
Vote dispersion, 1957				.61			.49
Percent coconut					−.60		.74
Percent cultivated land					−.74		.79
Percent Bicol					−.56		.34
Percent sugar						.79	.70
Percent Ilongo						.69	.54

NOTES: Percentage of overall variance explained by factors: 68; percentage of variance explained by last factor: 5.

[a] Variables with loadings less than .5 omitted from table. Percent tenancy loads +.42 on the sugar factor.

20

that the pattern of relationships of the "developed" sector has not varied greatly over time. The variables load in the same way in the composite factor analysis and in the 1960 factor analysis. Simple correlations of modern sector indexes suggest the same:

		1.	2.	3.	4.	Percent Urban 1960
1.	Percent modern labor force 1938	1				0.61
2.	Percent modern labor force 1960	0.64	1			0.65
3.	Percent farmers 1938	−0.84	−0.84	1		−0.59
4.	Percent farmers 1960	−0.69	−0.57	0.77	1	−0.74

Areas with a high fraction of farmers in 1938 have a high fraction in 1960, and the modern labor force is concentrated in the same provinces in both years. Also provinces with a high fraction of modern labor force have a high degree of urbanization.

THE PHILIPPINES IN 1938 AND 1960

Table 3 shows a factor structure for 1938 for 14 variables selected to represent our major areas of inquiry—economics, politics, crime, and dissidence. The data are mainly taken from the 1938 census.[16] We have identified four factors that account for 68 percent of the total variance in the data: (1) modern sector, (2) high growth, (3) tenancy/sugar, (4) coconut.

Only a limited number of variables can be used to represent economic development and growth in 1938. We use the fraction of workers engaged in modern activity by province as our index of economic "modernization."[17] The modern labor force and the labor force in transportation load positively on the modern factor and, as should be expected, proportion of farmers loads negatively.

The measures of growth do not load on the modern factor but cluster together on the growth factor. In fact, in 1938 growth was

[16] For 1938 we are short of political data. Data on crime about this time could be found only in the 1934 Governor General's report.

[17] We used data on occupation from the population census to exclude the traditional sector since no economic census data were available.

21

TABLE 3
1938 PROVINCIAL FACTOR ANALYSIS

Variable	Modern Sector	High Growth	Tenancy/ Sugar	Coconut	Commu- nality R^2
Fisherman/farmers	−.80				.80
Modern labor force[a]	+.90				.84
Percent labor force in transportation[a]	+.53				.31
Population growth		−.87			.80
Percent of population <10 years old		−.72			.74
Dissidence			−.86		.80
Tenancy			−.76		.78
Sugar			−.74		.56
Value of farm products per capita			−.75		.77
Coconut				−.73	.67
Irrigated land		.51		−.54	.67
Farmland/total land				−.64	.62
Unemployment				−.66	.63
Crime cases per capita, 1934				−.70	.54

NOTES: Percentage of overall variance explained by factors: 68; percentage of variance explained by last factor: 11.

[a] For definitions of these variables see Appendix B. Factor loadings below .5 omitted.

occurring in the relatively unsettled parts of the Philippines. If we examine the factor scores for 1938, the high growth provinces were Masbate, Lanao Norte, Misamis Occidental, and Davao, the last three provinces located in Mindanao.

Figure 4 shows two development axes. Two forty-five degree lines at one standard deviation from the means bound the region defined as indicating no relative change. Provinces above and to the left of these bounds have declined in their *relative* development position and those to the right and below have *gained* in the same sense. Camarines Norte is the primary loser. This is another case of the impact of changing international prices. The high score in 1938 was largely due to gold mining, which declined after the war.

Figure 5 is a cross plot of the growth rate factors for 1938 and 1960. The relative gains and losses are systematic and explainable. Northern Mindanao is a region of slower growth. Southern Mindanao is a region of relatively faster growth in 1960. As Northern Mindanao filled up, growth shifted to the south. In Ilocos growth was still slow in 1960 but not as slow as in 1938.

Basically, the separate factor analyses suggest much the same

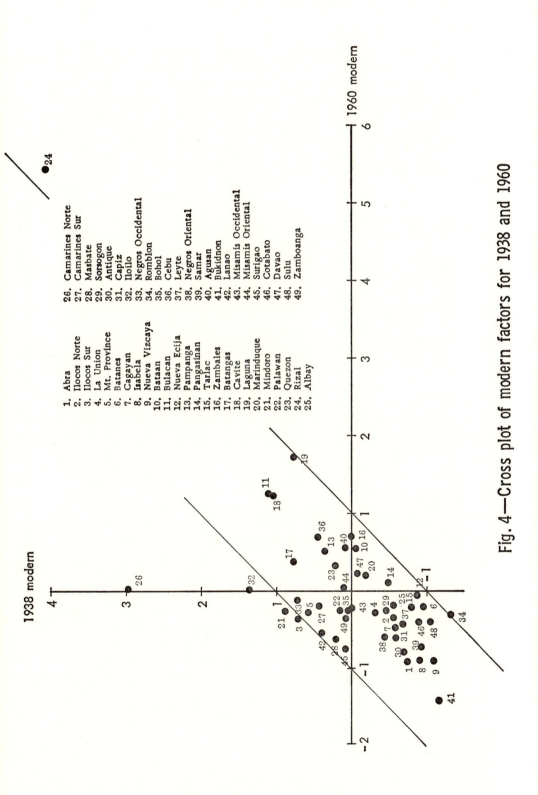

1938 modern

1960 modern

1. Abra
2. Ilocos Norte
3. Ilocos Sur
4. La Union
5. Mt. Province
6. Batanes
7. Cagayan
8. Isabela
9. Nueva Vizcaya
10. Bataan
11. Bulacan
12. Nueva Ecija
13. Pampanga
14. Pangasinan
15. Tarlac
16. Zambales
17. Batangas
18. Cavite
19. Laguna
20. Marinduque
21. Mindoro
22. Palawan
23. Quezon
24. Rizal
25. Albay

26. Camarines Norte
27. Camarines Sur
28. Masbate
29. Sorsogon
30. Antique
31. Capiz
32. Iloilo
33. Negros Occidental
34. Romblon
35. Bohol
36. Cebu
37. Leyte
38. Negros Oriental
39. Samar
40. Agusan
41. Bukidnon
42. Lanao
43. Misamis Occidental
44. Misamis Oriental
45. Surigao
46. Cotabato
47. Davao
48. Sulu
49. Zamboanga

Fig. 4—Cross plot of modern factors for 1938 and 1960

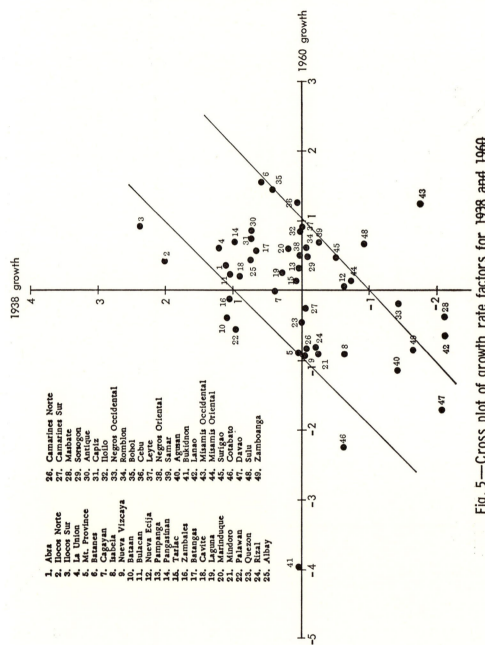

Fig. 5—Cross plot of growth rate factors for 1938 and 1960

pattern as does the composite factor analysis. The ethnic nature of Philippine politics and the relative economic development of various parts of the country have remained the same from 1938 to 1960, although the absolute level and tempo of economic and political activity increased greatly. Chapter 3 will explore how the Philippine people view this constancy within change.

3

Perceptions of the Philippine Political System

THE ATTITUDES of the public, politicians, and bureaucrats provide one measure of the performance of the government. If the government is habitually inept and unresponsive, these faults should be revealed in the way the people view the government or in the way politicians view the public. Filipinos appear reasonably well satisfied with the performance of their government. The politicians and bureaucrats, in turn, seem to perceive the desires of the public quite clearly and try to satisfy them. Politicians note the desire of the public for delivery of local goods and services or for a candidate who speaks their language. They respond by voting appropriations for numerous small projects and by carefully balancing party slates among the various ethnic groups represented in the population. This system does not satisfy any abstract notion of rational resource allocation, but it satisfies the desires of the participants and it is stable—hard to change and unlikely to disintegrate.

Perceptions of the Public

ATTITUDES TOWARD THE GOVERNMENT

We relied on several closed surveys to determine the attitudes and perceptions of the public, the politicians, and the bureaucrats.[1] It was our intention to find out whether the Filipinos feel the gov-

---

[1] The survey we funded in January 1969 is a stratified random sample of the major ethnic groups in the Philippines. See Appendix A for a more detailed discussion. Hereafter this survey will be referred to as Pegasus (*Philippine ethnic group attitude surveys*). In Pegasus we used several questions taken from G. A. Almond and S. Verba, *The Civic Culture*, Princeton University Press, Princeton, 1963, which compares the attitudes of citizens in the United States, Great Britain, Germany, Italy, and Mexico. Earlier data are drawn from surveys deposited at the International Data Library and Reference Service (IDLARS), Survey Research Center, University of California, Berkeley (National Science Foundation Grant GS1365). It is almost impossible to generalize from the large body of case study research done in the Philippines; thus we concentrated on structured interviews. See J. M. McKendry, M. S. McKendry, and G. M. Guthrie, *The Psychological Impact of Social Change in the Philippines*, Technical Report No. 857-R-2, HRB-Singer, Inc., State College, June 1967.

ernment can help them achieve a better life. In a 1963 survey, 1044 respondents answered the question: "Do you think the government can help you solve your problems?"[2] Seventy-six percent answered "yes." Of those who answered "no" or had no opinion (249), 66 percent cited unawareness of their problems by government officials. Those who believed the government could help solve their problems were asked if the government *had* taken any steps to solve their problems. Of those who responded, 84 percent answered "yes."

Regional tabulations of these responses are shown in Table 4.[3] Ignoring the small Cotabato sample, Ilocanos, the most politically

TABLE 4

BELIEF THAT GOVERNMENT CAN HELP SOLVE PROBLEMS,
BY REGION, 1963
(percent)

Region	Yes	No	SSR[a]
Ilocos	87	13	102
Pampanga	75	25	60
N. Ecija	84	16	56
Tagalog	63	37	107
Bicol	70	30	104
Cebuano	64	36	132
Cotabato	100	0	36
Davao	80	20	56
Ilongo	79	21	113
Greater Manila and other cities	80	20	278
DK: 3.7% out of 1084[a]			
$\chi^2 = 23.2$ with 9 D.F. without Cotabato			

NOTE:

[a] Hereafter in all tables *subjects responding* will be denoted SSR and subjects interviewed will be denoted as SS. DK will refer to the response "Don't know."

cohesive ethnic group, have the greatest belief in the government's ability to solve problems.[4] With respect to socioeconomic status (SES) a lower fraction of those in the lowest and highest groups (5 and 2) believe that the government can help solve their problems (Table 5). There may be rural-urban differences at work here. The rural segments of the population get help because they live in small groups and can go to their barrio captain; the upper

[2] IDLARS 416-59-002. The survey was conducted by the Robot Corporation for the Manila Times Corporation.

[3] In the survey regional classifications correspond almost exactly to ethnic groups.

[4] Although the President in 1963 was of Pampangan extraction, the Ilocanos had a strong voice in the government through then Senate President Marcos.

27

TABLE 5

BELIEF THAT GOVERNMENT CAN SOLVE PROBLEMS,
BY SOCIOECONOMIC STATUS, 1963
(percent)

| | SOCIOECONOMIC STATUS | | | | |
| | *Highest* | | | | *Lowest* |
Response	1	2	3	4	5
Yes	91	69	77	82	69
No	9	31	23	18	31
SSR	11	109	185	365	169

DK: 3.74% out of 1069

$\chi^2 = 14.0$ with 3 D.F. ignoring the small sample of SES 1.

urban strata can also get help, but those in between may not have the same access to the government.

The Pegasus survey measures attitudes of Filipinos today on a similar question. Table 6 shows that 73 percent of those responding

TABLE 6

PERCEPTION OF GOVERNMENT INFLUENCE, 1969

Response	Number Responding	Percent of Sample[a]	Percent of Respondents[a]
Yes	975	63	73
No	357	23	27
DK	217	14	0
SS	1550	100	100

NOTES: Actual text: "On the whole, do the activities of the national government tend to have any influence in your day-to-day life?"

[a] Percentages are calculated from responses weighted according to proper proportions of urban and rural in the population as well as the proper stratum proportions. See Appendix A. This practice will be followed in all tables from Pegasus. The notation SS or SSR in all tables means the actual numbers of subjects or subjects responding, not the weighted numbers.

to the Pegasus question about the influence of the government on daily life believe it does have an influence. Table 7 indicates that 57 percent of those responding "yes"—that the government has an effect—also believe that life would be worse without government activities.[5] Only 8 percent of respondents believe that life would be better without the government. If we can interpret the question about government help asked in 1963 as measuring the same at-

[5] The text of the questions in Tables 4 and 5 overlap deliberately. Thus we have a few respondents who believe inconsistently that the government has no effect on their lives but who also believe that life would be worse without the government.

28

TABLE 7

WORTH OF GOVERNMENT ACTIVITIES, 1969

Response	Number Responding	Percent of Sample[a]
Better without	77	8
Just the same	303	31
Worse without	559	57
DK	36	4
SS[b]	975	100

NOTES: Actual text: "Do you think your life would be worse, just the same, or better without these government activities?"

[a] Weighted percentages.

[b] Total number of SS consists of those who responded yes on the question concerning government influence on daily life.

titudes as in 1969, then Filipinos continue to believe that their lives can be changed—for the better—by government action.

We took several questions from *The Civic Culture* so we could compare Filipino attitudes with attitudes of people in other countries. Tables 8 and 9 show breakdowns for the Philippines as a whole and for Central Luzon, the latter area being the traditional site of dissidence. Concerning government impact on the individual,

TABLE 8

ESTIMATED DEGREE OF IMPACT OF NATIONAL GOVERNMENT ON DAILY LIFE
(percent)

Percent of Respondents Who Say National Government Has:	1960					1969	
	United States	United Kingdom	Ger-many	Italy	Mexico	Philip-pines	Central Luzon[b]
Great effect or some effect	85	73	70	54	30	63	59
No effect	11	23	17	19	66	23	23
Other	0	neg.[a]	neg.	3	neg.		
DK	4	4	12	24	3	14	18
SS	970	963	955	995	1007	1550	374

NOTES: Actual text for United States, United Kingdom, Germany, Italy, and Mexico: "Thinking now about the national government, about how much effect do you think its activities, the laws passed, and so on, have on your day-to-day life? Do they have a great effect, some effect, or none?" Actual text for Philippines: "On the whole do the activities of the national government tend to have any influence on your day-to-day life?" Weighted percentages.

[a] neg. = negligible.

[b] Includes Tagalogs south of Manila since dissident activity has been reported in these areas. Tagalog respondents seem most "alienated."

29

TABLE 9

CHARACTER OF IMPACT OF NATIONAL GOVERNMENT
(percent)

	1960					1969	
Percent Who Say:[a]	United States	United Kingdom	Ger-many	Italy	Mexico	Philip-pines	Central Luzon[a]
National government improves conditions	76	77	61	66	58	57	41
Sometimes improves conditions; sometimes does not; no difference	20	16	3	21	20	31	38
Better off without national government	3	3	3	5	19	8	9
Other	0	1	0	2	1		
DK	1	2	4	5	2	4	12
SS	821	707	676	534	301	975	211

NOTES: As described by those respondents who attribute *some* impact to the national government.
[a] Includes Tagalog areas south of Manila, since dissident activity has been reported in these areas.

the Philippine distribution resembles most closely responses obtained in Italy or Germany. Individuals in the Philippines do have political cognition[6] but not to as great a degree as people in the United States or United Kingdom.

In terms of whether government impact is good or bad—among those perceiving impact—the Philippines most closely resembles Italy and Mexico (Table 9).

The Filipino response to the *open* question: "What are you most proud of as a Filipino?" indicates a high fraction of persons who take pride in the "characteristics of the people." The replies range from "hospitality" to "respect for elders, women, and family," to "peacefulness and industriousness." A relatively low fraction of Filipinos responded with "government and political institutions" compared with the fractions for the United States, United Kingdom, and Mexico.[7] The fraction, though, is about the same as that for Germany.

[6] See Almond and Verba, *The Civic Culture*, pp. 79ff., for a discussion of "political cognition." As they use the term, "political cognition" is composed of (1) the importance attributed to national and local government, (2) awareness of politics and public affairs, (3) possession of political information, and (4) readiness to make choices or entertain opinions about political issues.

[7] Almond and Verba, *The Civic Culture*, p. 102.

The combined results of all our questions on political awareness suggest that Filipinos are interested in their government and believe that it is necessary.

ATTITUDES TOWARD GOVERNMENT OFFICIALS

Filipinos believe that graft and corruption are prevalent and constitute a major problem (Table 10). Some groups—Ilocanos, War-

TABLE 10

VIEWS ON WIDESPREAD GRAFT AND CORRUPTION AS A
NATIONAL PROBLEM, BY ETHNIC GROUPS
(percent of those responding)

	Not Prevalent	Prevalent Not Major Problem	Prevalent Major Problem	SSR
Greater Manila	10	9	80	148
Ilocanos	47	7	47	197
Pampangans	0	26	73	63
Pangasinans	2	12	86	65
Tagalogs	9	18	73	196
Bicols	12	25	63	133
Ilongos	8	15	78	142
Warays	49	41	10	68
Cebuanos	17	8	75	271
Magindanaos	50	5	45	48
Tausogs	0	17	83	50
Total sample	19	15	66	1381

NOTE: Actual text: "How do you feel about graft and corruption in the national government: do you think it is not prevalent at all, prevalent but not a major problem, or that is it prevalent and is a major problem?" Weighted percentages.

ays, and Magindanaos—differ somewhat from the general view (seeing graft to be either less prevalent or less of a problem though prevalent). Other ethnic groups, however, share a generally bleak view of the honesty of government officials. When we ask "Which officials are corrupt?" politicians come off the worst (Table 11). Nearly 40 percent of all respondents believe that most politicians are corrupt.

When we ask about local politicians, however, there is a shift from the "mostly corrupt" category to the "some corrupt" category. Local politicians are less likely to be considered corrupt for two reasons: first, because they are seen directly instead of through the mass media. The image of national politicians as corrupt is drawn in large measure from the press. Second, the activities of the local

TABLE 11

VIEWS ON CORRUPTION OF OFFICIALS
(percent of respondents)

	None/Few Corrupt (0)[a]	Some Corrupt (1)	Mostly Corrupt (2)	Mean Response	SSR
Government employees	20[b]	43	36	1.15	1394
Politicians in general	18	44	38	1.20	1404
Local politicians	16	62	22	1.06	1375
Lawyers (local)	35	56	8	0.72	1337
Policemen (local)	39	54	7	0.68	1432
Philippine Constabulary (local)	41	53	6	0.65	1294
Fiscals (District Attorney, local)	55	42	3	0.48	1255
Judges (local)	57	40	2	0.44	1303

NOTES:

[a] The numbers 0, 1, 2 in the table headings refer to the options of response on this question and are used to compute the mean response.

[b] All percentages weighted.

politicians probably seem to be attempts to deliver goods and services to local constituents, not corruption.

Judges and fiscals[8] appear to have the best image, followed by the Constabulary and the local police. This image seems consistent with the view of the *legal* system as generally honest. Out of 1269 respondents on the Pegasus question about the honesty of the court system, 70 percent answered that it was honest and efficient.[9]

Just as estimates of corruption varied across the country, views of politicians and government officials also vary across different groups of the population. Table 12 summarizes some of the most striking differences in opinions by group characteristics. The table shows coefficients that were significant at the .95 level or better in a multiple regression. For example, the first row indicates that Muslims and low SES individuals tend to say that politicians are

[8] Fiscals are equivalent to district attorneys.

[9] Text of question: "Do you think our courts are generally honest and efficient?" Respondents in Greater Manila had the lowest "yes" response rate—53 percent.

TABLE 12

VIEWS ON POLITICIANS AND GOVERNMENT OFFICIALS

	Ilocano	Muslim	Pam-pangan	SES	Higher on Ladder	Manila
Politicians						
Greedy		no	yes	no		yes
Honest	yes	yes		yes		no
Hard-working	yes			yes		no
Corrupt	no	no		no		yes
Nationalistic	yes	yes		yes		no
An example to follow	yes			yes		no
Expect equal treatment from government employee		yes			yes	no
Government employees						
Courteous	yes	yes		yes		no
Arrogant				no		yes
Efficient	yes			yes		no
Responsive	yes		no		yes	
Corrupt	no			no		yes
Helpful	yes			yes		no
Indifferent	no					

NOTE: The dependent variables are questions 4a to 4f, 17, and 18a-18g of Pegasus. See Appendix A. Each of these questions is coded so that 0 is "no" or "none/ few." The independent variables are dummies for Ilocano, Muslim, Pampangan, or Manilan; the values of the interviewer's estimate of the household's SES; and where the respondent places himself on a self-anchoring scale of welfare today (question 2b). Since SES is coded so that SES class A (highest) is equal to 0, a "yes" in this column means that low SES respondents show higher than average response values on the relevant question.

not greedy while Pampangans and Manilans tend to reply that they are.

Manilans clearly tend to have a negative view of the government and its representatives. Ilocanos, by contrast, are almost always significantly more favorable toward the government than the rest of the population. Muslims and respondents from low SES strata tend to resemble Ilocanos. Pampangans are significantly different from the rest of the population on only two of the 14 questions; they respond more frequently that politicians are greedy and less frequently that government officials are responsive.

Expectations of equal treatment in government offices and views of government employees mesh together consistently. Muslims expect equal treatment and feel that government employees are courteous. Manilans on the other hand do not expect equal treatment and feel that government employees are unhelpful, discourteous, and the like.

Table 13 shows expectation of treatment by nation, again adapted

TABLE 13

EXPECTATION OF TREATMENT FROM GOVERNMENT BUREAUCRACY,
BY NATION
(percent)

Percent Who Say:	United States	United Kingdom	Germany	Italy	Mexico	Philip-pines
They expect equal treatment	83	83	65	53	42	42[a]
They don't expect equal treatment	9	7	9	13	50	35
Depends	4	6	19	17	5	
Other	neg.	neg.	neg.	6	neg.	
DK	4	2	7	11	3	23
SS	970	963	955	995	1007	1550

NOTES: Actual text of the question: "Suppose there were some question that you had to take to a government office—for example, a tax question or housing regulation. Do you think you would be given equal treatment—I mean, would you be treated as well as anyone else?" "If you had some trouble with the police—a traffic violation maybe, or being accused of a minor offense—do you think you would be given equal treatment? That is, would you be treated as well as anyone else?" Actual text of the Philippine question: "Suppose there was some question you had to take to a government office . . . for example, a tax question or a housing regulation. Do you think you would be treated as well as anyone?" Only 3 responses were permitted, "yes," "no," and "DK"; which perhaps accounts for the relatively large DK in the Philippines.

[a] Weighted percentages.

from *The Civic Culture*, with the analogous tabulation from Pegasus. The Pegasus question is identical to that about bureaucrats in *The Civic Culture*. On this scale the Philippines appears to be roughly like Italy and Mexico.

Filipinos, however, are markedly *unlike* Italians and Mexicans in the degree to which their expectation of equal treatment is insensitive to measures of status. We find no significant relation between SES and expectation of equal treatment (see Table 12). The same appears to be true when we use education as a proxy for status (see Table 14). Comparable tabulations of Italian and Mexican responses reported in *The Civic Culture* show a strong relation between education and expectation of treatment. The least-educated Mexicans respond with an expectation of unequal treatment 81

TABLE 14

EXPECTATION OF EQUAL TREATMENT FROM GOVERNMENT
BUREAUCRACY, BY EDUCATION
(percent of those responding)

	No[a]	Yes	SSR
No schooling	41	59	87
Some primary	48	52	744
Some secondary	49	51	174
Some university	38	62	191
Total sample	46	54	1196

$$\chi_1^2 = 7.5 \text{ with 3 D.F.} \qquad \chi^2 = 7.3 \text{ with 3 D.F.}$$

NOTES: Weighted percentages.
[a] Text of question in Note, Table 13.

percent of the time as compared with a 32 percent response frequency from the most educated. The Italian responses ranged from
70 percent unequal (low education) to 41 percent (highest education).[10]

POLITICAL PARTICIPATION

In the Philippines about 60 percent of the adult population votes.
Political campaigns are intensive. Politicians battle for votes throughout the islands. For example, in a poll shortly before the 1965
election it was found that over 30 percent of the respondents had
personally seen or heard at least one of the presidential candidates
and close to 45 percent had seen or heard a senatorial candidate.[11]
In 1963 more than 65 percent claimed they attended political
rallies.[12]

The Civic Culture does not contain directly comparable data.
However, in Mexico 45 percent claim to pay no attention to political campaigns and another 38 percent indicate little interest. In
Italy these percentages are 54 and 25, respectively. On another
question 62 percent of the Italian sample claimed that they never
followed accounts of elections and 44 percent of the Mexicans indicated they never did.[13] The Philippines thus appears to have a relatively high percentage of political "participants," fewer than the

[10] Almond and Verba, *The Civic Culture*, pp. 110, 112.
[11] IDLARS 416-59-0010.   [12] IDLARS 416-59-0002.
[13] Almond and Verba, *The Civic Culture*, p. 89.

United States and the United Kingdom but considerably more than Italy or Mexico.[14]

Participants can be "content" or "alienated." If a person is aware of government impact and dissatisfied with that impact, then he is alienated. A larger proportion of Filipinos than of Mexicans and Italians feel that the government has a strong "positive" impact on life. At the same time, since the Philippines simply has many more participants, it outranks either of these countries in terms of the number of alienated persons.

THE ROLE OF POLITICIANS

Perhaps the most striking result of our survey is the demand for honest politicians. Ninety percent of all respondents say that they vote according to the perceived honesty of the candidate; no other criterion anywhere approaches the magnitude of this response. Yet paradoxically the people believe that politicians are the most corrupt of all officials. The tension between this demand for honesty and the perception of corruption may account for much of the turnover in national officials. Certainly the "outs" make no bones about the alleged graft and corruption of the "ins."

Honesty is not all that matters, however. Dialect and past help given to the voter's area are important, too, in both presidential and local elections (Table 15). Help promised but not yet delivered is valued much less than past aid; this difference is consistent with mild skepticism toward politicians.

TABLE 15

FACTORS CONSIDERED IN CHOOSING A CANDIDATE
(percent responding "very important")

Criterion	President	Mayor
Honesty of the candidate	90	90
Help given your area	65	65
General policy of the candidate	57	58
Candidate comes from your area or speaks your dialect	50	62
Promise of help to your area	32	33
Party of the candidate	32	32
Your close friends' or compadres' attitude toward the candidate	16	16

NOTE: Weighted percentages.   SS = 1550.

[14] Almond and Verba, *The Civic Culture*, use the term "parochial" for non-participant. A "parochial" is someone unaware of and unconcerned about the government.

Politicians, nevertheless, have their perceived functions in the Philippine system. For example, consider the following question: "If a friend of yours needed some help from a government office, would you advise him to go through channels, bring someone with the right connections, or try to use bribery?" Those in the lower SES groups have a greater propensity toward using the "right connections" (Table 16).

TABLE 16

ALTERNATIVE WAYS OF OBTAINING HELP FROM GOVERNMENT, BY SES

(percent of those responding)

SES	Seek Help Through Channels	Bring Right Connections	Use Bribery	SSR
High	69	28	3	172
Medium	55	38	7	542
Low	60	34	6	699
Total sample (including 15 Very High)	59	35	6	1428

$$\chi_1^2 = 22.5 \text{ with 4 D.F.}^a \qquad \chi^2 = 8.5 \text{ with 4 D.F.}$$

NOTES: Weighted percentages.

[a] The Bhapkar statistic χ_1^2 is highly significant. The χ^2 is significant at slightly less than .05. This suggests that there are offsetting differences in the strata.

In sum, for its level of development, the Philippines compares favorably with other polities in transition to a "civic culture." The general views of government and politics are not radically different from those in other relatively stable polities. There are, on the other hand, large differences in perceptions by ethnic or regional groups with Ilocanos and Muslims at the favorable end of the scale and Manilans and Tagalogs at the other. Manilans, in general, tend to view the political system, the government, and the legal system in far darker tones than do the rest of the population. This may help explain the pessimism expressed by foreign observers of the Philippines, whose observations are usually restricted to Manila.

The Perceptions of the Politicians

In any democratic society with a federal structure there will be a tension between the desires of various regions and the good of the country as a whole. Resources may be spread equally but thinly across the country or concentrated in a small number of more productive projects. The Philippines is hardly unique in often opting for the former. As we have seen, that choice accurately reflects the desires of the people, and Congressmen accurately perceive these desires.

To investigate what politicians think of the public and how they interpret the public's desires, we interviewed a randomly selected set of 66 of the 126 Congressmen and Senators.[15] These interviews show that Congressmen and the people rank national problems in a similar way.[16] Table 17 presents perceptions of legislators and the

TABLE 17

PERCEPTION OF NATIONAL PROBLEMS

Response	Legislators' Rank Order		Pegasus Respondents	
	On First Response	In All Responses	Mean Response[a]	Rank Order
Raising taxes ⎤			1.41 ⎤	
Increasing ⎫ General				
exports ⎬ economic	1	1	1.38 ⎬	1
High cost of ⎭ issues				
living ⎦			1.46 ⎦	
High crime rate	2	2	1.35	3
Rapid population growth	3	4	1.13	5
Widespread graft and corruption	4	3	1.37	2
Dissidence or the HMB problem		5	1.19	4
Treatment of minority groups			1.09	6

NOTES: Pegasus respondents were given a closed question concerning problems in the Philippines. They were asked to rank importance on a three point ascending scale—0, 1, 2. Congressmen were asked the question: "What do you think is the most serious problem facing the Philippines today?"

[a] From weighted percentages.

people. Even though the people and the Congressmen perceive these general problems, they do not believe that solving them is the key to political success. Table 18 lists the criteria Congressmen believe are important in winning elections and compares responses with Pegasus replies. The two predominant responses of constituents are "honesty" and "specific help given to home areas." Legislators also rank these as the two most important considerations, but in reverse order from

[15] There are 62 Congressmen and 4 Senators in the sample.

[16] We have included the legislators' responses on the dissidence issue because it looms so large in the eyes of U.S. decisionmakers. Dissidence was mentioned infrequently by the legislators relative to the other items on the list.

TABLE 18
PERCEIVED CRITERIA FOR WINNING ELECTIONS

Criterion	Percent First Response[a]	Rank of Congressional Respondents	Pegasus Rank
Honesty/personal qualifications	28	2	1
Help given to area in past/public improvements and services	41	1	2
Promised help to an area	4.5	4	6
Personal relationships, friends, money	3	6	7
General policy/stand on issues	6	5	3
A particular party affiliation	7.5	3	5
Candidate's dialect same as respondent's[b]	1.5	7	4

NOTES: Actual text of question for Congressmen: "What factors do you think determine the vote of your constituents?" Text for Pegasus shown on Table 15. Responses here are for presidential candidate. Weighted percentages.

[a] A computation based on all responses does not change the predominance of help given to local area and honesty.

[b] This may fail to appear important to the Congressmen (the bulk of the sample) because they usually represent ethnically homogeneous districts, and would as a matter of course speak the principal dialect of the area.

their constituents. Although the legislators recognize problems facing the nation as a whole at an abstract level, they feel that votes depend on the delivery of specific resources to their constituents. Voters prize honesty in a candidate; they also prize services. Neither the people nor the politicians recognize that these two criteria can be in conflict.

When asked why they enter politics, 56 percent of these legislators give "public service" as their first answer; 17 percent respond "gaining power and money" or "status and prestige." In second responses, legislators frequently list the protection of their own interests (26 percent of second responses).[17] The definition of public service must inevitably take on a local flavor given the perceived need to deliver goods and services and given the need to protect one's own interests. If Congressmen spent their energies solving the serious national problems they say they see instead of meeting demands of local constituencies, they would be vulnerable to challengers.

When Congressmen were asked whether they thought members of Congress were oriented toward the achievement of specific programs, they were ambiguous: 52 percent responded that most Con-

[17] Allegedly various important families or "blocs" attempt to have some of their members in important positions as a protective device.

gressmen were interested in achieving specific programs, 24 percent said some were, and 24 percent felt that few legislators were interested in specific programs. These answers, too, can be placed in some context by a cross-national comparison. In a survey of the Connecticut legislature, Barber noted a pronounced tendency to direct interview discussions to specific legislation and policy matters.[18] No tendency toward concreteness can be observed in the responses of Philippine legislators. We asked the question: "What policies do you think would best advance the social and economic development of the Philippines?" In Table 19 we have classified the responses ac-

TABLE 19

RESPONSES ON SOCIOECONOMIC POLICY TO HELP
DEVELOP THE PHILIPPINES
(percent)

| | *First Response*[a] | | |
	Economic	Social	Total
General	46	15	61
Specific	31	8	39

| | *All Responses*[b] | | |
	Economic	Social	Total
General	42	19	61
Specific	31	8	39

NOTES:

[a] This calculation is based on 59 respondents answering this question.

[b] This calculation is based on 66 interviews.

cording to whether they were specific or general and whether they fell into the economic or social categories. The dominance of the upper half of the table is striking. Policy is thought of in terms of generalities.

About 76 percent of the legislators in our sample say they believe that the government should exert less or much less control over the private sector. Yet the kind of legislation that passes is supposed to take the government into greater regulation of the private sector. In May 1969, while we were doing these interviews, the Congress unanimously passed a basic national economic policy. The joint resolution establishing the basic policy states: "Every encouragement shall be given by the government to *Filipino* private entre-

[18] James D. Barber, *The Law Makers*, Yale University Press, New Haven, 1965. See also James L. Payne, *Patterns of Conflict in Colombia*, Yale University Press, New Haven, 1968, p. 48. From Barber's presentation, Payne infers that the largest single group in the Connecticut legislature is oriented toward programs.

preneurs in the establishment and operation of basic and integrated industries. The *profit motive* shall, however, *not* be the principal consideration of national decisions affecting the establishment, dispersal, and location of socially and economically desirable basic and/ or integrated industries." Further on the legislators say: "Through *direct incentives, selective tariff, import credit*, and *foreign exchange restrictions*, the domestic market shall be conserved and enhanced primarily for products of local industries." And further: "The disposition of the nation's foreign exchange shall be subjected to a rigorous system of priorities."[19]

These aims cannot be achieved nor these policies implemented without much greater government control over business. Congressmen are able to uphold the schizophrenic position that both less and more control is needed.

We asked two questions designed to reveal legislators' program orientation:

(1) "Do you have any *specific* economic policy in mind?"
(2) "If so, under what circumstances would you initiate such measures?"

Of those who responded to the question on *specific* economic policy, 60 percent (26/43) again responded first with general policies. The following is a verbatim list of first responses on specific economic policy.

More General	*More Specific*
Economic independence	More private investment
Industrialization	More exports
Develop natural resources	More capital intensive industry
Agricultural development	More taxes
Science and technology	Manufacturing
More employment	Ease credit
More distribution of wealth	Tax exemption
Agro-industrial development	Import control
Agricultural production	More production of prime commodities
Exploit natural resources	Protect new industries
Filipinization	More government control
Give incentives	More labor-oriented industries
Magna Carta (refers to joint	Infrastructure program
resolution cited above)	Foreign exchange controls
Diversification	Ease foreign trade restrictions
Regional development	

[19] Sixth Congress of the Republic of the Philippines, fourth session, Special Committee on Social and Economic Planning, *Joint Resolution Establishing Basic Policies that Shall Govern the Nation's Endeavor Toward Economic Development and Social Justice.* Our italics in the quotation.

When legislators were asked under what circumstances they would initiate their preferred economic policies, there was a great tendency to say that the policy was already being implemented. There was very little explanation of procedural matters. Answers were extremely diverse, but very few saw themselves as taking political action to get bills implemented. One respondent replied, "When I become speaker"; another, "depends on the President"; and so on. Some legislators were waiting for external events: "the time the country is willing to sacrifice," "when people are willing to help," "under a Liberal administration," "executive-legislative cooperation."

Legislators see little payoff in acquiring expertise on national policy issues. Legislation affecting national policy is passed without intensive analysis or debate. The information necessary for such debate or analysis is not generated by reporting agencies.[20] Expertise gathers votes neither in the legislature nor in the barrios.

Most legislators believe that the current organization of Congress is "better than most." They have very few procedural changes to suggest. The debates about structure and procedure that periodically rock the U.S. Senate and House are unheard of in the Philippines. The most common suggestion for improvement was that attendance be required.

Nearly all the legislators felt that politics is "too prevalent in government budget decisions." But most blamed the situation on the executive, with the legislative branch playing a passive role. A few perceived that it was the negotiations over the budget that enabled the legislators to deliver the services and resources that permit them to play the game of politics.

We have no reliable data on how specific budget decisions are reached, but it appears that bureaucrats exchange jobs and resources with Congressmen for department budget.[21] Congressmen place enormous pressures on bureaucrats to allocate resources in a local, piecemeal fashion. At the same time, critics—many of them Congressmen—decry excessive political influence over the executive branch.

Philippine legislators, like the people, thus present a portrait of ambiguity and contradiction, which often go unrecognized. In practically the same breath a legislator can proclaim that he wants

[20] See Chapter 5 for a discussion of information and decisionmaking.
[21] See below on the problems of bureaucrats facing Congressional demands.

a free market economy and a planned economy or a solution to dissidence in Central Luzon but no interference with local political patterns. Yet even if politicians were clear about conflicting objectives, there may be no room for maneuvering to achieve national objectives. So long as local goods and services are a major criterion for winning office, the best information and expertise on economic and social problems will not suffice to solve these problems.

The Perceptions of the Bureaucrats

Between politicians and public stands the bureaucrat. We have already suggested the constant political pressure facing the bureaucrats. The Congress always passes a budget roughly three times the size of available revenues, but old appropriations never die. Bureaucrats and legislators are constantly skirmishing over the release of this enormous backlog.[22]

Our data on bureaucrats are not as fresh as our data on the people and the politicians. We were able to obtain data on 120 bureaucrats from a survey of higher civil servants carried out in 1960.[23] From a number of conversations with high-level bureaucrats and from the press, we believe that the opinions of bureaucrats cannot have changed very much. Bureaucrats in the Philippines have considerable longevity. In general they continue their traditional ways of behavior.

Table 20 shows the bureaucrats' beliefs about citizens' respect for the government. We have cross-tabulated "respect" by type of

[22] In particular the political pressure is extremely heavy on the Budget Commission which has the duty to release funds to the line agencies. Once funds have been released to the line agencies, then the politician has to see to it that the funds are actually expended at a time he considers appropriate. This is a difficult task because the typical line agency has very little knowledge of when an expenditure has actually taken place. It is the local representative of the line agency who knows about expenditures, but getting him to report to the upper echelons has been a very difficult task. And, in fact, what has happened is that *ad hoc* reporting systems are generated in the government for particular areas of interest.

[23] See Gregorio A. Francisco, Jr., *Higher Civil Servants in the Philippines*, College of Public Administration, University of the Philippines, 1960. The data were coded onto "unisort" cards permitting one way manual tabulations. Mr. Francisco kindly made these cards available to us, and we converted them to a regular IBM card deck. Unfortunately, Card 1 of the unisort deck has been lost. It contained the personal history and experiences of the respondents. Thus our ability to do cross-tabulations by bureaucrats' personal characteristics and experience is severely limited.

TABLE 20
BUREAUCRATS ON CITIZENS' RESPECT FOR GOVERNMENT
(percent)

	Little Respect	Moderate	Much	Very Profound	SSR
Type of agency					
Service or line	45	39	14	2	51
Regulatory	37	58	5	0	19
Staff	33	44	17	6	18
Government Corporation	48	29	19	5	21
Total sample	42	41	14	3	109

agency, since bureaucrats in agencies or bureaus that deal with the public all the time should differ from other bureaucrats. Most of our bureaucrats believe that citizens do not have a great deal of respect for their government. Bureaucrats in the line agencies and the government corporations take the dimmest view. When asked why they believe the citizen lacks respect for the government, the bureaucrats respond with "graft and corruption." Specific responses are shown in Table 21.

TABLE 21
BUREAUCRATS' REASONS FOR CITIZENS' NONRESPECT
(percent)

	Observed Graft-Corruption	Heard of Graft-Corruption	Government Failed Expectations	Discontent & Economic Plight	SSR
Type of agency					
Service or line	45	30	11	16	37
Regulatory	47	27	13	13	15
Staff	30	50	10	10	10
Government Corporation	45	18	18	18	11
Total sample	42	30	12	15	73

Francisco also asked the bureaucrats what a director would do if he had to choose between two economists applying for a position: one candidate is minimally qualified, but is the protégé of a Senator; the second candidate, with excellent qualifications, has the support of only a minor official. Thirty-six percent of those interviewed (44/123) thought the director would appoint the Senator's candidate and about 64 percent (79/123) said the most qualified candidate would be selected. Of those who thought that the Senator's candidate would be chosen, 84 percent said that the director would have to accede so as not to endanger his position and to avoid further political pressures. The other 16 percent said that their own personal observations led them to the belief that the Senator's candidate would be chosen.

When the bureaucrats were asked what would happen if the "most qualified" candidate were to be chosen, of those responding (61), 30 percent said that the director might lose his job or ruin his chances for promotion; 16 percent said that the bureau's budget might be cut and that the director would lose favor with the Senator; and 36 percent said there would be increased pressures from the Senator to get the post for his candidate. To avoid these pressures the bureaucrats believe that they have to conduct personal screenings for high-level positions to discover the extent of a candidate's contacts and to find ways around the civil service laws.[24]

Whenever political protégés do get jobs, the bureaucrats favor keeping them on regardless of effectiveness. Either they would try to retain them and give them some training, or reassign them, or give their work to others. Very few favor forced resignation or instituting administrative charges.

The public, the politicians, and the bureaucrats see each other accurately. They all know what to expect from one another. As a result the political system is responsive to the needs of the people, who vote the politicians in and out of office. The bureaucrats are responsive to the politicians, who provide the budget. Filipinos may not be proud of their political institutions, the mass media may blast the system daily, and visiting dignitaries may view it with alarm; nevertheless, the voters choose it every odd-numbered year.

[24] *Ibid.*, p. 200.

Politics in the Philippines

POLITICIANS need to allocate programs, budget, and talent toward winning voter approval.[1] Thus, if votes are determined by pork barrel, politicians have every incentive to require the delivery of "vote-getting" programs—for example, increased government employment—rather than "growth-achieving" programs.

Indirectly, the motives of bureaucrats are shaped by the same need because of their interactions with the politicians. To obtain budget, bureaucrats must bargain with the politicians, arranging and executing the programs the politicians choose.

The election is the central event in Philippine politics. It is through analysis of elections that we shall assess the prospects for political change, for the emergence of a style of politics more concerned with national issues, programs, and performance. We shall try to explain election outcomes in terms of important social and economic factors—for example, degree of poverty—and the traditional considerations of pork barrel and ethnicity. If voting can be explained almost wholly by these last factors, programs and governmental performance must have little effect on election outcomes.

The ethnic voting patterns that appear so sharply in political survey data are not declining in importance.[2] Furthermore, the de-

[1] Government sensitivity to popular pressures obviously differs among LDCs. "The general picture that emerges . . . is one in which the Brazilian government has had a substantial degree of autonomy from interest group or socio-economic class pressures in the making of economic policy" (Nathaniel Leff, *Economic Policy-Making and Development in Brazil, 1947-1964*, John Wiley & Sons, Inc., New York, 1968, p. 4). On Colombia, Robert Dix states: "The traditional parties have failed effectively to adjust their own internal structures and patterns *to a politics where socio-economic issues are central and the lower and middle classes are potentially participants.* The regime of the modernizing elite continues to lack the institutional channels through which participation of non-elite groups can effectively take place" (*Colombia: The Political Dimensions of Change*, Yale University Press, New Haven, 1967, p. 413. Our italics).

[2] Ethnicity and family traditions, of course, can contribute to political stability. The unsolved problem in LDCs is to get both stability and modernization. The breaking of old political and psychological commitments and the search for new ones has been termed "social mobilization." It is supposed to occur simultaneously with economic development. But we cannot say that it is necessary or sufficient or

46

livery of local services still appears to be a significant factor in national politics. However, groups with specific economic or social interests—for example, the poor, tenants, or the unemployed—vote by the same criteria as everyone else, rather than by their special interests.

We shall first examine some of the ecological and individual correlates of voter preference, dealing primarily with voting at the national level, keeping in mind, though, that the national level and the local level are interconnected.[3] Because our survey data go back only to 1963, this analysis will focus on the presidential election of 1965 and adult attitudes as revealed in 1963, 1965, and 1969 surveys. The results of this analysis will then be checked against regression models fitted to the earlier elections.

A Note on Parties and Elections

Before proceeding to the analysis of elections, we should introduce the characters and institutions of Philippine politics. The two current political parties have competed with each other since 1946. The first of these, the Nacionalista Party (NP), was founded in 1907 when a number of nationalist groups joined forces to campaign for independence. Leadership of the NP fluctuated between Manuel Quezon and Sergio Osmeña after 1916. In 1946 the NP split over the issues of wartime collaboration with the Japanese, Communism, and economic development policy. The splinter faction founded the Liberal Party (LP) and elected Manuel Roxas the first President of the Republic. Roxas soon died in office, however, and was succeeded by Elpidio Quirino. The Liberals under Quirino won the

---

both. See Karl Deutsch, "Social Mobilization and Political Development," *American Political Science Review*, 55 (September 1961), 493-514. See the elaboration by S. P. Huntington, *Political Order in Changing Societies*, Yale University Press, New Haven, 1968, pp. 34-49.

[3] Although there is some scholarly literature on Philippine politics, no systematic analysis of voting behavior yet exists. The roots of voting behavior are usually found in cultural factors and traditions, but these have not been systematically related to voting and politics. Often hypotheses about culture and politics are not tested rigorously but rest on impressions of data from small samples. The two standard works are Carl Landé, *Leaders, Factions and Parties: The Structure of Philippine Politics*, Yale University Press, New Haven, 1965; and Jean Grossholtz, *Politics in the Philippines*, Little, Brown and Co., Inc., Boston, 1964. Landé argues that Philippine voting behavior and politics are related to cultural factors, but does not test the hypotheses. Voting behavior is not discussed in the Grossholtz volume.

1949 election. In 1953 the Nacionalistas offered their nomination to Ramon Magsaysay (Quirino's defense minister), who was widely credited with discovering and applying the methods that cured the Huk insurgency. Magsaysay was elected by an enormous majority (about 67 percent of the vote). He died in office, and was succeeded by Carlos Garcia in 1957. Garcia was then elected to a full term. In 1961 Diosdado Macapagal, a Liberal who had been elected Vice President in 1957 with a larger vote than Garcia's, was elected President. Macapagal was defeated in 1965 by Ferdinand Marcos, originally a Liberal who switched to the Nacionalistas shortly before the election. In 1969 Marcos defeated Sergio Osmeña, Jr., becoming the first Philippine President to be twice-elected to a full term.[4]

Figure 6 shows the trends in percentage voter turnout and NP vote for the elections since 1946. Turnout is consistently between 70 and 80 percent. Voting at the presidential level has been fairly even with the exception of Magsaysay's lopsided victory in 1953.[5]

Analysis of Philippine elections is greatly simplified by the absence of an electoral college.[6] A candidate with a plurality wins. Unlike the case in the United States, all votes have the same value to a candidate no matter where they are cast.

Aggregate Models with Socioeconomic Variables

For the 1965 presidential campaign we specified two alternative voting models containing ethnic, political, and socioeconomic variables.[7] The general features of these models are sketched in Figure

[4] See Grossholtz, *Politics in the Philippines*, pp. 14-47, for a brief political history. For a history by Filipinos, see T. A. Agoncillo and A. M. Alfonso, *History of the Filipino People*, 2nd ed., Malaya Books, Quezon City, 1968.

[5] According to preliminary reports, Marcos received about 62 percent of the vote in 1969.

[6] See Grossholtz, *Politics in the Philippines*, p. 149, for a description of election procedures. On election day, a registered voter takes his ballot to the local polling place (the problacion—municipal capital—associated with his barrio) and *writes* in the name of his preferred candidate. There are no preprinted ballots.

After the disputed election of 1949, an independent Commission on Elections (COMELEC) was established to conduct registration of voters and to tabulate and certify outcomes. At the close of an election, votes are counted, sealed, and forwarded to COMELEC. With some lag, voting records are then compiled for the municipal, province, and city levels.

[7] The dependent variable in the regression analysis is percentage vote for specific parties or candidates. To normalize for differing populations in provinces, we have converted the dependent variables to percentages. The independent variables are cast as percentages, per capitas, or dummies with values of 1 or 0.

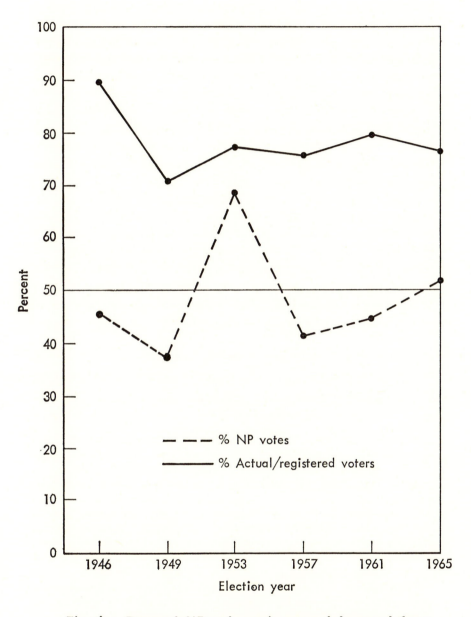

Fig. 6—Percent NP vote and percent turnout from
1946 through 1965 election years

7.[8] Both models attempt to explain the percent NP vote province by province as a function of the variables shown—percent Ilocano, percent Muslim, and so on. Each arrow shows the sign of the relationship we would expect to find between percent NP vote and the independent variable circled. These expectations are based both on the folklore of Philippine politics and on earlier studies by political scientists.

Ilocanos are alleged to constitute the most cohesive voting bloc in the Philippines whenever the candidate is an Ilocano or comes from an area near Ilocos. The NP candidate, Ferdinand Marcos, was a well-known Ilocano, so percent Ilocano should have a positive sign.[9]

Pampangans should vote for the incumbent Macapagal, a well-known Pampangan. Muslims have been alleged to constitute a well-defined ethnic and religious bloc, voting for incumbent administrations. Supposedly, the incumbent administration buys Muslim votes on a large scale in every election.[10] Muslim areas in 1965 should therefore go LP.

Mayors are an important source of political control. The mayor of a municipality is its most important official; he controls municipal resources and personnel, he is immediately visible to constituents, and he is ranked as important and influential by voters.[11] So the more NP mayors in a province, the larger we expect the NP presidential vote to be.

[8] The formulation of the "socioeconomic" model presented here was preceded by some earlier models where we were forced to use proxies for public works expenditure since there were no easily available data on public works by province. In these early models we explored the effects of unemployment. Any effect of unemployment on percent NP vote could be traced to Pampanga province, which reported 18 percent unemployed and gave Marcos only 15 percent of the vote. Much the same can be said for tenancy, so we have excluded these variables here.

[9] The Ilocano vote at Presidential level is specific to Ilocanos, not to parties. In 1953 when Ramon Magsaysay was the NP presidential candidate, the provincial mean percentage vote for Quirino, an Ilocano, was 32 percent. Quirino's mean percentage vote in heavily Ilocano areas was 47 percent. Quirino received over 90 percent of the vote in the pure Ilocano provinces.

[10] According to personal sources in the Muslim area, the flow of resources is to Muslim leaders who control votes rather than directly to the voter. Local Muslim leaders bargain with the national politicians, and voters follow the preferences of local leaders.

[11] See Mary Hollensteiner, *The Dynamics of Power in a Philippine Municipality*, Community Development Research Council, University of the Philippines, Quezon City, 1963.

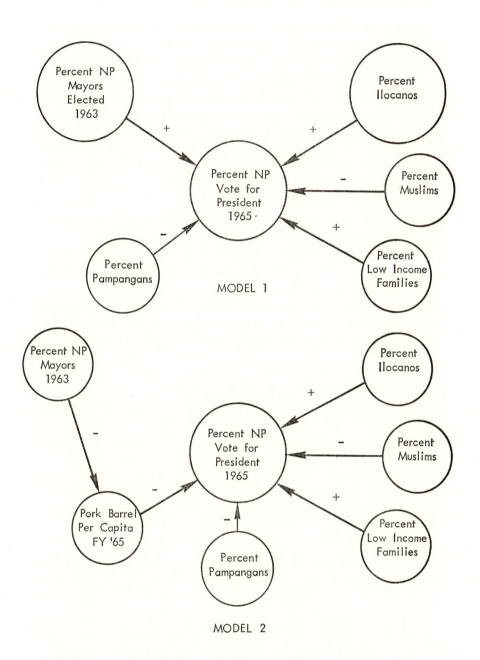

Fig. 7—Two alternative voting models

The poor in the Philippines are alleged always to vote for change. It is often claimed that the poor do not benefit enough from the economic and social structure. They therefore search for a man or a cause to alleviate their grievances. If the poor are really discontented and protest through their votes, this protest should be revealed in a strong positive relation between NP vote and "poverty" in 1965 (when the incumbent was LP).[12]

"Pork barrel"[13] is supposed to be an important determinant of voting.[14] If an incumbent administration has the means to control the allocation of public works expenditures across provinces—and whether it can is a question in the Philippines—then areas that have received more pork barrel should show their gratitude to the LP by voting against Marcos.[15]

Provinces with a larger fraction of NP mayors should receive less pork barrel from the LP administration. In Model 2, therefore, the sign of NP mayors should be negative in the pork barrel equation. The results of fitting these weighted regression models are shown in Table 22.[16] These equations indicate that the ethnicity and political control dominated the 1965 election.[17] At this level of

[12] Aggregate or ecological measures of poverty are scarce. For example, data on income distribution by province exist only for the year 1965. We have used fraction of low income families in a province—with less than 2000 pesos income—as a measure of aggregate poverty. But we can also test for a relation through Pegasus and other survey data.

[13] Every Congress passes a bill known popularly as "The Pork Barrel Bill." "Pork barrel" in this context refers to a specific, identifiable set of resources that politicians may allocate at their prerogative. However, all allocations of public works funds are subject to bargaining and political or bureaucratic coercion. See Ledivina Vidallon-Carino, *The Politics and Administration of the Pork Barrel*, Local Government Center, School of Public Administration, University of the Philippines, Quezon City, 1966.

[14] See Chapter 3.

[15] Past pork barrel, according to survey data, is more valuable to the voters than promises. Thus, we do not expect any particular relation between pork barrel *appropriations* and voting behavior even if voters were aware of the appropriation process.

[16] The reason for using weighted regression is that evaluated at the mean of all the independent variables it gives us an estimate of the national proportion for the NP plus a confidence interval, and also the coefficients have smaller variance. The weights are the ratio of voting age population of each province to the total voting age population in 1960.

[17] The models of voting behavior developed here do *not* predict who will win an election but show provincial and regional differences in voting behavior. By

TABLE 22

WEIGHTED REGRESSIONS OF ALTERNATIVE VOTING MODELS[a]

Model 1[b]	$PCT\ NPV_{65} = 37.9 + .39\ PCT\ ILOC - .31\ PCT\ PAMP - .20\ PCT\ MUS +$
	$(.04)^c \qquad\qquad (.07) \qquad\qquad (.06)$
	$.068\ LO\ INC + .19\ NP\ MAY, \qquad R^2 = .76, F = 31.0\ with\ 5,49\ D.F.$
	$(.054) \qquad (.05)$
Model 2	$PCT\ NPV_{65} = 49.7 + .36\ PCT\ ILOC - .37\ PCT\ PAMP - .24\ PCT\ MUS +$
	$(.05) \qquad\qquad (.08) \qquad\qquad (.07)$
	$.004\ LO\ INC - 1.15\ PB\ CAP, \qquad R^2 = .69, F = 21.8\ with\ 5,49\ D.F.$
	$(.057) \qquad (4.2)$
	$PB\ CAP = .38 - .0035\ NP\ MAY, \qquad R^2 = .07, F = 4.0\ with\ 1,53\ D.F.$
	$(.0018)$

NOTES:

[a] The general linear model is:

$$PCT\ NPV_{65} = 41.8 + .39\ PCT\ ILOC - .27\ PAMP - .22\ PCT\ MUS + .03\ LO\ INC +$$
$$(.04) \qquad\qquad (.08) \qquad (.06) \qquad\qquad (.05)$$
$$1.15\ PB\ CAP + .20\ NP\ MAY, \qquad R^2 = .77, F = 22.4\ with\ 7,47\ D.F.$$
$$(3.79) \qquad\quad (.05)$$

Here we postulate a political control factor via mayor and a direct pork barrel factor. It does not give results different from Model 1.

[b] $PCT\ NPV_{65}$ = Percent NP vote, 1965   LO INC = Percent of families with less
    PCT ILOC = Percent of Ilocano voters, 1960   than 2000 pesos annual in-
    PCT PAMP = Percent of Pampangan voters, 1960   come, 1965
    PCT MUS = Percent of Muslim voters, 1960   NP MAY = Percent of NP Mayors
    PB CAP = Public works per capita, FY 1965   elected in province, 1963

The data exclude chartered cities. However, the correlation between the vote by province including cities and excluding cities is .998. If we fit the models with chartered cities included, the coefficients are nearly identical in magnitude and always identical in significance.

[c] Numbers in parentheses are standard errors.

aggregation the effects of economic variables cannot be detected; all of their coefficients are insignificant. Even the role of pork barrel is undetectable at province level; the signs of the pork barrel relation in both models are as expected, but the coefficients are not significant. The relation between pork barrel and NP mayors is weak, at the margin of significance, but only about 5 percent of the variation in pork barrel can be explained. Nor is pork barrel significant in the voting equation. In both models, ethnic variables alone explain the vote.

In Pegasus, respondents claimed that help given by a candidate

pooling data for all years it might be possible to explain variation over time, but we have not attempted this.

to their area was an important factor in deciding their vote. Yet pork barrel allocations did not significantly affect the vote, according to our equation. This paradox may rest on a "cancellation effect," NP and LP pork barrel offsetting each other. Even though public works are theoretically under the control of the incumbent administration,[18] some allocations go to opposition congressmen. Regressions therefore correctly show no relation at province level. But neither side could unilaterally stop delivering pork barrel without losing votes.

Polling Results

The regression model of the 1965 election is based on highly reliable data: voting records, Census materials, reports of the Auditor General, and the like. Survey data, on the other hand, may be less reliable. We can get some estimate of the reliability of the surveys by checking information from a poll and from an election. Table 23 gives the results of a poll taken in November 1965 just before the election. The percentages for each category saying they were going to vote for the three candidates are cross-tabulated against region. We have also put the actual percentages recorded in the regions. The results of this poll appear to be fairly close to the actual outcome. We also show retrospective information from Pegasus. It is clear that a memory bias here accounts for a 10 to 20 percentage point increase in the reported vote of the winner. The pattern of the vote, however, is broadly consistent with the observed election returns. In the waning days of the campaign there seems to have been a shift from Manglapus to Marcos. At the time Marcos was the perceived winner in the mass media, and the shift from Manglapus was probably the result of a "bandwagon" effect.

[18] The reporting system in the Department of Public Works delivers highly aggregated information. It seems doubtful that incumbent decisionmakers would know with any precision when and where the pork barrel public works go. For the period 1958-1961 we have a measure of the total NP pork barrel appropriated to the provinces. The correlation between percent NP vote for President in 1961 and *appropriated* NP pork barrel per capita is —.01. On a per capita basis measures of public works correlate well only with each other. On an absolute basis provinces with greater population get more public works. On a per capita basis, appropriations are highest in wealthy provinces. Appropriations per capita for a given year correlate highly with those for earlier years suggesting constancy in allocation patterns.

54

TABLE 23

PREDICTED AND ACTUAL VOTE, BY REGION
(percent)

	November 1965 Poll				Actual				Pegasus 1969[a]			
	Maca-pagal	Mar-cos	Mang-lapus	SSR	Maca-pagal	Mar-cos	Mang-lapus		Maca-pagal	Mar-cos	Mang-lapus	SSR
Muslim[b]	51	40	9	215	57	40	4	Muslim (Cotabato, Sulu)	68	32	0	89
Mindanao (Cebuano)	51	36	13	124	48	45	8	Cebuano	24	75	1	103
Leyte[e]	56	36	8	245	47	52	2	Samar	23	75	2	52
Ilongo	46	44	10	254	46	49	5	Ilongo	29	71	0	111
Bicol	43	43	14	148	45	50	5	Bicol	22	78	0	103
Southern Tagalog	37	55	8	158	41	52	7	Tagalog	33	64	3	154
Bataan, Manila, Bulacan	33	48	19	223	28	61	12					
Central Luzon[d]	60	38	2	170	49	50	2	Pampanga	48	52	0	33
Mixed Ilocos	18	75	7	156	18	79[e]	3	Pure Ilocos	2	99	0	183
Mean percent	44	46	11		42	53	5					
Percent DK 14.35												

NOTES:

[a] Only the Pegasus regions corresponding roughly to those on the polls are shown here. Weighted percentages.

[b] This particular breakdown includes two provinces that have very low fractions of Muslims. Excluding these two, Macapagal had 60.3 percent of the vote, Marcos 36.5, and Manglapus 3.3.

[e] This area is the home of President Marcos' wife. Her family is very strong there which may account for the deviance of actual from predicted vote.

[d] How Macapagal's home province of Pampanga was weighted in the survey would be important in determining the survey outcome.

[e] In the pure Ilocano provinces Marcos received about 95 percent of the votes. If we use our regression model to predict the percentage vote for, say, the Mixed Ilocos region above we predict 77 percent for Marcos.

Ethnic Differences in Voting

Ecological regression models implicitly state, and the polls shown in Table 23 confirm, that individual political preferences vary sharply across ethnic groups. Areas with high fractions of Ilocanos then tend to show up in the regression as voting more heavily than the average for the NP candidate in 1965—in this case a well-known Ilocano.

Results from earlier surveys enable us to pursue ethnic differences in political attitudes further. The following tabulations are from the 1963 IDLARS survey cited in Chapter 3. The number of respondents in each region is small, but the results are nonetheless suggestive. The sample is designed to give regional attitudes; however, this is equivalent to ethnic attitudes in most cases.[19]

Ilocanos and Pampangans value sincerity and "keeping promises" more than other ethnic groups (Table 24). Muslims also seem to

TABLE 24

REGIONAL CRITERIA FOR "GOOD CANDIDATE," 1963
(percent)

Response	Ilocos	Pampanga	*Muslim* Cotabato and Davao	Rest of Country
Honest, humble	14	3	43	46
Patient, intelligent, good leader	30	59	31	45
Keeps promises, sincere	38	32	18	4
Helps poor	16	7	1	4
No lies, loyal to party	1	0	1	4
DK	0	0	0	2
SS	104	60	96	737

SOURCE: IDLARS 416-59-0002.
NOTE: Actual text of question: "What do you like in a candidate?"

place a higher than average value on keeping promises. Ilocanos say they like a candidate who "helps the poor." One way that a politician can keep his promises is to deliver "community develop-

[19] This particular survey did not record the mother tongue of respondents. In mixed ethnic areas such as Nueva Ecija we do not know whether we have a respondent whose mother tongue is Ilocano, Tagalog, or Pampangan. Similarly, in Cotabato in 1960 about 35 percent of the population listed their religion as Muslim but the survey under discussion did not record religion.

ment" projects before the election. The view of Ilocanos toward this activity is consistent with the high value they place on pork barrel: Ilocanos tend to view such projects as vote buying but also as "good and natural" (Table 25).[20]

Ilocanos say they turn out to vote for *their* candidate (Table 26).

TABLE 25

ATTITUDES TOWARD "COMMUNITY DEVELOPMENT" BEFORE ELECTIONS, 1963
(percent)

Response	Ilocos	Pampanga	Muslim Cotabato and Davao	Rest of Country
"Illegal," "should be prohibited," "bad," "dirty"	24	60	46	55
Brings trouble[a]	3	0	2	0
Buys vote	38	0	8	6
Good, natural	33	2	22[b]	22
DK	3	38	21	18
SS	104	60	96	737

SOURCE: IDLARS 416-59-0002.
NOTES: Actual text of question: "What can you say about the practice of engaging in 'community development' before elections?"
[a] Complete response is "Brings trouble since candidates will fight over certain projects."
[b] In Cotabato proper 28 percent of respondents give this reply.

TABLE 26

REGIONAL REASONS FOR VOTING, 1963
(percent)

Reasons Given	Ilocos	Pampanga	Muslim Cotabato and Davao	Rest of Country
Duty, privilege	15	62	81	84
My candidate	60	22	5	6
Express opinion	18	0	1	4
Family relative	6	15	7	3
No answer	1	2	1	2
NA	0	0	4	1
SS	104	60	96	737

SOURCE: IDLARS 416-59-0002.
NOTE: Actual text of question: "Do you vote? Why do you vote?"

[20] Closed political surveys in the Philippines do not usually record incomes, perhaps because of the time required to establish income from all sources. The category "socioeconomic status" based on housing type (SES) is a more accurate indicator of income than responses about income. About 32 percent of those in the lowest SES categories respond with "good and natural" compared with 23 percent for middle SES and 8 percent with high SES.

They appear to be less influenced by the abstract notions of duty and privilege.[21] Thus their greater political cynicism is matched by a higher level of direct personal identification with candidates.

These data underscore the importance of ethnic factors in Philippine politics. Ilocanos appear to be a cohesive bloc trading their votes for promise and delivery of material reward. Since other ethnic groups do not appear to be as cohesive in their voting patterns, a candidate who comes out of the Ilocos region with a very large majority stands a good chance of winning the election.

If the responses on community development are further broken down, they suggest, although weakly, that the traditional pattern of trading votes for pork barrel is most prevalent in economically stagnant areas. For example, 49 percent of Bicol, 37 percent of Ilongo, and 28 percent of Cotabato respondents also felt that "community development" was good and natural; these are traditionally depressed areas.[22] The study by the McKendrys and Guthrie cited earlier also suggests this pattern in the southern Tagalog region. They contrasted four stagnant towns with four "changing" towns and found that persons in the stagnant areas tended to have a much higher regard for traditional protective political relations than did persons in the changing areas.[23]

Later survey material on political attitudes by ethnic groups confirms that ethnic differences remain strong. Table 27 presents the Pegasus mean responses to a question concerning criteria for a presidential candidate. Ilocanos, Muslims, and Pangasinans value past aid most highly among all groups, and they rank high in their valuations of promises of aid. They also rank high on preference for a candidate who speaks their dialect. These 1969 data suggest that ethnic politics is still very important. Pegasus data yield the following analogy to our aggregate regression models. This time

[21] To a much lesser degree this is true of Pampangans, but this may be because President Macapagal was a Pampangan.

[22] In 1965 median family income for the Philippines as a whole was 1648 pesos. In Ilocos Norte it was 1095; in Iloilo and Ilongo provinces, it was 1315; in Cotabato, it was 1397 (Bureau of Census and Statistics, Special Tabulation, *Survey of Family Income and Expenditure*, 1965; courtesy of Census Director T. Mijares). For a brief description of the Bicol area, see Tillman Durdin, "Philippine Region Pursues Progress," *The New York Times*, January 19, 1969.

[23] McKendry et al., *The Psychological Impact of Social Change in the Philippines*, p. ix.

TABLE 27

MEAN RESPONSE ON CRITERIA FOR PRESIDENTIAL CANDIDATE, 1969

Criterion	Overall	Ilocos	Pampanga	Pangasinan	Tagalog	Bicol	Samar	Cebu	Ilongo	Muslim	Greater Manila
Candidate's dialect	1.31	1.61	1.27	1.64	1.16	1.57	1.34	1.29	1.14	1.59	1.13
Candidate's honesty	1.92	1.98	1.71	1.94	1.92	1.94	1.82	1.88	1.99	2.00	1.93
Candidate's policy	1.48	1.59	1.69	1.80	1.60	1.74	1.17	1.56	1.08	1.73	1.63
Compadres' and friends' opinions	.66	.79	.57	1.46	.83	.76	.37	.60	.54	1.43	.60
Candidate's past aid	1.58	1.83	1.73	1.82	1.69	1.62	1.22	1.48	1.54	1.87	1.43
Candidate's promise of aid	1.01	.97	1.20	1.41	1.17	.83	.95	1.12	.86	1.43	1.14
Candidate's party	.91	1.23	.76	1.24	.84	1.19	.67	.88	1.02	1.46	.75

NOTE: Exact text of question: "I will read to you some factors that people take into account when selecting a candidate for the Presidency of our country. In your own case do you consider this factor not important . . . somewhat important . . . or very important?" The answers were scaled 0 = not important, 1 = somewhat important, 2 = very important. Mean responses based on weighted percentages.

the notation refers to individual characteristics (figures in parentheses are standard errors):

1965 RETROSPECTIVE NP VOTE $= .61 + .31$ ILOCANO $+ .02$ PAMPANGAN

$$(.04) \qquad (.03)$$

$$- .33 \, \text{MUSLIM} + .03 \, \text{SES} + .05 \, \text{N MAY}$$

$$(.05) \qquad (.02) \qquad (.03)$$

$$R^2 = .12, F = 28 \text{ with } 5{,}1041 \text{ D.F.}$$

This is surprisingly close to the analogous ecological equation, considering the memory bias in survey data. The equation again suggests that ethnic factors are the most powerful explanations of votes with socioeconomic variables playing a lesser role.[24] Thus in the interval 1963 to 1969 there seems to have been little overall change, although as we shall show, voters more oriented toward programs than pork barrel were emerging in the urban areas.[25]

[24] Values for the independent variable are 1 if NP, 0 if LP; SES runs from 0 as highest to 4 as lowest; N MAY $= 1$ if respondent lives in a town that elected a Nacionalista mayor in 1963. We expect that N MAY should have a positive sign and it does. Using a one-tailed test it can be considered significant. If SES is considered a measure of poverty, and we expect that the poor should be voting NP, then SES is barely significant.

[25] See Chapter 5 for a discussion of the modern labor force.

TABLE 28

VOTER PREFERENCES, BY SES

(percent)

	Macapagal	Marcos	Manglapus	SSR
1. June 1964				
High	27	56	17	147
Medium	30	54	16	773
Low	31	56	13	1421
				2341
2. November 1965				
High	38	43	18	60
Medium	44	46	10	507
Low	44	46	10	754
				1321
3. 1965 Voter Preferences in 1969				
High	27	66	7	138
Medium	23	74	3	425
Low	25	74	1	514
				1077

SOURCES: June 1964: IDLARS 416-59-0003. From voters who had a preference. November 1965: IDLARS 416-59-0010. From voters who had a preference. 1965 Voter Preferences in 1969: Pegasus. Among those who say they voted in 1965. Weighted percentages.

Poverty, Tenancy, and Voting

Table 28 shows voter preferences in June 1964 and November 1965 broken out according to socioeconomic status. Voter preferences are similar across socioeconomic classes. For comparison we also show the same election viewed four years later. There is a general shift in favor of the winner, but again there is no difference by socioeconomic class.

Table 29 shows a finer breakdown of the vote by SES and region. Low and middle SES Ilocanos are overwhelmingly for Marcos. Residents of Central Luzon in these two classes are for Macapagal. In Muslim and Cebuano areas they are for Macapagal also. The poor were not voting for change; for the most part they were just

TABLE 29

1965 PRESIDENTIAL PREFERENCES, BY AREA AND SES
(percent)

	Maca-pagal	Marcos	Mang-lapus	SSR
Relatively poor (*Lower middle SES*)				
Ilocos	14	78	7	56
Central Luzon	56	44	0	95
Bataan, Manila, Bulacan	31	52	17	112
Southern Tagalog	45	51	4	51
Bicol	43	40	17	30
Ilongo	56	33	12	52
Leyte	58	35	6	62
Mindanao (Cebuano)	62	23	15	26
Muslim	56	34	10	23
All relatively poor	44	46	10	507
The poorer (*Lowest SES*)				
Ilocos	18	74	8	77
Central Luzon	66	28	6	50
Bataan, Manila, Bulacan	31	46	23	26
Southern Tagalog	31	61	8	61
Bicol	42	42	16	94
Ilongo	43	49	8	152
Leyte	54	37	9	94
Mindanao (Cebuano)	48	40	12	65
Muslim	52	40	8	135
All poorest	44	46	10	754
All SES	43	44	13	1499

SOURCE: IDLARS 416-59-0010.

61

like everyone else. Any differences that did appear within strata offset each other in the total.

It is often argued that poor tenants are a potential source of unrest, although tenancy is concentrated in only a few areas. It follows that their attitudes and voting patterns should be different from those of other voters. Table 30 shows the attitudes of tenants on Pegasus questions concerning national government. We have bro-

TABLE 30

VIEWS ON GOVERNMENT, BY TENANTS, FARMERS,
AND NONFARMERS
(percent)

	None/Few	Some	Most	SSR
1. Politicians Greedy				
Farmers (nontenants)	23	46	30	133
Tenants	7	62	31	138
Nonfarmers	16	45	39	1127
$\chi^2_1 = 33.1$ with 4 D.F. $\quad \chi^2 = 18.9$ with 4 D.F.				
All Farmers	14	55	31	271
Nonfarmers	16	45	39	1127
$\chi^2_1 = 13.0$ with 2 D.F. $\quad \chi^2 = 12.2$ with 2 D.F.				

	No	Yes	SSR
2. Get Action from Government			
Farmers (nontenants)	40	60	105
Tenants	48	52	113
Nonfarmers	50	50	1028
$\chi^2_1 = 8.18$ with 2 D.F. $\quad \chi^2 = 7.90$ with 2 D.F.			
All Farmers	44	56	218
Nonfarmers	50	50	1028
$\chi^2_1 = 4.86$ with 1 D.F. $\quad \chi^2 = 4.5$ with 1 D.F.			

	No	Yes	SSR
3. Get Equal Treatment from Government			
Farmers (nontenants)	40	60	126
Tenants	54	46	106
Nonfarmers	45	55	1010
$\chi^2_1 = 8.20$ with 2 D.F. $\quad \chi^2 = 8.25$ with 2 D.F.			
All Farmers	47	53	232
Nonfarmers	45	55	1010
$\chi^2_1 = .78$ with 1 D.F. $\quad \chi^2 = .57$ with 1 D.F.			

NOTE: Weighted percentages.

ken out tenants, farmers who are not tenants, and the rest of the sample. By collapsing the tenant category back into the farmer category we can obtain differences in rural versus urban views.

The table shows that farmers are different in one important respect from the "urban" population. They have a more *favorable* impression of the politician than the rest of the population. Relatively more of the farmers and tenants believe they can get action from the government. On equal treatment farmers and nonfarmers do not differ, but a somewhat larger fraction of tenants do not expect equal treatment; the difference is not large, but it is significant.

The expectation of unequal treatment does not seem to translate into less reliance on traditional voting criteria, however. Table 31

TABLE 31

MEAN RESPONSE ON CRITERIA FOR PRESIDENTIAL ELECTION
CANDIDATE AMONG FARMERS, TENANTS, AND NONFARMERS

Criterion	Farmers, Non-tenants	Tenants	Non-farmers	χ^2_1 with 4 D.F.	χ^2 with 4 D.F.
Dialect	1.64	1.47	1.19	104.9	89.3
Honesty	1.98	1.86	1.90	157.3	21.3
Policy	1.57	1.65	1.42	36.5	30.5
Compadres	.84	.72	.56	39.8	38.2
Past aid	1.76	1.77	1.50	99.6	69.5
Promises of aid	1.22	1.06	.94	27.0	26.1
Party	1.20	1.03	.87	53.8	38.5

NOTE: Based on weighted percentages. χ^2_1 and χ^2 refer to the underlying contingency tables.

shows the mean response on voting criteria used by tenants, farmers who are not tenants, and the rest of our sample, which is essentially urban. Tenants do not differ from other farmers in the criteria they use. They are basically the familiar criteria of dialect and past aid. There are strong differences, however, between the farm respondents and the nonfarm respondents. These differences may be seen most clearly in Table 32, where we have aggregated all the farmers and compared them with nonfarmers. Nonfarmers are much less oriented to the criteria of dialect and past aid.

As we shall see in Chapter 5, the nonfarm modern labor force has been growing rapidly. Thus, the difference we observe here between farmers and nonfarmers should have been growing in importance over the past two decades.

TABLE 32

MEAN RESPONSE ON CRITERIA FOR PRESIDENTIAL
CANDIDATE AMONG FARMERS AND NONFARMERS

Criterion	Farmers	Non-farmers	χ^2_1 with 2 D.F.	χ^2 with 2 D.F.
Dialect	1.55	1.19	86.2	74.2
Honesty	1.92	1.90	2.6	2.4
Policy	1.61	1.42	36.5	28.6
Compadres	.78	.56	25.9	28.2
Past aid	1.77	1.50	78.3	68.5
Promises of aid	1.13	.94	18.9	19.4
Party	1.12	.87	30.6	29.0

NOTE: Answers scaled (0), not important; (1) somewhat important; (2), very important. χ^2_1 and χ^2 refer to the underlying contingency tables.

Other Elections

THE 1953 ELECTION—MAGSAYSAY (NP) VERSUS QUIRINO (LP)

Earlier elections appear to have been dominated by the same considerations of ethnicity that we have found important in the 1965 election. In regression models of the elections of 1953, 1957, and 1961 much the same variables are important. The 1953 election, pitting a charismatic, popular hero, Ramon Magsaysay, against an incumbent Ilocano, Elpidio Quirino, provides another test of the ethnic components of our regression model. Here we use 1948 census data rather than 1960 data. Unfortunately we do not have exactly the same data available in the 1948 census, nor were the issues exactly the same. Tenancy was allegedly a far more powerful issue in 1953 than it was in 1965. We do not have a measure of the fraction of tenants for 1939 or 1948, but we do have the percent of farm area cultivated by tenants. The latter was used for the 1953 equation. We have the following weighted regression:[26]

$$\text{PCT NP VOTE}_{53} = 69 - .27 \text{ PCT ILOCANO}_{48} - .17 \text{ PCT MUSLIMS}$$
$$(.06) \qquad\qquad (.09)$$
$$+ .07 \text{ PCT TENANT FARM AREA}$$
$$(.07)$$
$$R^2 = .35, F = 8.1 \text{ with } 3,45 \text{ D.F.}$$

The ethnic coefficients as we now expect are important: Ilocanos vote for Ilocanos irrespective of party. Quirino's vote probably would have been higher in the mixed Ilocano provinces except that Mag-

[26] The weights are the fraction of voting age population in the province in 1948.

saysay himself was partly of Ilocano extraction. Muslims tended to vote for the incumbent administration in 1953 as well as in 1965.

The role of tenancy in the 1953 election has been disputed. Starner writes: "It is quite apparent from a comparison of the statistics . . . that there is no correlation between the distribution of Magsaysay's voting strength in 1953 and the incidence of tenancy either in the Philippines as a whole or in Central Luzon specifically."[27] Our weighted regression supports this view—provided our measure of tenancy is accurate. Starner attributes Magsaysay's relatively poor showing either to his inability to reach the peasant or to the peasant's unwillingness to listen to or believe Magsaysay's appeals. The assumption is that somehow tenants see things differently or have different interests from other Filipinos. There is no way to prove this conclusively for 1953. In 1969 we have seen that tenants do not really differ from the rest of the population in their voting criteria.

The 1957 Election—Garcia (NP) versus Yulo (LP), Manahan, and Recto

Practically all knowledgeable observers agree that Magsaysay would have been reelected. After Magsaysay's death in March 1957, Vice President Carlos Garcia, a Cebuano, succeeded him. He became the Nacionalista candidate in 1957. Arrayed against Garcia were three distinguished Senators: Yulo, a Tagalog; Manahan, an Ilocano; and Recto, also a Tagalog.

The 1953 model fitted to the 1957 election, but including Cebuanos and Tagalogs, gives the following weighted regression:[28]

$$\text{PCT NP VOTE}_{57} = 49.6 - .08 \text{ PCT ILOCANO} - .13 \text{ PCT TAGALOG}$$
$$(.06) \qquad\qquad (.04)$$
$$+ .30 \text{ PCT CEBUANO} + .01 \text{ PCT MUSLIM} - .22 \text{ PCT TENANTS}$$
$$(.04) \qquad\qquad (.10) \qquad\qquad (.08)$$
$$R^2 = .79, F = 31.9 \text{ with } 5,43 \text{ D.F.}$$

Here tenancy is significant, but the sign is anomalous. Areas with high tenancy tended to vote against Garcia—who inherited the mantle of Magsaysay. Compared with Magsaysay, one contemporary observer felt, Garcia failed to demonstrate a sense of identifica-

---

[27] Frances Lucille Starner, *Magsaysay and the Philippine Peasantry: The Agrarian Impact on Philippine Politics*, University of California Publications in Political Science, vol. 10, University of California Press, Los Angeles, 1961, p. 67.

[28] The independent variables for this election model are 1960 values, so the measure of tenancy is people rather than area.

tion with the poor in the barrios.[29] Aside from this, the model is once again purely ethnic, a battle between Tagalogs and Cebuanos.

The 1961 Presidential Election—Garcia (NP) versus Macapagal (LP)

The 1961 election does not differ in any great respect from the election we examined earlier. Again it appears to be a straight ethnic battle—Ilocanos versus Cebuanos.[30] Percent Muslim is not significant, but it might have been had we not had to exclude Lanao Sur, which is 69 percent Muslim, because data were unavailable. Percent NP governors elected in 1959 was not significant. Unfortunately we were unable to obtain data on NP mayors elected in 1959. The explanatory power of the model is somewhat less than the model for 1965 where we have data on mayors. Our equation for 1961 is:

$$\text{PCT NP VOTE}_{61} = 41.3 - .14 \text{ PCT ILOCANOS} + .21 \text{ PCT CEBUANOS}$$
$$(.05) \qquad\qquad (.03)$$
$$+ .06 \text{ PCT MUSLIMS} + .73 \text{ NP GOV}$$
$$(.08) \qquad\qquad (2.2)$$
$$R^2 = .64, F = 19.5 \text{ with } 4,44 \text{ D.F.}$$

Prospects for Performance-Oriented Politics

In the preceding sections we have tried to assess the potential appeal of national issues, programs, and performance in Philippine elections. The method we used was indirect—comparing the strength of social and economic explanations of elections with ethnic and purely political factors. In both regression analysis and survey data the latter dominate the former.[31]

Further Pegasus results tell us that the groups ranking lowest in SES use traditional criteria in selecting their candidates—honesty, of course, language, and past aid to the constituent's area. And they value the opinions of their friends more highly than do those in

---

[29] Lawrence Olson, "After Magsaysay, What?" *American University Field Staff Reports*, October 17, 1957.

[30] Macapagal, a Pampangan, won 71 percent of the vote in Ilocos; some of his success may be due to his wife's Ilocano extraction.

[31] Using different methods, H. Ando noted the same results. See "A Study of Voting Patterns in the Philippine Presidential and Senatorial Elections, 1946-1965," *Midwest Journal of Political Science*, 13 (November 1969), 567-587.

the high group. Party ranks as an unimportant criterion with all groups.

If we cross-tabulate the criteria for presidential and mayoralty candidates against occupational groups—professional, white collar, farmer, modern blue collar, and nonmodern blue collar—only a few differences from traditional criteria currently emerge. Voters in the modern labor force—noncraft manufacturing, transportation, power generation—are the single exception.[32]

If there is a voter less oriented to ethnicity and pork barrel he should be found concentrated among the young and mobile, but our analysis shows no strong difference emerging between younger and older voters.[33] If we cross-tabulate voting criteria against migrant/nonmigrant status, migrants still appear attached to the old criteria.

In general, whichever way we look at voters they prefer generalized honesty, past aid, and a candidate who speaks their dialect. No voters appear to be demanding a different kind of politics.[34] Without such a demand, it is very difficult for any politician anywhere to be an innovator. Yet politicians continue to deliver the rhetoric of social mobilization and rapid industrial development.

As far as our data take us—to early 1969—prospects for dramatic

[32] If we examine the vote for Manglapus' third party (PPP) in 1965, we can find a significant correlation ($+.27$) between PPP vote and the fraction of modern labor force in a province. Fraction of modern labor force is collinear with fraction of low income families and with unemployment rate. According to our survey data, Manglapus was relatively popular with professionals, white collar workers, and the "not gainfully employed," which are correlated with the modern labor force. And our factor analysis in Chapter 2 suggested that modern areas vote a little differently from traditional areas.

Yet the PPP vanished after 1965. Although Manglapus tried to revitalize his supporters through the formation of the Christian Social Movement, it does not, at this time, appear to be a political force.

[33] At least in 1965, young voters (21-29) had a slight preference for Macapagal. Marcos scored most heavily with those in the 30-44 age bracket (IDLARS 416-59-0003). In a nationwide survey done in 1970 students were found to hold many of the same views of the government and of officials as the rest of the population. Where there were significant differences, student opinion was generally *more* favorable. Jose P. De Jesus and Jose C. Benitez, *Sources of Social Unrest*, Citizenship and Research Foundation, Inc., Manila, 1970.

[34] Paul Hammond of Rand suggests that political and economic development often occur with social mobilization that is nationalistic, emotional, and xenophobic; but we did not ask whether people would prefer such a policy.

changes in voting behavior are hard to find. The substantive choices offered the voters, however, have not differed very much. Nonetheless, our best estimate—buttressed by the 1969 election outcome —is that the structure of electoral politics will remain roughly the same, because it satisfies the mutual needs of the participants.

The Lurching Economy

5

ALTHOUGH it is hard to find evidence of rapid political change in the Philippines, economic growth is proceeding at a respectable rate and, as we shall see, is spread broadly across the country. Paradoxically, though, the image of the Philippines as a nation muddling along is drawn at least as much from dissatisfaction with the performance of the economy as it is from criticism of the political system. Criticism centers on high unemployment, an allegedly inadequate rate of growth of GNP accompanied by an exploding population, the erratic lurching of the economy, and the periodic balance of payments difficulties. In the face of such problems the government appears to hesitate and vacillate.

Much of the criticism, however, reflects little more than the realization that the country is poor. By American standards, most people *are* poor, badly housed, and badly fed. The population *is* growing rapidly, and unemployment *is* higher than in developed countries. Income *is* distributed very unequally by the standards of Europe and North America; upperclass homes contrast sharply with squatters' shacks not far away. To deplore these conditions is easy; it does not, however, contribute much to the design of policy.

The resources that the government can command—both financial and administrative—are limited. To allocate those resources effectively, policymakers need to be able to sort out the problems that must be attacked today from those that can wait a year, a decade, or a generation. If every aspect of the nation's poverty is taken to represent a crisis, then this sorting out is impossible.

Although proclamations of crisis are common, it is unusual for them to be accompanied by specific programs. Usually the problem is seen as justifying a call for fundamental reform when, in fact, some specific incremental measures could cope with the problem. But devising a measure tailored to a specific situation is difficult unless the situation itself is well understood.

"Well understood" is vague language. When is a problem understood well enough that a policymaker can decide intelligently? The answer obviously depends on what the decision is. GOSPLAN requires more detailed information on the functioning of the Soviet economy than the Council of Economic Advisers needs to suggest U.S. macro-economic policy. Sensible policymakers may do well with only modest information.[1] So we must be careful about making a priori judgments that the information available for decisions is "adequate" or "inadequate."

Nonetheless, the problem of improving the flow of organizational intelligence and tightening the articulation of information and analysis with policymaking appears to be a necessary but not sufficient condition for improving the performance of the Philippine government. Since this is not a proposition that can be tested a priori, we shall examine several areas—unemployment, stagnation, the unevenness of growth—that are alleged to be major problems and determine whether fine-grained analysis would change perceptions, toss up politically feasible alternatives, or squelch proclamations of crisis.

As we shall see, problems do look different when they are examined closely. Sharpened perceptions, however, are not likely to change the behavior of the Philippine political system substantially. As we saw in Chapters 3 and 4, the Philippine political system satisfies the needs of the participants. It is not enough that people and politicians understand their problems better. If votes continue to be determined by ethnic patterns and the delivery of favors and jobs, we should not be surprised to find politicians spending little time addressing more general issues.

The Image and Structure of Unemployment

THE IMAGE OF UNEMPLOYMENT

Rampant unemployment is a constant theme in evaluations of the Philippine economy. A recent report of the Congressional Economic Planning Office, in a catalogue of the ills of the country, called attention to a "deteriorating unemployment situation which now finds one million of the country's labor force fully unemployed and

[1] For general arguments that decisionmakers can, do, and *should* function without attempting to gather complete information, see David Braybrooke and Charles E. Lindblom, *A Strategy of Decision*, The Free Press, Glencoe, 1963. For an empirical study of successful use of crude information, see John E. Koehler, *Economic Policymaking with Limited Information: The Process of Macro-Control in Mexico*, The Rand Corporation, RM-5682-RC, August 1968.

approximately seven million of said labor force in a condition of underemployment and disguised unemployment."[2]

The problem is not new. Former President Macapagal noted in his memoirs: "Unemployment has been ominously serious in the Philippines for too long a period. The employment opportunities are unable to catch up with the increase in the labor force. The youth come out of colleges and universities only to join the "intellectual unemployed." A total of one and a half million unemployed and over two million underemployed would be a fair figure out of the divergent and inaccurate statistics on unemployment."[3] The response of the Macapagal administration to the unemployment crisis was the Emergency Employment Administration, which expired under a cloud of scandal in 1966 after putting thousands to work cutting grass and raking leaves before the 1965 election.

The Magsaysay administration, too, confronted the crisis. Estimating that approximately *one-half* of the Philippine labor force was unemployed, Magsaysay promised that the criterion of the economic policy of his administration would be the reduction of unemployment.[4]

Filipinos' image of unemployment is a mixture of Nurkse, Agee, and Dickens: a family's breadwinner tramps the streets of Manila looking in vain for work; young men just out of college and high school, having searched for jobs for months without success, succumb to left-wing rabble-rousers; farmers, having nothing to do except at planting and harvest, sit idly most of the year, gossiping, smoking, grooming their birds for Sunday's cockfight. But such images, by and large, are inaccurate. That they are inaccurate could have been known more than a decade ago.

THE STRUCTURE OF UNEMPLOYMENT

There is no shortage of raw data on unemployment. Since 1956 the Bureau of the Census and Statistics (BCS) has conducted large sample surveys of households twice every year. The sample design has been judged to be quite good, although there have evidently

[2] Quoted in *The Manila Times*, February 22, 1969, p. 11-a.

[3] Diosdado Macapagal, *A Stone for the Edifice*, Mac Publishing House, Manila, 1968, p. 189.

[4] See Frank Golay, *The Philippines: Public Policy and National Economic Development*, Cornell University Press, Ithaca, 1963, p. 227.

been problems with maintaining control of the field staff.[5] Defects notwithstanding, the surveys are a rich source of information on the labor force and could have helped to determine who the unemployed are, where they are, and what characteristics they have.[6] If the unemployed are mostly urban females older than 40, a program of construction of feeder roads in the wilds of Bukidnon will obviously have little impact on unemployment. If unemployment is concentrated in rural areas far from Manila, promoting industries in Rizal Province is not a sensible direct attack on the problem.

Unemployment in the Philippines is not a formless, general problem of all areas and all types of people; it is a very specific problem heavily concentrated in particular demographic groups. Table 33 shows who the unemployed are, decomposing the aggregate unemployment figure into more specific demographic categories. In each cell the numerator is the number of "totally unemployed," the denominator is the number of people in the labor force with those characteristics. The third figure in the cell is the numerator as a percentage of the denominator, the rate of unemployment of that part of the labor force. For example, the last square in the bottom row refers to young (ages 10-24) urban males who have previously worked for at least two weeks ("experienced"). There are 654,000 young, experienced, urban males in the labor force, of whom 43,000 were totally unemployed (6.6 percent) in the survey week in May 1968. (Since all of the "inexperienced labor force" is by definition unemployed, no percentages are given in the blocks for that part of the labor force.)

As the table shows, most of the unemployed have never held a job before. This is not terribly surprising since nearly 75 percent of the unemployed are under 25 years of age and over half are under 20. Nearly half of the unemployed are women, and half of the unemployed women are really girls under 20. Over half of all *rural* unemployed (272,000 out of 511,000) are females.

Even looking at inexperienced unemployed aged 10-24 overstates

---

[5] On the sample design and execution see Burton T. Oñate, *Estimation of Population and Labor Force in the Philippines*, International Rice Research Institute, Journal Series No. 43 (revised, 1966); Emmanuel Levy, *Review of Economic Statistics in the Philippines*, Interim Report B, World Bank Resident Mission, Manila, May 1964 (mimeo), pp. 46-48.

[6] We should note, too, that BCS has usually presented some analysis and discussion of the structure of unemployment with its published statistics.

The Structure of Unemployment, 1968

Total
7.5%
$\dfrac{1022}{13529}$

Rural
5.4%
$\dfrac{511}{9420}$

Urban
12.4%
$\dfrac{511}{4109}$

Rural branch:

Female
8.1%
$\dfrac{272}{3344}$

Male
3.9%
$\dfrac{239}{6076}$

Female — Old
4.6%
$\dfrac{90}{1958}$

Female — Young
13.1%
$\dfrac{182}{1386}$

Male — Old
1.4%
$\dfrac{49}{3624}$

Male — Young
7.7%
$\dfrac{190}{2452}$

Old (Female): Inexp. 36 / Exp. 2.8% $\dfrac{54}{1922}$

Young (Female): Inexp. 121 / Exp. 4.7% $\dfrac{60}{1265}$

Old (Male): Inexp. 16 / Exp. 0.9% $\dfrac{34}{3608}$

Young (Male): Inexp. 133 / Exp. 2.4% $\dfrac{56}{2319}$

Urban branch:

Female
13.2%
$\dfrac{213}{1612}$

Male
11.9%
$\dfrac{298}{2497}$

Female — Old
7.2%
$\dfrac{67}{932}$

Female — Young
21.5%
$\dfrac{146}{680}$

Male — Old
4.4%
$\dfrac{73}{1661}$

Male — Young
26.9%
$\dfrac{225}{836}$

Old (Female): Inexp. 38 / Exp. 3.1% $\dfrac{28}{894}$

Young (Female): Inexp. 125 / Exp. 3.8% $\dfrac{21}{555}$

Old (Male): Inexp. 25 / Exp. 2.9% $\dfrac{48}{1636}$

Young (Male): Inexp. 182 / Exp. 6.6% $\dfrac{43}{654}$

SOURCE: Tabulations of the May 1968 BCS Labor Force Survey done at Rand.
NOTE: Absolute numbers are in thousands.

Total young, inexperienced unemployed = 571

the magnitude of the unemployment problem somewhat. Table 34 shows a finer breakdown by age groups. About 12 percent of

TABLE 34

INEXPERIENCED UNEMPLOYED, BY AGE, MAY 1968
(thousands)

Age	Male	Female
10-14	55	35
15-19	162	122
20-24	98	89
25+	41	75

SOURCE: Tabulations of the May 1968 BCS Labor Force Survey done at Rand.

all unemployed are less than 15 years old. Unemployed children are not ordinarily defined as a major social problem.

So far, we have merely followed the definitions of "employment" and "labor force" used by the Philippine BCS. But unemployment is an elusive concept in an LDC. The BCS definitions match those used in developed countries: the unemployed have no job at all and are either actively looking for a job or are not looking because they believe no jobs are available. In a developed country, where economic activity is organized into visible, formal structures, application of this definition divides the population into two categories that have fairly well-defined implications for individual welfare: the employed have a regular income; the unemployed do not. In an LDC much economic activity is informal and irregular. If a man spends a few days tending his fields, a few days weaving nipa mats, a few days idle, is he to be regarded as employed or unemployed? The application of the BCS definition places him into the category "employed."

The conceptual difficulties are most acute when one measures the inexperienced unemployed. Half of those assigned to this group qualify although they are not looking for jobs. They give as their reason for not searching that they believe no jobs are available or that they have no backer, no recommendation, no one to approach, and so on. It would be possible for someone to spend considerable time in the category "inexperienced unemployed" without either finding a job or hunting for one. Such a person may move in and out of the labor force without any intervening period of employment. That this must be the case with many people is indicated by the size of the pool of inexperienced unemployed and the length of time those who hunt for jobs say they have been looking. In 1968 the labor force probably did not grow by more than 4 percent—about 600,000. Our data show 571,000 inexperienced unemployed. On the average, the inexperienced unemployed have spent less than eight weeks looking for work as measured in both the May and October *Survey* rounds.[7] If the length of search and the number of unemployed were "steady state" levels, the labor force would have to be growing much more rapidly than it is. So movement out of the labor force from the category "inexperienced unemployed" must be substantial—movement to marriage, to helping with housework, to school, and the like. Such desultory participation in the labor force is an available option since only 3 percent of the inexperienced unemployed are heads of households. Conversely, some of the group may be delaying household formation because of failure to find jobs.

In short, unemployment in the Philippines does not fit the usual metaphor. It is not formless and general; rather it is concentrated in quite specific groups of the population. Furthermore, many of the inexperienced unemployed have but an ambiguous commitment to the labor force, and the extended family system shields them from the impact of joblessness.

The problem of seasonally unemployed farmers is likewise ambiguous. Most of the emergency employment measures—road construction and such—have been aimed ostensibly at the problem of putting them to work usefully. Table 35 shows a decomposition of the underemployed by age, sex, and urban or rural residence. Most of the really seriously underemployed (working less than 20 hours per week and wanting more work) are rural females. The underemployed who are already working more than 20 hours per week cannot be considered to be available for full-time work. The most striking aspect of underemployment is that most of those who want more work are already working 40 hours or more per week. Of all rural males in the labor force, 16.1 percent fall into this category. This is hardly consistent with the image of farmers loafing away the slack season.

[7] The median number of weeks the inexperienced unemployed have spent looking for work depends in part on the relation between the end of the school year and the date of the *Survey* round. In 1965 and 1966 both the May and October *Survey* rounds showed a median on the order of 5.5 to 7.7 weeks. Our tabulations of the May 1968 *Survey* show a median of four weeks.

TABLE 35

UNDEREMPLOYMENT, 1967

(thousands wanting more work by hours worked)

	Rural	Urban		Rural	Urban
Working less than 20 hours			*Working 20-29 hours*		
Male					
Number	146	49		265	52
Percent	2.4	2.0		4.4	2.1
Female					
Number	240	63		229	42
Percent	7.2	3.9		6.8	2.6
Working 30-39 hours			*Working 40 hours and over*		
Male					
Number	300	75		976	364
Percent	4.9	3.0		16.1	14.6
Female					
Number	194	45		164	110
Percent	5.8	2.8		4.9	6.8

NOTE: Percent in this table refers to fraction of labor force with the specified attribute; for example, of the 6,076,000 rural males in the labor force, 146,000 (2.4 percent) work less than 20 hours a week and want more work.

The image of rural underemployment is clearly a stereotype drawn both from the Philippine intellectual tradition and the writings of professional economists. Rizal himself wrote a series of essays on *The Indolence of the Filipino,* and even contemporary intellectuals still take pains to explain the laziness of the Filipino peasant in terms of the deadening effect of the colonial past. But the intellectuals are explaining too much. The image is simply inaccurate.

Although he may not be busy farming all of the year, the rural Filipino engages in many supplementary activities: nipa mat weaving, tailoring, petty trading, and a host of other such occupations. The 1965 *Survey of Income and Expenditure* shows that the typical rural household in the Philippines has 3.1 different sources of income.[8] This is an understatement of the real range of activities since, for example, each individual in the household may receive

[8] Taken from tabulations of 1965 *Survey.* The count excludes rental value of owner-occupied homes, pensions, gifts, and other nonfactor income. This broad range of rural activities is confirmed in various anthropological studies. McKendry et al., *The Psychological Impact,* pp. 123-125.

"nonagricultural wage and salary income" from more than one activity.[9] Here, too, the details of reality cast doubt on the metaphor.

THE POLITICS OF THE UNEMPLOYED

We have been applying the strict BCS definition of unemployment in the preceding analysis. Filipinos, evidently, do not think in terms of such a strict definition of unemployment. As we saw above, the rate of "unemployment" measured by BCS definition was 7.5 percent in May 1968. The Pegasus survey asked the question, "How many people are there in the household willing to work but jobless?" The tabulated answers to this question imply an "unemployment" rate of about 38 percent.[10] Evidently the Pegasus respondents took everyone who did not have a regular, well-defined job to be "jobless."[11] This, of course, includes many people who are, by Philippine standards, far from destitute, so unemployment measured this way does not yield immediate conclusions about economic welfare.

The large difference between the strict definition of unemployment and the common view may explain why Philippine politicians see employment as an important issue, even though officially measured unemployment does not appear to be a widespread and mount-

[9] The May 1957 *Survey* found that 15 percent of rural households engaged in one or more "home industries" and that each such household produced on the average about 130 pesos of output. See *The Philippine Statistical Survey of Households Bulletin*, Department of Commerce and Industry, Series No. 6, Manila, June 1960. This range of rural activities suggests that much of the debate among economists on the existence of real surplus rural labor is beside the point. Even if agricultural output were unaffected by the withdrawal of a portion of the rural labor force, it is unlikely that these supplementary activities—which clothe, house, and equip a large fraction of the population—would continue at their previous level. In this case the debates of economists have obscured rather than clarified the real issues. For a theoretical discussion of the role of nonagricultural production in development, see Stephen Hymer and Stephen Resnick, "A Model of an Agrarian Economy with Nonagricultural Activities," *American Economic Review*, 59 (September 1969), 493-506. See also Bent Hansen, "Employment and Wages in Rural Egypt," *American Economic Review*, 59 (June 1969), pp. 298-313.

[10] The respondents were also asked, "How many people are there in the household with jobs?" This unemployment rate of 38 percent is calculated by dividing the number given as jobless by the sum of the number jobless and the number with jobs.

[11] McKendry et al., *The Psychological Impact*, suggest that, although intermittent employment is common in the Philippines, their respondents tended to view employment as "an either-or affair" causing considerable confusion in reports of employment status.

ing economic problem. Unemployment may still be a political problem if the unemployed are alienated and strongly dissatisfied with the "system."

We saw above (Chapter 4) that officially measured unemployment did not appear to be a significant determinant of voting in the 1965 election. One possible reason for the absence of any political manifestation of unemployment is that most of the unemployed, measured officially, are too young to vote.

A large fraction of the voting-age population *perceive* themselves to be unemployed, but they appear not to be alienated and dissatisfied. By and large the opinions of the self-perceived unemployed are much like the opinions of the rest of the population. In the cases where there are significant differences between the opinions of the two groups, the unemployed respond *more* favorably toward the government and politicians than do the employed. Tabulations of the Pegasus questions on the importance of various national problems show no difference between the employed and the unemployed except that the unemployed are less concerned about the treatment of minority groups and about crime.[12] When questioned on their impressions of politicians, the unemployed responded more often that they thought politicians were honest, hardworking, nationalistic, and an example to follow, and less often that they felt politicians were corrupt.

It is possible that the large number of housewives who appear in the category "unemployed" might be masking some significant differences in these tabulations. When we eliminated female respondents from the sample, all of the significant differences in views on national problems and perceptions of politicians disappeared. The opinions of unemployed men are indistinguishable from the opinions of employed men.

Do the unemployed value government development activities more highly than the employed? The differences are not striking. Both the unemployed and employed feel that government activities

[12] These are questions 1a through 1f of Pegasus. See Appendix A for text. Ignoring crime and minority treatment, the largest χ^2 derived in testing for a difference between the employed and unemployed was only 4.6 with 2 degrees of freedom, which does not show a significant difference between the two groups even below the .90 level of confidence. On the treatment of minority groups, 43.5 percent of the unemployed responded that it was a very important problem versus 54.3 percent of the employed. On crime, the corresponding percentages were 59.7 and 67.0.

providing employment are very important; but the unemployed do not reply more strongly on this point. The unemployed men do, however, place significantly more value on building roads, which is the traditional manner of providing supplemental government employment. On building schools, which is another activity used to provide rural jobs, the two groups do not differ (see Table 36).

TABLE 36

VIEWS ON THE ORDER OF IMPORTANCE OF GOVERNMENT ACTIVITIES, BY EMPLOYED AND UNEMPLOYED MEN
(row percentages)

	4[a]	3	2	1[b]
1. Building Schools[c]				
Unemployed	9	16	35	40
Employed	10	17	34	39
$\chi^2_1 = .58$ with 3 D.F. $\chi^2 = .51$ with 3 D.F.				
2. Building Roads[c]				
Unemployed	29	29	32	11
Employed	36	30	26	8
$\chi^2_1 = 6.19$ with 3 D.F. $\chi^2 = 6.5$ with 3 D.F.				
3. Providing Employment[c]				
Unemployed	32	13	13	42
Employed	20	11	20	49
$\chi^2_1 = 18.71$ with 3 D.F. $\chi^2 = 18.2$ with 3 D.F.				

NOTES: Actual text of question: "Here are some activities of our government. Which of these do you feel is the most important to you and your family? Which is the next one? And after that?"

[a] Least important.

[b] Most important.

[c] SSR for 1, 2, 3: 452 unemployed, 642 employed. Weighted percentages.

The employed and unemployed both say they base their votes for president on the same considerations: honesty, language, and past help given to their area in roughly that order. There are no significant differences between the two groups.[13] Unemployment does not appear to underlie any political crisis. There is no evidence that the unemployed are alienated from Philippine politics, or angry, or even that they are demanding some special attention to their problem.[14]

[13] Based on questions 6a-6g on Pegasus. See Appendix A for text of the questions.

[14] This appears to apply to the unemployed as measured by *both* definitions. Unemployment, according to the official measure, is heavily concentrated among the

The apparent failure of the unemployed to articulate any demands for special programs and the fact that unemployment is concentrated among the nonvoting young suggest also that the government is unlikely to do anything about unemployment except, perhaps, to continue the old pattern of expanding road-building around election time. In part, this reflects a failure of the political information system: the self-perceived unemployed do not draw any particular attention to themselves or to their problem. They think the government should provide employment, but so does everyone else. They think the government should build roads, and the government does build roads. They do not, however, form a readily definable group consistently demanding some special policy response from the political system.

The unemployment of the young and inexperienced is an ambiguous problem. In part, it appears to be a result of the delay between leaving school and finding a job. Programs aimed at reducing this delay—job counseling, better information on availability of jobs, and the like—might significantly reduce the officially measured rate of unemployment. This kind of specific solution, however, is not likely to be tossed up in political debate in the Philippines.

Economic Growth: Pace and Pattern

THE AMBIGUITY OF AGGREGATE DATA

Most foreign judgments that the Philippine economy is only a mediocre performer are based on aggregate economic statistics—when they are based on any data at all. Filipinos themselves have, of course, other sources of information: the farmer knows the price he gets for his crop and what he pays for his purchases; the businessman knows how his business is faring; the politician can see if the country appears prosperous. Foreigners, however, are forced to rely on summary statistics: GNP, population, balance of payments, and the like. The Philippine government generates all of the standard statistics and reports them to the UN and IMF, who duly reproduce the data in their statistical publications.

Aggregate economic statistics also shape *Filipinos'* perceptions of their country. The rate of growth of GNP is announced in news-

---

young, who were excluded by the Pegasus sample design. The earlier survey data cited in Chapter 4 suggests, however, that the young in the labor force differ little from the rest of the population. See above, p. 67.

paper articles and appears in the rhetoric of politicians and high-level bureaucrats. Filipino economists write for the general press explaining why the rate of growth of GNP is not high enough and what policies should be adopted to raise it.

The inaccuracy of Philippine national accounts has long been a subject of public controversy. In the late 1950s and early 1960s criticism centered on the plausibility of the investment magnitudes produced by the National Economic Council (NEC). Drawing on special surveys and the examination of financial data, several studies demonstrated that the official estimates of capital formation were undoubtedly understated.[15] A report by a member of the World Bank resident mission in Manila went further and concluded that the accounts were so inaccurate (both in level and annual changes) as to be "useless for most purposes of analysis and projection."[16] In 1968 an open controversy between the NEC and a group from the University of the Philippines and the BCS, over the input-output tables each had produced, cast further doubt on the validity of the official estimates.[17] The controversy produced articles and editorials in the local press. In an article in *The Philippines Herald*, Bernardo G. Bantegui, director of the statistical branch of the NEC, protested that the NEC was doing a good job and that such "ad hoc pilot studies" should not be used "to harm the established orderly system of statistics which economists, bankers and businessmen could use with continuing confidence."[18] *Business Day* carried articles and

[15] See Clarence L. Barber, "National Income Estimates in the Philippines," *The Philippine Economic Journal*, 4, no. 1 (1965), 66-67; Ruben Trinidad, "An Inquiry into the Sources and Methods of National Income Accounting in the Philippines," M.A. thesis, University of the Philippines, Quezon City, August 1958, and also his "Some Proposed Improvements in the Estimation of Capital Formation in the Philippines," *The Statistical Reporter*, 4 (April 1960), 28-40; David Cole, *Growth and Financing of Manufacturing in the Philippines*, University of the Philippines, Institute of Economic Development and Research, Quezon City, 1963; R. W. Hooley, "A Critique of Capital Formation Estimates in Asia with Special Reference to the Philippines," *The Philippine Economic Journal*, 3, no. 2 (1964), 114-129, and *Saving in the Philippines, 1951-1960*, University of the Philippines, Institute of Economic Development and Research, Quezon City, 1963; Gerardo P. Sicat, "On the Accuracy of the Philippine National Accounts," *Philippine Review of Business and Economics* (October 1964); Ramon B. Cardenas, "A Re-estimation of the Philippine National Accounts, CY 1953-1963: A Description and Evaluation of the Alternative Estimating Methodology," M.A. thesis, Cornell University, Ithaca, June 1967.

[16] Levy, *Review of Economic Statistics*, p. 7.

[17] See Appendix D for details.

[18] June 19, 1968, p. 20.

editorials on the conflict for two weeks, complaining, "along the business cocktail circuit, the joke now goes: 'You don't like the figures you get, go to another office.' "[19]

As Appendix D shows, NEC did in fact undertake revisions to take account of some of the criticisms, but these look more like attempts to fend off criticism than real improvements. Even after the revisions and improvements there remains a great deal of uncertainty about the precise magnitude of Philippine GNP and its rate of growth. Within the range of uncertainty, NEC lies on the low side of the range with respect to both level and long-run rate of change.

Even though the defects of the accounts are well known, recent interviews of economic decisionmakers indicate that they rely on the national accounts when making judgments about the state of the economy (see Table 37). Political statements about the condition

TABLE 37

ECONOMIC DATA USED BY POLICYMAKERS

Type of Information	Order of Response			
	First	Second	Third	Fourth
National accounts	6	1	1	1
Price indexes	1	3	3	4
Balance of payments	5	3	2	1
Production indexes	1	2	2	1
Public debt	0	1	1	0
Foreign exchange holdings	2	1	0	0
Other data	3	4	2	3

SOURCE: See Appendix E.

of the economy often include a long list of percentage increases. But if policymakers really believed that the data made a difference to real decisions, would they view the known uncertainty of the data with equanimity? If the data are important, the uncertainty of the data must a fortiori be vital. But when asked what new data or improvements in the old data they most desired, none responded specifically that he wanted the uncertainties in the national accounts to be resolved (see Table 38). In fact, most of the responses were simply diffuse requests for "better" or "faster" data.

The inference that is usually drawn from the national accounts is that the Philippine economy is only a mediocre performer. If we

[19] See Jess Estanislao, "Divergent Estimates," *Business Day*, vol. 2, no. 17, June 13, 1968, p. 12, and "A Contradiction in Figures," vol. 2, no. 19, June 20, 1968, p. 8, and editorial, "A Statistical Joke," same issue, p. 10.

TABLE 38
ECONOMIC DATA DESIRED BY POLICYMAKERS

| | | Order of Response | |
Information Desired	First	Second	Third
"Better everything"	5	1	0
"Faster everything"	1	0	0
Better credit data	1	0	0
Anticipations data	2	0	1
Unification of statistical system	6	1	0
Other	6	1	0

SOURCE: See Appendix E.

examine some of the underlying data in detail, the case becomes quite ambiguous.

MEASURES OF THE GROWTH OF MANUFACTURING

Table 39 presents various estimates of the growth of manufacturing between 1960 and 1966.[20] An examination of the manufacturing

TABLE 39
DATA AMBIGUITY: ALTERNATIVE ESTIMATES OF THE
GROWTH OF MANUFACTURING, 1960-1966

	1960	1966	Rate of Growth Percent per Year 1966/1960
		Current Prices	
NDP in manufacturing (NEC National Accounts, $ millions)	2141	3472	8.4
Census value added (Survey of Manufactures, $ millions)	1763	3097	9.9
		Constant Prices	
NDP in 1955 prices (NEC National Accounts, $ millions)	1791	2346	4.6
CBP index of the physical volume of production in manufacturing	150.5	263.7	9.8
		Employment	
Employment in manufacturing (Survey of Manufactures, thousands)	249	328	4.7
Employment in manufacturing (Labor Force Survey; thousands)[a]	1069	1326	3.6

NOTE: [a] The figure 1,113,000 is the official estimate based on the May 1960 Labor Force Survey. The 1960 Census figure for employment in manufacturing is only 838,000. With different interviewers and slightly different concepts, we can arrive at a significantly different number. If we took the 1960 Census figure as the base the rate of growth of employment in manufacturing would be 7.9 percent.

[20] This spans as much of the period of "stagnation of manufacturing" as is possible with the data.

83

sector is especially relevant since the slow growth of this sector is most often cited as the reason for the disappointing performance of the country. As the rates of change show, the national accounts are conservative. The Central Bank index is known to be biased downward because it is based on a fixed sample of "cooperating firms" concentrated in Manila.[21] There is considerable evidence that the growth of manufacturing outside the Manila area has been substantial since 1960.[22] Yet the national accounts' constant price series lies *below* the Central Bank data. Although the rate of change of employment in manufacturing measured in the *Survey of Manufactures* is similar to that shown in the *Labor Force Survey*, the levels are vastly different. The gap between the two employment estimates represents workers employed in very small firms; although such small-scale employment has grown rapidly, the output of these workers has never been measured.[23]

We cannot conclude unambiguously that manufacturing is growing very slowly. We know that the manufacturing estimates are ambiguous because we have multiple data sources. Would these sources reveal the same ambiguity in other sectors? Closer examination of the labor force data suggests strongly that the Philippine economy has actually been progressing quite rapidly.

ALTERNATIVE MEASURES OF GROWTH: THE MODERN LABOR FORCE (MLF)

Ultimately the process of economic development implies a shift of the center of gravity of an economy from agriculture and craft activities to more "modern" activities.[24] The theoretical formulations of development models are usually vague on how this shift is to be measured. Nonetheless, the concepts must refer to something like a shift from relatively casual, perhaps intermittent activity performed with the aid of little capital to activity performed with more capital equipment and more formal organization; that is, performed in something approximating a modern business establishment. We

---

[21] See Levy, *Review of Economic Statistics*, pp. 42-44.

[22] See Table 42. See also Malcolm Treadgold and R. W. Hooley, "Decontrol and the Redirection of Income Flows: A Second Look," *The Philippine Economic Journal*, 6, no. 2 (1967), 115.

[23] See Appendix D.

[24] John C. H. Fei and Gustave Ranis, *The Labor Surplus Economy*; and R. R. Nelson, "A 'Diffusion' Model of International Productivity Differences in Manufacturing Industry," *American Economic Review*, 58 (December 1968), 1219-1247.

have no such current measure of economic activity in the Philippines, but we can approach it by manipulation of reported data on employment by industry and class of worker.

The problem of data can be defined in the following way: we need the sort of information on employment that could be found in an economic census. As of this writing, the *1967 Economic Census of the Philippines* is still unavailable. We do, however, have the May 1968 *Labor Force Survey*. We can extract the appropriate workers from the *Labor Force Survey* to approximate those who would be engaged in modern activities as measured in a proper economic census.

The economic censuses are drawn from the universe of business establishments; they count activities that take place in regular, visible establishments but omit informal and craft activities taking place in households. Economic census definitions, therefore, correspond approximately to what we mean by modern activities. Population censuses and labor force surveys, on the other hand, are drawn from the universe of households and classify craft and modern workers in the same industries. For example, weavers of nipa mats are placed in manufacturing by the population census but are simply omitted from the economic censuses because they rarely pursue their occupation in well-defined establishments. The nipa mat weavers, however, will probably be listed as "self-employed" in the population census, while factory workers will be "employees." Workers in public utilities and other highly visible activities should probably *all* be counted as modern; the electric utility industry, for example, will probably not contain any craft firms.

Thus, by counting all workers in "visible" industries and wage and salary workers in industries with a large craft sector, we should be able to estimate the *Economic Census* MLF, using *Population Census* data. As Table 40 shows, it is possible to achieve a reasonably close match between the estimates of MLF derived from the two sources.

Since we were able to match the MLF derived from the 1960 *Population Census* with the MLF derived from the 1961 *Economic Census* by choosing appropriate combinations of industry and class of worker, we ought to be able to approximate an economic census measure of MLF by choosing the same combinations of industry and class of worker from the labor force surveys. We can, moreover, produce a series of such estimates from the various labor force

TABLE 40

CORRESPONDENCE BETWEEN ECONOMIC AND
POPULATION CENSUSES:
EMPLOYMENT, BY INDUSTRY, MODERN LABOR FORCE

Industry	1960 Population Census	1961 Economic Census[d]	
Forestry and logging	53,740[a]	28,083	
Mining and quarrying	23,610[b]	25,218	
Manufacturing	346,520[a]	358,799	
Construction	36,658[c]	20,751	
Electricity, gas, water	12,770[b]	13,104	
Commerce	160,520[a]	364,963	(252,901)[e]
Transport, storage	162,080[a]	129,377	
Communication	4,000[b]	8,393	
MLF	799,898	948,688	(836,626)[f]

NOTES:

[a] Counts only "Wage and salary" workers.

[b] Counts "Total employed persons" which included employees, employers, self-employed, and unpaid family workers.

[c] Counts only "Heavy construction, total employed persons."

[d] *Economic Census* definition: "Number of persons engaged, payroll period nearest November 15." The *Economic Census* did not count the sector "finance, insurance, and real estate." The *Population Census* "commerce" category showed 23,580 workers for this sector, so this number was added to the *Economic Census* "commerce" figure yielding the total shown.

[e] Of the 365,000 "persons engaged" in the *Economic Census* estimate for commerce, 112,000 are working owners and unpaid family workers in sari-sari stores, small neighborhood grocery and general stores. Such employment, although measured in the *Economic Census*, does not correspond to what we mean to include in the MLF, so here it is excluded.

[f] *Economic Census* MLF total with commerce adjusted as explained in footnote e.

surveys available. These estimates are shown in Figure 8 together with estimates for 1948 and 1938, which are roughly, but not exactly, comparable. The growth of the MLF since 1960 has been quite rapid; this has been the period of alleged stagnation. By our measure this period looks like one of rapid transformation.

Although it appears that aggregate growth has been substantial, change has proceeded at very different rates across the country. This is true not only when measured by factor scores, as in Chapter 2, but also when measured directly by estimates of median family income by region. Figure 9 shows the growth of median family income by census region over the period 1956-1965. Some regions have grown very rapidly, while others have stagnated.

The patterns of economic change across the country may have consequences for the shape of politics. We shall see below that the political attitudes of the MLF appear to differ somewhat from

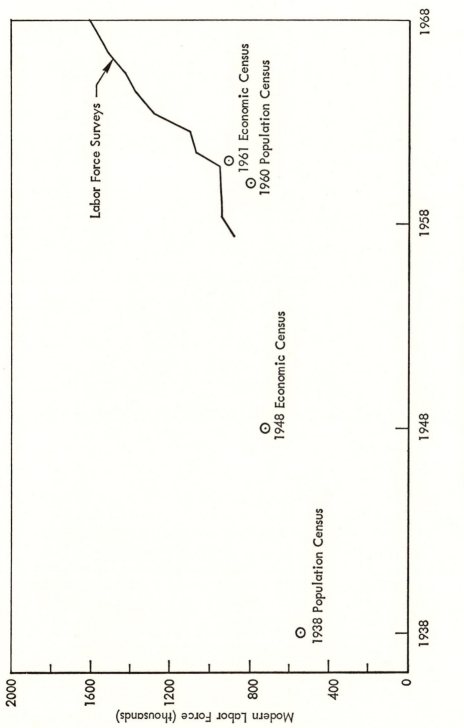

Fig. 8—Estimates of the Modern Labor Force

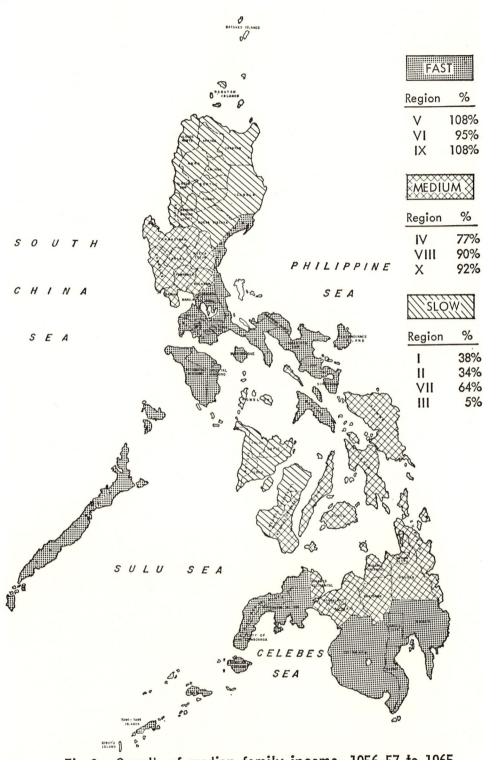

FAST

Region	%
V	108%
VI	95%
IX	108%

MEDIUM

Region	%
IV	77%
VIII	90%
X	92%

SLOW

Region	%
I	38%
II	34%
VII	64%
III	5%

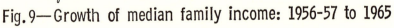

Fig. 9—Growth of median family income: 1956-57 to 1965

the attitudes of those who remain in traditional occupations. If it were true, for example, that modern activities became highly concentrated in one part of the country, we could expect regional cleavages to develop also in politics. So it is important to try to find where the MLF is located and where it is growing.

THE DISTRIBUTION OF THE MODERN LABOR FORCE, 1948-1961

The period 1948-1961 is bounded by the Economic Censuses of 1948 and 1961, so data are immediately available that will enable us to track the changes in the distribution of the MLF between those dates. Since the Economic Censuses measured employment in *establishments*, the workers they counted correspond to what we defined as "modern" employment. Because of inconsistencies in definition and coverage between the two censuses, the closest we can come to our previous definition of the MLF is the sum of establishment employment in manufacturing, forestry and logging, commerce, and transportation; in 1961 these industries accounted for 92 percent of the MLF. Since consistent definitions of the total labor force are not available for the two censuses, we will normalize this measure of the MLF for the size of the province by dividing it by the population in the province more than 20 years old. Thus, our index of modernization is the MLF expressed as a percentage of the population over 20.

Figure 10 plots the index of modernization by province for 1948 and 1961. Increasing modernization, as defined here, tended to be concentrated in a small number of provinces, particularly in the Manila-Rizal-Bulacan area, with only a few provinces in the rest of the country showing any increase in the index at all.

The concentration of employment in establishment manufacturing is even more striking. Of the total increase in paid employment in manufacturing establishments between 1948 and 1961, 71 percent occurred in the same three provinces—Manila, Rizal, and Bulacan (see Table 41).

TABLE 41

WAGE AND SALARY EMPLOYEES IN MANUFACTURING
ESTABLISHMENTS, 1948-1961

	1948	1961	Increase
(1) Philippines	90,000	301,400	211,400
(2) Manila-Rizal-Bulacan	38,600	188,000	149,400
(3) (2) as a percentage of (1)	43	62	71

SOURCE: Economic Censuses of 1948 and 1961.

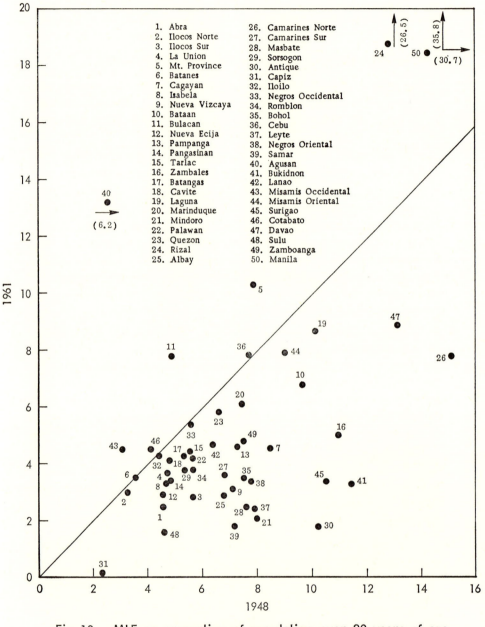

1. Abra
2. Ilocos Norte
3. Ilocos Sur
4. La Union
5. Mt. Province
6. Batanes
7. Cagayan
8. Isabela
9. Nueva Vizcaya
10. Bataan
11. Bulacan
12. Nueva Ecija
13. Pampanga
14. Pangasinan
15. Tarlac
16. Zambales
17. Batangas
18. Cavite
19. Laguna
20. Marinduque
21. Mindoro
22. Palawan
23. Quezon
24. Rizal
25. Albay
26. Camarines Norte
27. Camarines Sur
28. Masbate
29. Sorsogon
30. Antique
31. Capiz
32. Iloilo
33. Negros Occidental
34. Romblon
35. Bohol
36. Cebu
37. Leyte
38. Negros Oriental
39. Samar
40. Agusan
41. Bukidnon
42. Lanao
43. Misamis Occidental
44. Misamis Oriental
45. Surigao
46. Cotabato
47. Davao
48. Sulu
49. Zamboanga
50. Manila

Fig. 10 —MLF as proportion of population over 20 years of age,
1948 - 1961

THE DISTRIBUTION OF THE MODERN LABOR FORCE, 1960-1968

This pattern has changed. Figure 11 plots the MLF as a proportion of the population over 20 for 1960 and 1968. Here the data are drawn from the May 1968 *Labor Force Survey* and the .5 percent sample of households enumerated in the 1960 *Census of Population*.[25] MLF is defined as the combination of employees by industry and class of worker shown above in Table 40. Although the Manila area has continued to show an increase in the proportion of MLF, a large number of provinces outside this area have registered even more substantial increases. The same shift is shown in the data on wage and salary employees in manufacturing. Although the Manila-Rizal-Bulacan area has continued to show substantial increases in manufacturing employment, the proportion of the increase in total employment that occurred in these provinces between 1960 and 1968 is not as large as their corresponding proportion over the period 1948-1961 (see Table 42).[26] Thus, although growth con-

TABLE 42

WAGE AND SALARY EMPLOYEES IN MANUFACTURING, 1960-1968

	1960	1968	Increase
(1) Philippines	321,000	753,200	432,200
(2) Manila-Rizal-Bulacan	119,400	330,000	210,600
(3) (2) as a percentage of (1)	37	44	49

SOURCE: Tabulations of the .5 percent sample of the 1960 *Census of Population* and May 1968 *Labor Force Survey* done at Rand.

tinues to be uneven and some parts of the country lag behind, it is no longer accurate to identify the Manila area as "modernizing" and the rest of the country as "traditional." Change is both substantial and widespread.

The point of these arguments, however, is *not* that the rate of growth of GNP is 6 or 7 percent rather than 5 percent. We do not

[25] The sample of the 1960 Census was made available to us through the courtesy of the Population Institute, University of the Philippines, and its director, Professor Mercedes B. Concepcion. The tape of the 1968 Labor Force Survey was made available through the courtesy of Census Director Tito A. Mijares.

[26] M. Treadgold and R. Hooley, on the basis of data from the *Survey of Manufactures* from 1956 to 1962 concluded that the shift of manufacturing growth from the Manila area to the rest of the country that was visible in that period could be traced to the impact of decontrol and devaluation. See "Decontrol and the Redirection of Income Flows: A Second Look," *The Philippine Economic Journal*, 6, no. 2 (1967), 109.

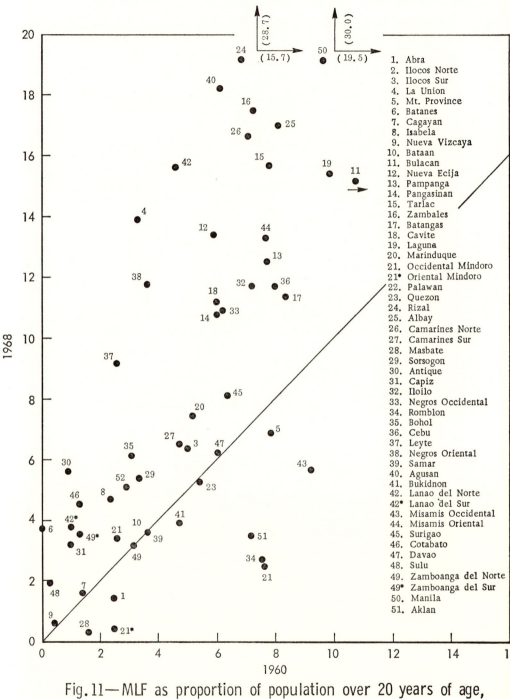

Fig. 11—MLF as proportion of population over 20 years of age,
1960-1968

know. The data strongly suggest—but do not conclusively prove—that the country has done a good deal better than common opinion holds. But the economic nostrums proposed for the Philippines really *assume* that some fundamental change is required before the country can achieve anything like satisfactory performance. If that assumption is incorrect, prescriptions of fundamental change are not only beside the point but run the risk of reducing a satisfactory performer to a poor performer. Revolutionizing a success would be much more costly than revolutionizing a failure.

THE POLITICS OF THE MODERN LABOR FORCE

We saw in Chapter 4 that the poor appear to differ little from other Filipinos. We saw above that the unemployed seem to bear no special grievance against the political system. These observations do not prove that dissatisfaction and tensions would not appear if the economy failed to grow for some length of time. If the Philippines did in fact stagnate, political troubles could very well follow. But the country does not appear to have stagnated, so announcements that slow growth has pushed the country to the brink of revolution are premature. Even by the official NEC figures, the performance of the economy is impressive; and these figures, as we noted, probably understate the true growth of GNP.

If we do not expect to find protest against the alleged slow rate of growth of the economy, it is possible that the Philippines faces precisely the reverse problem: social disorganization and political alienation arising from the process of growth itself. The literature on economic development commonly asserts that tensions will rise as people move rapidly from traditional to modern styles of life.[27]

We can identify the opinions of the MLF by extracting from Pegasus those respondents who are engaged in modern occupations.[28] This is the group whose life-styles presumably represent more modern rather than more traditional patterns. And it is a group that is growing rapidly.

[27] See Huntington, *Political Order in Changing Societies*, Chapter 1.
[28] The Pegasus MLF is defined occupationally. The following occupation classes are *excluded*: proprietors of sari-sari stores; farmers, farm laborers, fishermen, hunters, and related workers; weavers of hats, mats, baskets, and other handicrafts; spinners, weavers, and related workers; dressmakers, seamstresses, tailors, shoemakers, and related workers; food, beverage, and copra workers; manual workers and laborers; service and related workers; housewives; and not reported.

By and large, the MLF is different in ways we would expect. When compared with the non-MLF they are more worried about crime, population growth, dissidence, and treatment of minorities and equally concerned about taxes, the cost of living, and graft.[29] As Table 43 shows, however, they are slightly more skeptical of

TABLE 43

IMPRESSIONS OF POLITICIANS, BY MLF AND NON-MLF
(row percentages)

	None/Few	Some	Most	SSR
1. Greedy				
MLF	11	45	43	424
Non-MLF	16	50	34	623
$\chi_1^2 = 9.51$ with 2 D.F.		$\chi^2 = 8.4$ with 2 D.F.		
2. Nationalistic				
MLF	24	51	25	417
Non-MLF	20	46	34	617
$\chi_1^2 = 9.68$ with 2 D.F.		$\chi^2 = 8.8$ with 2 D.F.		

NOTE: Actual text of question: "From your impressions of politicians, is the word I will read to you descriptive of none or very few politicians . . . some of them . . . or most of them?"

There were no significant differences between MLF and non-MLF on the other questions of this group, 4a-4f of Pegasus.

politicians. The differences here, although statistically significant, are not overwhelming. The MLF also profess to weigh candidates for president according to somewhat less "traditional" measures than does the rest of the population. Although the differences here are not sharp, they weakly support the contention that members of the MLF represent the emergence of a new kind of voter (see Table 44). The MLF say they consider the candidate's dialect, party, and promises of help to be somewhat less important, while honesty is much less important to them than it is to the non-MLF. The absence of sharp differences in voting behavior, however, is corroborated by the failure of percent MLF in a province to add anything to the explanation of election results in the regression models of Chapter 4.[30]

[29] Tabulation of questions 1a-1h of Pegasus. The criterion of significant difference is a χ_1^2 or χ^2 significant at .95.

[30] MLF was used as a variable in the 1961 and 1965 voting equations reported in Chapter 4 but it was not significant.

TABLE 44

FACTORS CONSIDERED IN DECIDING ON VOTE FOR PRESIDENT,
BY MLF AND NON-MLF

(row percentages)

	Not Important	Some Importance	Very Important	SSR
1. Candidate's dialect				
MLF	29	24	43	422
Non-MLF	17	30	53	642
$\chi^2_1 = 18.89$ with 2 D.F. $\quad \chi^2 = 21.9$ with 2 D.F.				
2. Honesty				
MLF	1	7	92	438
Non-MLF	neg.	9	91	673
$\chi^2_1 = 3.71$ with 2 D.F. $\quad \chi^2 = 5.8$ with 2 D.F.				
3. Promises of help				
MLF	41	31	28	436
Non-MLF	30	41	30	676
$\chi^2_1 = 14.03$ with 2 D.F. $\quad \chi^2 = 14.0$ with 2 D.F.				
4. Party				
MLF	54	19	27	434
Non-MLF	37	30	33	674
$\chi^2_1 = 39.96$ with 2 D.F. $\quad \chi^2 = 40.0$ with 2 D.F.				

NOTE: Actual text of question: "I will read to you some factors that people take into account when selecting a candidate for the presidency of our country. In your own case, do you consider this factor not important . . . somewhat important . . . or very important?"

The Biennial Lurch

THE UNEVENNESS OF GROWTH

Although it is growing rapidly, the Philippine economy also appears to be rather unstable. At least until 1966, the reported rate of growth of real GNP alternately rose and fell in a two-year cycle (see Table 45).[31] Furthermore, the Philippine balance of payments position has been repeatedly precarious: net foreign exchange reserves have fluctuated sharply, but with a strong downward trend since 1960 (see Table 46). The unevenness in the growth rate and the recurring foreign exchange crises have tended to obscure perceptions of the real progress of the Philippine economy and have bred pessimism about the country's long-run prospects.

[31] The apparent break in the pattern after 1966 will be discussed below.

TABLE 45

PERCENTAGE RATES OF GROWTH OF GNP,
IN CURRENT AND 1955 PRICES

Year	Current Prices	1955 Prices
1957	9.1	5.8
1958	6.1	3.8
1959	8.7	6.9
1960	6.7	1.3
1961	9.3	6.5
1962	10.6	6.1
1963	15.4	7.4
1964	7.3	2.5
1965	8.3	5.5
1966	10.3	6.0
1967	6.2	6.0
1968	6.4	6.3

SOURCE: NEC, *The National Accounts of the Philippines with Supporting and Analysis Tables, CY 1946 to 1967* (mimeo).

ELECTIONS AND FISCAL POLICY

Every Philippine president—except Magsaysay, who died in office —has sought reelection. What does a president have to do to be reelected? The survey data cited in Chapters 3 and 4 suggest that both politicians and voters perceive election strategy in terms of allocating public works, jobs, and various other payoffs to maximize votes. If this is how a candidate perceives his strategic problem, then the needs of a politician playing the role of rational campaigner are clear: he must capture as many resources as possible, allocate them to projects that will bear his name, and distribute as many jobs and bribes as possible to the voters.

We shall argue in this section that the unevenness we observe is in part the consequence of fiscal and monetary policies that work together to destabilize the economy. The instability does not reflect the impact of uncontrollable events but is built into the Philippine political system. As Philippine policymakers pursue and *achieve* their goals, they generate the cycles we have observed.

To speak of "the goals of policymakers" over nearly a decade is to bend reality somewhat. Institutions have come and gone: the Program Implementation Agency supplanted NEC in some roles and was in turn transmuted into the Presidential Economic Staff, only to lose its major functions to the new Board of Investments. The same institution may behave differently under different directors: the Central Bank, for example, fought the administration's spending program less vigorously under Castillo than under Cua-

TABLE 46

INTERNATIONAL RESERVES, 1956-1967

(in U.S. $ millions)

End of Period	Total Reserves[a]	Net Reserves[b]
1956	225	225
1957	140	100
1958	145	105
1959	163	155
1960	192	179
1961	103	36
1962	141	94
1963	147	135
1964	38[c]	9
1965	92[c]	−19
1966	151	23
1967	221	−13
1968	195	−87[d]

SOURCE: CBP. Taken from Armand V. Fabella, *An Introduction to Economic Policy*, Philippines Executive Academy, College of Public Administration, University of the Philippines, Manila, 1968, Appendix Table 9.

NOTES:

[a] Gross reserves of the Central Bank plus net reserves of the commercial banks (net of foreign exchange liabilities). This is the Central Bank definition of the international reserves.

[b] Total reserves (as defined above) less short-term foreign obligations of the Central Bank. A minus sign means that the total reserves are less than the combined short-term liabilities of the Central Bank and the commercial banks.

[c] Revised as of November 22, 1966, to include deferred payments liabilities previously unreported by commercial banks. These revisions supersede those previously made on end of 1964 data. Thus, the international reserves from 1964 on would not be directly comparable to pre-1964 figures.

[d] Our estimate. Computed by substracting Liabilities to the IMF and "Loans Payable—Foreign" found in the 1968 Statement of Condition of the Central Bank from the Total Reserves figure.

derno. Nevertheless, much of the change is more apparent than real. Although the players change, many of the roles remain the same: the President must present an expenditure program; the Congress must pass appropriations; the Treasury must raise the required funds; and the Central Bank must finance the deficit. The structure of the government spending process defines these roles, and they have remained the same over the decade. The convergence and divergence of the various actors' goals, how they perceive their roles and how vigorously they play them, define the policy outcome.

Expenditures must be financed in one way or another, and all the possible methods of raising the money entail political costs. The political costs of higher tax rates or improved collection at present rates seem obvious. Since many voters perceive the high cost of living as a very important problem, recourse to inflationary finance may be self-defeating beyond fairly narrow limits.[32] If the administration cannot raise taxes, noninflationary financing is available from only three sources: foreign borrowing, running down foreign exchange reserves (accompanied by an import surplus), and capturing more of the savings of the private sector through the financial system. Capturing domestic savings for government expenditures requires tightening credit for business investment and is likely to alienate an influential segment of the electorate (and another source of campaign financing). The ability of the government to borrow abroad is also limited, although the limits are not rigidly defined. And, of course, foreign exchange reserves are also limited.

The Central Bank was not set up to say no to the needs of the administration. Indeed, the Secretary of Finance is chairman of the Monetary Board, the Bank's policymaking body, and the Board itself has often held other prominent politicians, past or future. On the other hand, the Bank also has another constituency: foreign bankers, the IMF and IBRD, and other proponents of "sound" policy. If the CB hopes to negotiate satisfactorily in the future with this foreign constituency, the amount of inflationary finance or foreign borrowing it can provide should not exceed the limits judged "prudent" by this community. Also, there are several checks on inflationary financing written into the CB organic act, Republic Act 265: direct advances to the government are limited to 15 percent of the average of government income of the previous three years; the CB is required to explain whenever either the money supply rises by more than 15 percent or the consumer price index rises by more than 10 percent over any 12-month period.[33] The limit on direct advances can, of course, be circumvented in various ways, and the reporting requirement is little more than a source of potential embarrassment; but the two constraints may exert some restraining influence on government decisions to finance a deficit by inflationary means, and they may be used as counters in CB bargaining with the administration.

THE FISCAL CYCLE

We are postulating the existence of a two-year cycle in fiscal policy, corresponding to the biennial elections. In order to detect

[32] See Table 17.
[33] See Republic Act 265, Secs. 95, 66.

such a short cycle, we should have quarterly or monthly data on taxes and expenditures, and the data should be defined in a fashion consistent with national income-accounting definitions. The Philippine budget process is not designed to generate such data—either for us or for policymakers.

Appropriations from Congress must be released in quarterly allotments by the Budget Commission to the operating departments. Allotments release funds to the agencies by allowing them to draw treasury warrants to replenish their cash balance with commercial banks or the Philippine National Bank. At this point we lose track of the funds. Appropriations, Budget Commission releases, and transfers from treasury to department accounts are all reported regularly. But the actual departmental purchases from the economy may be delayed into succeeding fiscal years if, as has been common practice, the department certifies that unexpended releases are obligated in order to prevent their reversion to the Treasury.[34] In FY 1962, for example, these accumulated obligations were run down 360 million pesos, accounting for over 16 percent of all actual expenditures.[35]

Thus, there are no fully satisfactory data.[36] All that we can use to judge the cyclical impact of fiscal policy are the figures on operating receipts and disbursements. These figures, however, do have the virtue that they are the data actually taken by the Treasury and CB to represent the impact of fiscal activities. They are as close to actual expenditures as we can get. Figure 12 shows a monthly plot of net government operating receipts. This is essentially government tax and entrepreneurial income less government expenditures.[37] The data show a strong annual cycle, but deficits appear to be unusually large in the months immediately preceding elections. The government surplus as measured here does tend to decline in election years and increase in nonelection years. The relationship

[34] Since 1967 the action office of the infrastructure program has been gathering data on expenditures and unexpended appropriations, quarterly by project. This information, however, is tightly held and not available to other branches of the government.

[35] See R. V. Tiaoqui, "The National Budget System of the Philippines," *The Philippine Economic Journal*, 2, no. 1 (1963), for the best description of Philippine budgeting and FY 1962 data.

[36] Which is, of course, symptomatic of the Philippine government's general problem of poor command and control.

[37] The figures exclude government borrowing and debt repayments.

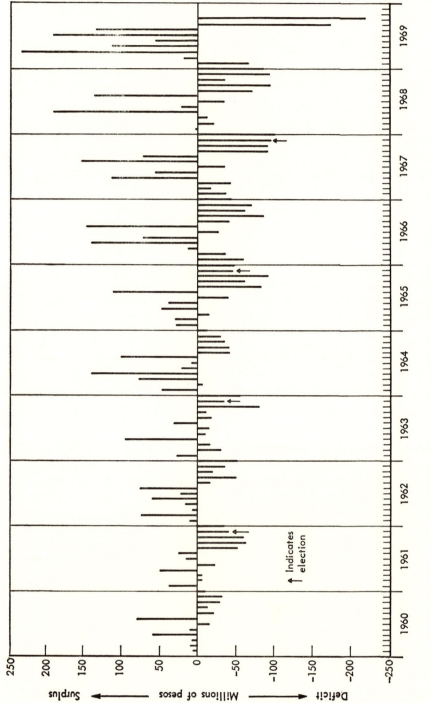

Fig. 12 —Net government operating receipts

Source: Central Bank of the Philippines

between changes in government net operating receipts and elections is shown in Table 47. In each of the five election years, the level of net receipts declined.[38]

TABLE 47

THE RELATION BETWEEN GOVERNMENT NET RECEIPTS
AND ELECTIONS, 1957-1968

| | Change in Net Receipts | |
	Positive	Negative
Election Year	0	5
Nonelection Year	6	0

| | Data | |
Year	Net Receipts (million pesos)	Change in Net Receipts (million pesos)
1957 election	−123.4	
1958	17.8	141.2
1959 election	−60.7	−78.5
1960	46.9	107.6
1961 election	−159.2	−206.1
1962	88.8	248.0
1963 election	−110.0	−198.8
1964	75.3	185.3
1965 election	−208.2	−283.5
1966	−86.7	121.5
1967 election	−120.8	−34.1
1968	−85.3	35.5

SOURCE: Central Bank of the Philippines, *Statistical Bulletin*, various issues.

The use of annual data to test for this relationship is somewhat arbitrary, however. The hypothesis is really a statement about the months surrounding elections; the annual pattern, for example, could be produced by a bulge in expenditures *after* the elections, which could not be explained by the need for election finance. We tested for this by experimenting with a variety of periods, testing to see, for example, if the relation between elections and changes in net receipts remained if we looked at the sum of net receipts for the months of February through June of each year. The results conformed generally to the annual results, but the strongest relation

[38] We can test the relationship formally, using Fisher's exact test. If there were in fact no relationship between election years and changes in net receipts, the probability of finding a relationship this strong by random drawing is only .0022. Thus, the hypothesis that there is in fact a relation is strongly confirmed. See Frederick E. Croxton, *Elementary Statistics with Applications in Medicine and the Biological Sciences*, Dover Publishing Co., New York, 1959, pp. 276-278.

101

(perfect correspondence between election vs. nonelection and change in net receipts) appeared in *any* combination of initial and terminal months that ended in either May, June, or July; that is, in any set of months ending three or four months before the election.[39]

This observation is easy to explain ex post. The public works acts always specify that employment of casual workers on government projects must cease 45 days before the election, that is, by mid-September.[40] And the data we have measure releases rather than actual expenditures, so their peak should lead the peak in construction activity by a month or so.

This political cycle in fiscal policy is not news. The CB in its *Annual Reports* has often commented on fiscal policy in ways that suggest awareness of the two-year cycle.[41] And Sixto Roxas, a well-known economist and sometime government official, has described the cycle at some length.[42] But the predictability of the cycle and its monetary and foreign payments consequences have not been considered in formal analyses of the Philippine economy.

THE MONETARY-POLICY CYCLE

The Central Bank could adjust monetary policy to offset the impact of the fiscal cycle. In general, however, the bank has moved with, rather than against, the fluctuations in spending. Table 48 shows a selection of the Bank's own evaluations of the net impact of monetary policy. Although there are some differences in emphasis from year to year and an apparent shift from the pattern in 1967, the Bank has generally surrendered to the demands of election finance by expanding credit rather than by capturing bank reserves.

In general, we find that the CB, *in its own evaluation*, behaves pro-cyclically. The pattern, however, has been somewhat modified in recent years as the Marcos administration has continued to increase expenditures rapidly in off years. In 1967 the CB offered the following critique of Philippine fiscal policy:

[39] We also experimented inconclusively with spectral analysis of the monthly series. The strength of the annual and quarterly cycles swamped attempts to estimate the density of the spectrum at a frequency of two years.

[40] See Republic Act 5187, Sec. 9, "Suspension of Work Done by Administration Before General Elections."

[41] See Table 48.

[42] See "The Economics of Politics," *Business Day*, vol. 2, no. 79, January 16, 1969, pp. 1-2.

TABLE 48

CENTRAL BANK EVALUATIONS OF POLICY

Year	Fiscal Policy	Monetary Policy
1961[a]	Fiscal measures of restraints adopted in 1959 as part of the stabilization program were relaxed in mid-1961 and continued to ease up during the second half of 1961. The emphasis placed on the objective of monetary stability began to be reduced during the course of 1961 *in response to election demands.* This shift in budgetary policy was reflected in the sharp increase in cash deficits and borrowings from the banking sector. *CB Annual Report,* 1961, p. 44.	Money supply expanded by 17 percent during 1961, whereas it had remained relatively stable during the two preceding years. This change occurred despite the substantial decline in the international reserve in 1961 as against an increase in the earlier years, and an unusually large increase in time and savings deposits. The monetary expansion was due principally to the shift in fiscal and credit policies from restraints to ease. The continued adoption of expansionary monetary measures [was] designed to meet the liquidity requirement of banks in particular and the economy as a whole. *CB Annual Report,* 1961, p. 62.
1962	The policy of ease which was adopted in 1961 and which contributed to disturbances in the domestic and external equilibrium gave way in 1962 to one of restraint. Although the general tone was one of monetary restraint, the Government nevertheless undertook larger expenditures especially in the last four months of 1962 to implement essential and strategic projects involved on the first phase of the Five-Year Socio-Economic Development Program. The development in the spending program placed emphasis on the availment of Treasury cash balances built up through an intensification of tax collections rather than on public borrowings, in order to minimize generating any new inflationary tendencies in the economy. *CB Annual Report,* 1962, p. 55.	In the light of the excessive monetary expansion and the decision to lift controls on foreign exchange transactions at the beginning of 1962, the Central Bank reversed its policy of ease to one of restraint at the beginning of 1962. *CB Annual Report,* 1962, p. 36.
1963[a]	Fiscal operations during 1963 were characterized by a reversal of the	Monetary and credit developments during 1963 continued to reflect the expansionary

Table 48 (continued)

Year	Fiscal Policy	Monetary Policy
	surplus position attained in the preceding year. Compared to the P16 million surplus of 1962, cash transactions of the Treasury resulted in a deficit of P468 million in 1963. Excluding debt repayments of P196 million the current cash deficit of the Treasury amounted to P272 million during the year. This deficit was brought about by an upward bias of programming expenditure levels. Another contributory factor was the large settlement of accounts payable during the year. . . . The increased deficit was brought about largely by the expansion in government operations and subsidies to temper the price effect of the decontrol program. *CB Annual Report,* 1963, p. 29.	pressures that emerged during the last quarter of 1962. As it became increasingly evident that the expansionary trend in money would continue in 1963, the Central Bank moved to counter this development by shifting to a policy of mild restraint during the first nine months and a further tightening of credit towards the end of the year. *The movement of money supply mirrored these changes in monetary policies. From 13 percent in 1962, the annual rate of growth of money supply reached 20 percent in March 1963, 24 percent in May, and 26 percent in August* before money supply went down to the December level of P2,954 million which was 18 percent over the figure in December of last year. *CB Annual Report,* 1963, p. 8.
1964	A policy of fiscal restraint was pursued in 1964 to bring about a better balance between expenditures and revenues. As revenues at existing rates failed to come up to expectations, budgetary authorities adopted retrenchment measures in expenditures in spite of the larger financial requirement of strategic and essential projects embodied in the five-year fiscal plan. The shortfall in anticipated revenues concomitant with the deterioration in the tax collection machinery at customs, the enactment of a number of tax-exemption laws which considerably narrowed the current tax base and the approval of the law transferring 50 percent of the specific tax on locally manufactured Virginia cigarettes into a special fund for the tobacco industry constrained fiscal	Monetary and credit developments during 1964 were governed by the Central Bank's policy of restraint prevailing since the closing of 1963. The heavy withdrawal of government deposits from private commercial banks, although implemented by the National Government rather than by the Central Bank, also emerged as one of the significant influences on the monetary situation. In the external field, the foreign exchange deficit plus the 20 percent surrender requirement continued to exert a disinflationary effect on money supply. As commercial banks began to feel the pinch in their liquidity position towards the middle part of the year, the Central Bank amended some of its credit measures to relieve the low reserve position of the commercial banking system. *CB Annual Report,* 1964, p. 7.

Table 48 (continued)

Year	Fiscal Policy	Monetary Policy
	authorities to reduce planned expenditures. Infrastructure projects financed to some extent by bond issues were likewise deferred as inflationary financing was held down to a minimum. *CB Annual Report,* 1964, p. 31.	
1965[a]	Government budgetary operations in 1965 did not adhere to the fiscal discipline of 1964. This turn-about conformed to the biannual pattern of fiscal transactions where a year of excessive expansionary operations is followed by a year of discipline and restraint. Such extreme swings in fiscal policy tend to hinder economic advancement as the brunt of efforts to restore stability is likely to fall on growth expenditures due to the irreducible character of current outlays (mostly for salaries and wages). *CB Annual Report*, 1965, p. 30.	Although the monetary authorities were perceptibly more liberal in supplying reserves to the banks than they were last year, forces operating beyond their sphere of influence prevented the monetary measures from exerting their intended effects fully. *CB Annual Report*, 1965, p. 5.
1966	Fiscal policy in 1966 was directed at overcoming the shortcomings of previous years which came to a head in 1965. Policy direction was therefore aimed at improving efficiency in revenue administration and, on the expenditure side, placing emphasis on infrastructure and food production projects by instituting economy measures on current outlays. The government, in addition, instituted measures establishing a bills market to mobilize and obtain domestic resources at competitive rates for its funding requirements. . . . The substantial improvement in revenue collections reduced the cash gap in the operational budget to P153 million	The year 1966 saw a relaxation of the policy of credit restraint that had been maintained since late 1963 as a complementary measure to the removal of virtually all restrictions on international trade and payments. Measures were adopted starting January 21, 1966 to increase the availability and lower the cost of credit, the more important of which were the decrease in reserve requirements against savings and time deposits, the reduction of the rediscount rate and the sizeable increase in the volume of Central Bank credit which the commercial banks could avail of. These changes were effected shortly after the interest rates on savings and time deposits had been raised and the exchange rate finally unified in November 1965. . . .

Table 48 (continued)

Year	Fiscal Policy	Monetary Policy
	in 1966, or 44 percent smaller than the operational deficit in the previous year. Administrative reorganization, intensified efforts to contain activities on contraband commodities as well as the revenue impact of the devaluation in late 1965 appeared to be the principal factor in raising the collections of the customs and internal revenue bureaus. *CB Annual Report*, 1966, p. 33.	The large expansion in credit, *however*, did not give rise to a significant increase in money supply as it was matched by a heavy inflow of private savings and time deposits, probably in response to the rise in deposit interest rates of November 1965. *CB Annual Report*, 1966, p. 4.
1967[a]	Following a year of restraint and consolidation, the government moved vigorously in 1967 to implement its infrastructure and expanded food production projects. In the process, the gap between receipts and disbursements widened and the volume of new debt instruments to finance the deficit increased substantially. *CB Annual Report*, 1967, p. 30.	The rapid expansion of domestic credits and imports which started during the third quarter of 1966 continued through the first three quarters of 1967. In the light of these developments, the Central Bank adopted several measures in June and October which changed the direction of monetary policy from credit ease in force since January 1966 to restraint. These measures were designed to moderate the credit expansion and to redirect the application of credit resources away from import financing and into domestic production particularly rice and processed export commodities. However, seasonal and cyclical factors, reinforced by speculative activities against the payments system and the momentum of the rice production program, operated in opposition to the direction of monetary policies during the latter part of the year. As a consequence, the expansion in domestic credits continued and the increase in import payments persisted during the last quarter of the year. These developments gave rise to a depletion of the net foreign exchange assets of the Central Bank and commercial banks in the amount of $65 million and a P411 million or 12.2 percent increase in money supply during the year. *CB Annual Report*, 1967, p. 4.

Table 48 (continued)

Year	Fiscal Policy	Monetary Policy
1968	In 1968, the government proceeded further with the expansion of its infrastructure facilities and the social improvement program at a pace that pushed expenditures beyond anticipated levels. Moreover, because the growth of revenues during the year was smaller compared to 1967, the acceleration in government expenditures resulted in a revenue gap that exceeded the deficits of previous years. *CB Annual Report*, 1968, p. 35.	In the light of the persistent high level of import demand and the sharp rise in domestic prices during the preceding year, the Central Bank in 1968 reinforced its measures of restraint adopted since mid-1967, and adjusted certain selective features of the monetary measures in response to the evolving situation. Among the important measures instituted in 1968 were increases in the rediscount rate and in the special time deposit requirements on import letters of credit, the establishment of ceilings on the portfolios of commercial banks and the regulation of certain aspects of foreign exchange transactions. *CB Annual Report*, 1968, p. 4.

NOTE:

a Indicates election year. Italics added.

Developments in 1967 again point to a deficiency in the economic policy mix which is found not only in developing countries but, as brought out at international monetary meetings, also appears to be quite common among developed countries. Basically the trouble lies in over-dependence on monetary policy for the regulation of economic activity. This has led on a global level to alternate periods of speed-up and slowdown, and to a secular rise in interest rates. On the national level, when credit is liberalized in order to stimulate growth without however instituting complementary fiscal measures, the consequent rise in demand leads to a drain on a country's foreign exchange position, forcing an eventual slowdown in development spending. The balance of payments effects of increased domestic demands must be absorbed by increased foreign exchange resources, in the form of higher exports which however take time and investment to generate, and in the form of substantial international financing for development projects. But international development loans are often linked with the institution of appropriate fiscal policy by recipient countries. *The conclusion is, therefore, inescapable that much greater reliance will have to be placed on appropriate fiscal policy measures for economic adjustment and relatively less on an already over-loaded monetary policy.* The tax proposals for 1968, if finally approved, should go a long way toward helping the government extend the limits to which it can pursue its development efforts. The alternatives to such fiscal legislation are either a slower growth rate or alternating periods of high and low economic activity.[43]

After June 1967 the CB relied on specific measures to restrict imports rather than on general credit contraction. In keeping with the normal election-year pattern, the Central Bank began to loosen credit in April 1969, then in June placed an absolute ("voluntary") ban on the opening of new import letters of credit. By September government net receipts showed an unprecedented deficit. The balance of payments deteriorated until the peso was unpegged again in February 1970; it quickly went to a "free market" rate of about 6 pesos per dollar from the old rate of 3.9 per dollar.

Until the first Marcos administration, the relation between the rate of growth and monetary and fiscal policy was exactly as we would have expected: alternating years of expansionary and contractionary policy produced matching cycles in the growth rate. The cycles in the growth rate have been accompanied by foreign exchange losses. In the analysis of the CB, the loss of foreign exchange follows from the rapid expansion of credit and money supply. This analysis is only partly true; as Table 48 shows, expansionary policy in election years did not always result in foreign exchange losses. For example, in 1959 and 1963, reserves increased. In 1963 the impact of fiscal expansion was offset by the effects of the 1962 devaluation; why reserves increased in 1959 remains a mystery. On the other hand, the sharp decline in reserves in 1961 was partly the result of short-term capital outflows, as well as of fiscal and monetary policy. These outflows should have been expected because the government had simultaneously announced its intention to devalue in stages and removed all controls from capital movements. In these circumstances rational wealth-holders had a powerful incentive to shift out of pesos to ride out the staged devaluation. In 1961 and 1965 the requirements of electioneering also placed further burdens on the current account as the government imported large

---

[43] *CB Annual Report,* 1967, p. 3. Our italics.

quantities of "basic commodities"—principally rice—to stabilize prices.

In general, however, it appears either that exchange crises or reimposition of foreign exchange controls are to be expected every election year. The strain on the balance of payments generated by elections will probably increase. Philippine election campaigns are becoming increasingly capital-intensive: the well-equipped campaigner now travels the country by personal helicopter and distributes masses of posters and campaign materials printed abroad and imported as "educational materials."

Since the pattern is regular and predictable and rooted in the functioning of the political system, foreign policymakers should hardly be surprised and disturbed (as they are) every time a foreign exchange crisis occurs. The crises ought not be interpreted as evidence of a fundamental disequilibrium. If exports and foreign exchange reserves were larger, the Philippine government would probably be unable to resist the temptation to sacrifice all of the increased foreign exchange to try to win the election. The motivations are powerful. *At any level of foreign exchange availability,* "crises" are inevitable.

Consequences and Sources of Ambiguity

Filipinos feel that economic problems are important. In the interviews of Congressmen, the crime rate emerged as the second most serious problem facing the Philippines; various economic problems held first place.[44] That the most frequent response was the vague "economic problems" rather than something specific is itself suggestive: the perception is one of general malaise rather than specific problems. A problem can be attacked and beaten back; what policies will alleviate anxiety? In any event, Congressmen do not have specific policies in mind. Even those who responded that some specific economic problem was important did not later reply that they desired some specific policy change.[45]

Ordinary Filipinos interviewed in the Pegasus survey also responded that economic problems were on the whole "very important."[46] This result, however, is hard to interpret. It seems highly unlikely that "increasing exports" should be a salient personal con-

[44] See Table 17.   [45] See Table 19.   [46] See Table 17.

109

cern of a farmer in Ilocos Norte. Perhaps the most we should make of this set of responses is that ordinary Filipinos, like their representatives, seem vaguely to feel that the economy is not performing as it should.[47]

Even professional economists are gloomy. In a long article on economic policy issues of the 1970s, Gerardo P. Sicat of the University of the Philippines concluded:

> The Philippines has the underpinnings of a very healthy economy . . . [but] the growth of the last 10 years has not been generally satisfactory. . . . The structure of economic incentives adopted in our post-war history have not opened up avenues for industrial export expansion and further import substitution in more intermediate manufactures. . . . I doubt very much if we can push the country's industrial development potentials, create a higher rate of employment absorption, and cure our balance of payments difficulties without taking a closer look at what is basically wrong with the structure of economic incentives implied by our economic policies.[48]

Economists' analyses of the economy center on the low rate of growth of manufacturing and exports, on the "colonial structure" of the economy, on the failure to plan "effectively," and so on. These professional criticisms, in turn, influence the thinking of policymakers, both foreign and Filipino.

But the malaise and the analyses remain ambiguous, because the data that underlie diagnosis and prescription are contradictory, partly because of the behavior of the official reporting systems. In the field of unemployment there has been no shortage of raw data; the failure is one of analysis and interpretation.[49] On the question of the aggregate performance of the economy, the producers of competing input-output estimates, BCS and NEC, denounced each other, but these denunciations failed to illuminate important causes of the inconsistencies between the two estimates.[50] And the foreign

[47] There are, of course, political postures that capitalize on diffuse anxiety. The rhetoric of Philippine politicians caters to the anxiety and contributes to it.

[48] *The Manila Chronicle*, April 30, 1969, p. 7-A.

[49] Recall, for example, the confusion on the magnitude of unemployment in the statements of Presidents Magsaysay and Macapagal cited above, p. 71.

[50] For example, the debate between NEC and BCS failed to reveal that a substantial part of the difference between the two tables was due simply to the different exchange rate conventions used. See Appendix E.

exchange crises are misperceived, at least by foreigners, because of a failure to view the functioning of the economy in its political context.

The persistence of ambiguity, however, is partly due to the failure of politicians and bureaucrats to demand that inconsistencies be resolved. If politicians are not very interested in specific programs aimed at the economic problems of the country, they may even find data inconsistencies politically useful because, with careful selection of data, it is possible to "prove" any politically convenient point.[51] But even if politicians were interested in specific programs, the ambiguity would make it difficult to design relevant and efficient policy.

In large measure, these failures are built into the Philippine economic information system, which is structured to provide the data necessary for macro-economic policy. National accounts play a key role. Gathering together raw data from other agencies and transforming them into GNP estimates is the main function of the Office of Statistical Coordination and Standards—a branch of the NEC—which stands by law at the focus of the information system. The national accounts and Central Bank data are the only economic indicators that appear promptly and are circulated widely.

This focus on macrodata may represent a fundamental error.[52] As we saw above, the government does not pursue the stabilizing fiscal and monetary policy that prompt national income data are expected to guide, nor does it pursue a coherent tax and expenditure policy for development. So the resources expended on generating the data produce little return in terms of improved policy performance, not because the data are bad, but because the Philippine government does not pursue the policies to which the data are relevant.

The government does pursue many micro-economic policy objectives. Decisions of the Board of Investments on industrial priorities, of the Department of Agriculture on rice production and distribu-

---

[51] For example, although nearly all other indicators show a substantial rise in real income per capita, the CB Indexes of Real Wage Rates in Manila are stagnant or declining. Because of fairly obvious problems of sample design and weighting, these indexes are particularly poor measures of what is going on in the whole nation. Yet they are continually cited as evidence that the country is going to pot.

[52] For a thorough discussion of various problems of information systems in LDCs see Albert Waterston, *Development Planning: Lessons of Experience*, The Johns Hopkins Press, Baltimore, 1965, Chapter 6.

tion strategy, of the Tariff Commission, in fact of nearly all government agencies rest on judgments requiring very specific, timely data providing information with a spatial and sectoral dimension. Such information is rarely available.

In 1966, Executive Secretary Rafael M. Salas noted that:

> The Executive Office has for some time now identified certain problems and inadequacies in the national statistical system. To name only a few and to quote from the draft of the NEC 4-year program and the reports of other executive agencies, these are:
> 1. The significant time lag between the collection and release of census, survey, and other data-processing results:
> 2. The lack of more detailed and adequately indicative statistics, and the almost complete absence of data for geographical areas below the national level. . . .[53]

The points are well taken. Census results have usually been delayed five years or more. The last complete Survey of Manufactures was taken in 1962; subsequent surveys have only now reached the worksheet and summary stage.[54] The Labor Force Survey of May 1968 was not even punched onto cards until June 1969. The shortage of regional data is even more striking than these examples of tardiness. The latest available regional establishment data are found in the 1961 Economic Census; the 1962 Manufacturing Survey, which appeared in 1968, contains some regional data on manufacturing. Although there has been some improvement in the Philippine information system in the last few years, Salas's evaluation is still true.

The absence of regional data may be particularly important because it relates back to questions of political change. Different parts of the country show sharply different patterns of growth, which can be traced in part to differential impacts of government policy, particularly exchange rate policy. Yet these impacts may not be perceived well. By the same token, observers may extrapolate the performance of one region to an estimate of the performance of the whole

[53] Rafael M. Salas, "Statistics and the Decision-Making Process," *The Philippine Statistician*, 15 (March-June 1966), 62.

[54] Surveys were taken in 1963, 1965, and 1966. The 1963 data can be found only in BCS worksheets; the 1965 and 1966 data were published only in summary form, with no spatial information and detail only at the two-digit level.

112

country without realizing that what he sees in one area may be atypical.

Prospects for the Future

The central economic problem of the Philippines is *not* the balance of payments, nor is it unemployment, nor is it stagnation, nor is it any other of the large number of candidates that have been offered. The central problem is misperception. The announcements of crisis that continually assail decisionmakers fail to clarify real issues or to suggest real options. "Fundamental structural reform" is not a live option. The country has economic problems, and government action could make a real contribution to national welfare in many areas; but no one knows where these areas are, what the structure of the problems is, or what the impact of programs is likely to be.

We have examined three alleged crises in detail, and we have found that they look different from those proclaimed in the press and in Congress: (1) unemployment is concentrated in a special portion of the population; (2) the manufacturing sector is not stagnating, and judgments that it is are based on dubious inferences from highly uncertain data; (3) the lurching of the economy and the recurring foreign exchange losses are rooted in the behavior of the political system.

The information system produces data that are late, aggregative, inconsistent, and badly matched with the needs of policymakers. Even if politicians were interested in specific programs—and the evidence is that they are not—their ability to devise intelligent programs would be severely limited by the nature of the information system. The bureaucracy, parts of which may be interested in devising programs, must deal with the same ambiguities.

The successful execution of the administration's rice program may offer a hopeful sign that policymaking capabilities are increasing: the government perceived a manageable problem, seized the technological opportunity offered by the development of the new strains of rice, and successfully organized and executed a complex program to alleviate the problem of rice shortages. In a sense, though, the rice program was easier than most of the problems facing the country: the problem was well-defined, noncontroversial, basically technological. Few other problems are likely to prove so inherently manageable.

113

Even if the ability of the government to attack and solve problems remains slight, no prophecy of disaster follows. The unemployed do not seem likely to rebel; the economy will continue to grow, and the Central Bank, having helped create balance of payments crises, will continue to manage them intelligently. In short, the problems facing the Philippines do not appear to be greatly in excess of the government's capacity to solve them. Greatly improved economic performance, however, will be very difficult to achieve unless the information systems begin to produce effective, politically feasible alternatives as well as reliable knowledge of the consequences of innovation.

6

Crime in the Philippines

Introduction

FILIPINOS AND FOREIGNERS alike view the Philippines as a violent society beset by murder, robbery, and theft. The impression is hard to escape—at least in Manila where armed guards, lurid newspaper headlines, and "check your firearms" signs are everywhere.[1] Violent crime, like the lurching of the economy, appears to be related to politics and to the same considerations of ethnicity that were so important in the political realm. Here, too, our first problem is to untangle the basic information about the prevalence of crime. Then we have to test for social and economic relationships. Finally, we have to see if policy instruments exist to control crime as the country develops.

Perceptions of Crime

Do the Filipinos really see crime as imposing major social costs? Do they see a crime wave? In Pegasus we asked the respondents about major problems facing the Philippines. The list of issues included items such as "need to increase exports," "high cost of living," "increasing crime." Sixty-four percent of all respondents indicated that crime was a very important problem, 14 percent indicated it was of some importance, and 25 percent indicated little or no concern. This response frequency gives crime the fifth most important spot among the eight issues listed, comparing the national mean responses.[2]

[1] See John Mecklin, "The Philippines: An Ailing and Resentful Ally," *Fortune*, 80 (July 1969), 119. According to Mecklin, "Morally, after only twenty-three years of independence, the islands are decaying, beset by crime and outrageous corruption." Examination of the Manila press indicates a continuous perception of a crime wave for at least ten years. President Marcos, in his 1968 *State of the Nation* Address to Congress, had the following to say about peace and order (January 22, 1968, pp. 31-32): "When I assumed office in 1966, smuggling, criminality, and other forms of lawlessness were rampant, sapping our national will and capacity to progress. . . . Despite [measures to reduce crime] the incidence of crime index [major crimes per 100,000 population] continues to show an upward trend."

[2] Congressmen, on a free response basis, did rank crime second most important, however. They are quite thoroughly exposed to Manila and the mass media. In 1968 one congressman barely survived an assassination attempt. These factors may explain some of the concern over crime found in our congressional sample.

Typically, there is much regional variation in the response on "crime as a problem." Table 49 shows the response patterns from Pegasus on crime as a problem. Comparing within-region means, only in Manila and Pangasinan did the respondents give crime the

TABLE 49

REGIONAL VARIATIONS IN "CRIME AS A PROBLEM"
(percent)

Region	Mean Response	Position of Mean Crime Response in Interval Scale[a]	Rank as Problem Within the Region[b]
Greater Manila	1.72	1.00	1
Ilocos	0.97	.08	7
Pampanga	1.68	.84	2
Pangasinan	1.88	1.00	1
Tagalog	1.56	.82	4
Bicol	1.35	.68	5
Waray (Samar)	0.74	.43	5
Cebuano	1.42	.45	5
Ilongo	1.77	.96	2
Magindanao	1.18	.48	5
Tausog	1.83	.75	3

NOTES: Actual text of question: "I will read to you some problems facing our country. For each problem I read will you please tell me if you think it is not important . . . of some importance . . . or very important to the welfare of our country." Weighted percentages. See Frontispiece for a map of these regions.

[a] Calculated as (a-b)/(c-b) where a is the mean response on "crime as a problem," b is the minimum within-region mean response on questions 1a-1h, c is the maximum within-region mean response.

[b] Using within-region mean responses.

highest rating. Beyond a 100-mile radius of Manila, crime was consistently rated as fifth or lower, except in Sulu.

In the Pegasus questionnaire we also asked each respondent the degree to which he was fearful of being the target of a crime—of being killed or robbed. We formulated the question as the "danger of being killed or robbed in your neighborhood." Permitted responses were very low, low, moderate, and high. The distribution of responses in the total sample was as follows:

	FREQUENCY[3]	
Response	Being Killed	Being Robbed
Very low	0.57	0.55
Low	0.19	0.27
Moderate	0.17	0.12
High	0.05	0.07

[3] Weighted percentages.

116

Crime does not appear to be greatly feared, although the 22 percent who feel a moderate to high probability of being killed probably reflect the high violence rate.

Regional variations, as usual, are quite large. The following mean values are computed by scoring the responses from 0 (very low) to 3 (high).

	MEAN RESPONSE[4]	
Region	Killed	Robbed
Greater Manila	1.21	1.51
Ilocos	0.35	0.33
Pampanga	0.16	0.20
Pangasinan	0.21	0.63
Tagalog	0.61	0.81
Bicol	0.47	0.49
Waray (Samar)	0.32	0.41
Cebuano	0.88	0.65
Ilongo	0.71	0.57
Magindanao	1.45	1.27
Tausog	1.17	1.17

Manilans and the Muslims in the Magindanao and Tausog areas indicate the greatest concern about violence. Pampangans and Pangasinans feel little concern.

Overall, people in a few areas appear to be disturbed about crime while most feel that their neighborhoods are quite peaceful.[5] The large differences we see in concern about crime are matched by large differences in reported rates of crime.

The Structure of the Reporting System

Before we can make inferences about crime and its causes we must understand the reporting system, how it has changed, and the relation between the reporting system and the actual amount of crime. Prior to 1964 there apparently were no nationwide data on crime. Beginning in 1964, the National Bureau of Investigation (NBI) began reporting crime statistics by province. The first NBI report was backdated to cover 1962 and 1963, utilizing "police reports" as basic data.[6] At that time, however, there was no uniform

[4] Derived from weighted percentages.

[5] This was true earlier. For example, in 1963, 82 percent of the respondents in IDLARS 416-59-0001 reported that their community or barrio was peaceful, contented, or orderly.

[6] See *Philippine Crime Report*, 1962 and 1963, National Bureau of Investigation, Republic of the Philippines, Department of Justice. Subsequent years have the same title.

format for police reports. The NBI obtained actual crimes reported by municipality and city. These were aggregated to province level and projected according to the fraction of population represented in the reporting municipalities.

From 1962 through 1965, the NBI was making a systematic error in its province projections and consequently for the country as a whole. Whenever there was a large fraction of population not reporting, the NBI's *actual* method substantially understated the correct estimated crime rate.[7] Thus, the national crime rates for 1962-1965 were all understated. In 1966, the NBI started using the correct computational method. As a consequence, in 1966 there is an arithmetically induced rise in crime rates. The judgment that national peace and order have deteriorated during the Marcos Administration depends partly on this splicing of the early, incorrect NBI series to later, more accurate data.

In the left-hand column of each category in Table 50 we show the reported NBI national rates for three categories of crime.[8] The

TABLE 50

PHILIPPINE CRIME RATES, 1962-1967

Year	Murder/Homicide Rate		Robbery		Theft	
	Reported	Corrected[a]	Reported	Corrected	Reported	Corrected
1962	20.7	31.6	18.3	30.1	57.5	86.6
1963	24.5	33.9	18.3	24.0	50.8	66.9
1964	25.0	36.6	21.3	25.1	57.7	64.2
1965	27.0	36.3	20.1	24.0	61.5	77.2
1966[b]	37.9	37.9	27.5	27.5	75.8	75.8
1967	42.4	42.4	53.0	53.0	129.2	129.2

NOTES:

[a] Note that here we have only corrected the arithmetic error. The "corrected" figures include no adjustment for improved reporting.

[b] Marcos Administration begins.

[7] NBI used $\frac{C}{P} \times [1 + (1-F)]$ instead of the correct $\frac{C}{P} \times \frac{1}{F}$ where C = actual crimes reported, F = fraction of population in the districts reporting, and P = total population in 100,000s. For example, let C = 100,000; P = 50,000; F = .2; then the NBI method gives a crime rate of 3.6 compared with the correct 10.

[8] The NBI sums the projected absolute number of crimes by province and then divides this sum by the total population to get national rates. Since 1966 the Philippines has had three reporting systems—NBI, Police Commission, and Philippine Constabulary. They each use the same reporting form, but at any given time the set of municipalities reporting in each system is different.

right-hand column shows the corrected national rates. Beginning with the Marcos Administration, there is a definite change in the reporting system. Splicing the rates generated by the new system to the old incorrect rates leads to mistaken conclusions about a rapidly deteriorating crime situation in the Philippines. The corrected national 1967 robbery and theft rates still deviate markedly from 1966, and even with the corrected statistics there seems to be a slight increase for homicide.[9]

The question is whether these differences are real—caused by an upswing in crime—or whether they are quirks of the reporting system. For example, consider the 1967 mean robbery rate, since it shows a 100 percent increase over 1966. If we disaggregate the data —much as we did for the unemployment data in the previous chapter—we find the large increase in mean robbery rate can be attributed to a few very deviant cases. The following four provinces are among the most striking:

	ROBBERY RATE		THEFT RATE		
Province	*1966*	*1967*	*1966*	*1967*	*Comments*
Mountain	49.44	89.90	172.01	244.90	Baguio City investigated by the Police Commission.
Zambales	92.83	590.88	128.30	538.78	Constabulary control of Olongapo City. Olongapo for 1967 reports 600 robberies alone.
Cavite	54.27	168.60	174.57	367.77	Investigated by the Police Commission.
Rizal	64.40	231.77	115.37	333.42	CRUSAC (Crusade against Crime). All of Rizal investigated by the Police Commission.

In each of these provinces, it seems reasonable to assume that the reporting system and behavior of the police were sharply changed by Police Commission or Constabulary intervention. If we remove these four provinces and recalculate, the 1967 mean robbery rate falls to about 25 and the mean theft rate falls to 83.

[9] The rise in the homicide rates for 1965, 1966, and 1967 is partly accounted for by a large upsurge of reported homicides first in Manila and then in Rizal province (surrounding Manila). In Manila there were 672 reported homicides in 1965 compared with 1,969 in 1966 and 1,150 in 1967. In Rizal province there were 723 reported homicides in 1965 and 1,112 in 1967. A real question is raised when reported rates double in a year. Such a phenomenon probably involves a change in statistical procedures.

119

These data then fall into line with those for previous years. Allowing for the recently improved reporting procedures, it can be argued that there is no crime wave or even perhaps that there has been a slight decrease in crime. This judgment is buttressed by the attitudes and perceptions cited earlier. *Nevertheless, we judge the level of violence relatively high, whether increasing or decreasing.* And it is violent crime that needs to be explained.[10]

Province Analysis

In the analysis that follows we have separated provinces and chartered cities for two reasons. First, we believed that cities might differ sharply from the rest of the country in the pattern of determinants of crime. The regression models presented below suggest that this is indeed true. Second, some types of data are available at one level that are not available at the other. For example, detailed data on police departments and the characteristics of police are available for cities but not for provinces; on the other hand, a great deal of the socioeconomic data reported for provinces is unavailable for cities.

Provinces differ enormously in the level of violent crime reported. In 1967 murder/homicide rates in provinces ranged from 7 to 120 per hundred thousand. We have tried to explain some of this variation in terms of ethnic and socioeconomic variables.[11]

We believed that the crime rate should be negatively related to

[10] The Philippine national homicide rate in 1965 was about 35 per 100,000. For the same year Thailand had a rate of 29; Burma, 28; Colombia, 25.

[11] There is very little theoretical or empirical work on the relation of crime and development, so we had little guidance in model specification. We were interested in the effects of economic variables such as population growth and density, of the differences among ethnic groups, and in policy variables such as number and pay of police. For a discussion of crime and development see R. G. Ridker, "The Economic Determinants of Discontent," *Journal of Development Studies*, 4 (January 1968), 174-219; A. L. Wood, "Crime and Aggression in Changing Ceylon: A Sociological Analysis of Homicide, Suicide, and Economic Crime," *Transactions of the American Philosophical Society*, 51, pt. 8 (December 1961), 5-126; J. H. Straus and M. H. Straus, "Suicide, Homicide, and Social Structure in Ceylon," *American Journal of Sociology*, 58 (March 1953), 461-469; E. D. Driver, "Interaction and Criminal Homicide in India," *Social Forces*, 40 (December 1961), 153-158; M. Bacon and H. Barry, "A Cross Cultural Study of Correlates of Crime," *Journal of Abnormal and Social Psychology*, 66 (1963), 291-300.

arrest rate—at least for some classes of crime.[12] We also believed the higher the crime rate the more thinly police resources would be spread. Consequently, arrest rate might decline as the crime rate rises. Because of these expected relations we were obliged to compare simultaneous equation models with single equation models. The exogenous variables consist of the now familiar ethnic ones, "fraction of Ilocanos and Muslims," since these groups are alleged to be especially violent, and the socioeconomic variables "population growth" and "population density." We also had data on police per thousand by province. It was ambiguous whether "number of police" should be considered as responsive to other variables or as exogenous. We therefore examined this variable both ways.

The two province models are shown in diagrammatic form in Figure 13. The arrows and the signs on the arrows show the expected direction and sign of the relation. Essentially the first model says that the crime rate in a province is influenced in the specified direction by each variable independently. The second model postulates that there is interaction between the crime rate and police per capita in a province. The crime rate influences the number of police per capita and vice versa.

Population growth could affect the crime rate in two ways. It may be related to social disorganization, which presumably increases crime; it may influence police per capita, which influences the crime rate. We are uncertain about the sign of the relation between police per capita and population growth. Fast growing areas may be able to tap resources to expand public services; or public services, including police, may simply lag far behind the growth of an area.

As Table 51 shows, most of the relations we expected do not appear in the equations. In Model 1 only percent Ilocano and population density are significant.[13] In Model 2, as we expected, the murder/homicide rate is related to the number of police per thousand but the number of police is not in turn related to the murder/homicide rate. Essentially Model 2 is able to relate only

[12] As used here the arrest rate is the proportion of all crimes reported that are cleared by an arrest.

[13] In the single equation context the ratio of the coefficient to the standard error has the usual t-distribution. In the simultaneous equation context this same ratio has approximately a standard normal distribution (z). See Carl F. Christ, *Econometric Models and Methods*, John Wiley & Sons, New York, 1966, p. 598.

121

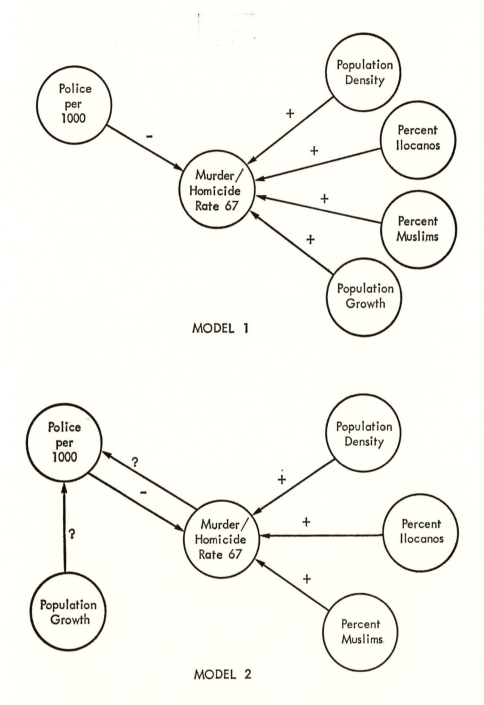

MODEL 1

MODEL 2

Fig. 13—Alternative provincial crime models

TABLE 51

FITTED MODELS OF PROVINCIAL MURDER/HOMICIDE RATES
(observations weighted by population)

Model 1 $\text{HOM RT}_{67} = 46.3 + .20 \text{ PCT ILOC} + .03 \text{ PCT MUS} - 4.6 \text{ POP GRO}$
$(.08)^a$ $\quad\quad\quad (.13)^b$ $\quad\quad\quad (6.9)$
$- 6.3 \text{ POP DEN} - .007 \text{ POL THOUS}$
(3.0) $\quad\quad\quad (.08)$
$R^2 = .22, F = 2.71 \text{ with } 5{,}48 \text{ D.F.}$

Model 2 $\text{HOM RT}_{67} = 54.1 + .18 \text{ PCT ILOC} - .04 \text{ PCT MUS} - 4.15 \text{ POP DEN}$
$(.09)$ $\quad\quad\quad (.14)$ $\quad\quad\quad (2.9)$
$- .21 \text{ POL THOUS}$
$(.29)$

$\text{POL THOUS} = 107.9 - 1.06 \text{ HOM RT}_{67} + 7.3 \text{ POP GRO,}$
$(.50)$ $\quad\quad\quad (9.8)$
$F = 1.56 \text{ with } 2{,}2 \text{ D.F.}^c$

Model 3 $\text{HOM RT}_{67} = 37.4 + .21 \text{ PCT ILOC} - 5.4 \text{ POP DEN,}$
$(.08)$ $\quad\quad\quad (2.3)$
$R^2 = .21, F = 6.8 \text{ with } 2{,}51 \text{ D.F.}$

NOTES: Our notation will be as follows:

HOM RT_{67} = Joint murder/homicide rate for 1967 as reported by the Philippine Constabulary.
PCT ILOC = Percent Ilocano in province (1960)
PCT MUS = Percent Muslim in province (1960)
POP GRO = Population growth (1960/1948)
POP DEN = Population density (1965)
POL THOUS = Police per thousand in province *not* including chartered cities. *Constabulary* province crime data excludes the chartered cities.

[a] Numbers in parentheses refer to the standard error of the coefficients.
[b] Ordinary least squares estimates of the homicide rate and murder rate by themselves show that fraction of Muslims is significantly negatively related to the homicide rate and positively related to the murder rate. Fraction of Ilocanos is positively related both to the homicide rate and the murder rate.
[c] Phoebus Dhrymes' F. In two stage estimates, the F statistic is that derived in P. J. Dhrymes, "Alternative Asymptotic Tests of Significance and Related Aspects of 2 SLS and 3 SLS Estimated Parameters," *Review of Economic Studies* (April 1969), 213-226. This statistic is defined only for overidentified equations.

Ilocanos to the crime rate. Eliminating variables that are not significant determinants of the murder/homicide rate leaves us with Model 3. This has relatively little explanatory power but does suggest a "rural-Ilocano" image of violence.

The failure of our socioeconomic models and the discrepancy between the positive impact percent Ilocano has on the homicide rate and the failure of Ilocanos to worry greatly about crime suggest explanations of violence as an organized activity. For example, some areas of Ilocos are noted for their political violence. (One municipality in Ilocos Sur had a rate of 134 reported murders per 100,000 for 1967.) Ilocos Sur is, allegedly, the most politically volatile of all provinces. Figure 14 shows the monthly trend in actual homicides in Ilocos Sur as well as a three-month moving average. Violence does peak at the time of elections and a little after, when political scores are settled. Then there is a large downswing followed by an upward trend beginning each election year. This political violence may cause a relatively high homicide rate while placing only a small fraction of the population at risk, thus resolving the paradox of perceived security in areas with high violence rates.

City Analysis

Crime rates vary widely across Philippine cities. Some cities report virtually no crime. Others report crime rates as high as any in the world. Table 52 lists some illustrative cases.

TABLE 52
SAMPLE CITY CRIME RATES PER 100,000 POPULATION, 1967

City	Murder Rate	Homicide Rate	Robbery Rate	Theft Rate
San Carlos (Negros Occ.)	0.6	0	0	4.3
Bacolod	83.3	12.7	76.0	210.1
Paranaque	8.9	137.9	296.0	538.9
Olongapo	11.9	55.9	1157.0	652.2

Cities provide some advantages over provinces as units of observation.[14] They are smaller and more homogeneous than provinces. Reporting is probably better than in municipalities, and we can take a better look at the role of the police. However, as we have noted before, some socioeconomic data cannot be obtained by city.

[14] In our analysis the city category includes chartered cities and the primary non-chartered suburbs of Manila. We have excluded Manila, Trece Martires, and Tagatay cities from our sample. The latter two are actually municipios under tight political control, reporting almost no crime. On the other hand, Manila reports large amounts of crime and on most variables is at least 50 times as large as any other city. These three cities can create many spurious relations. We have 51 cities left.

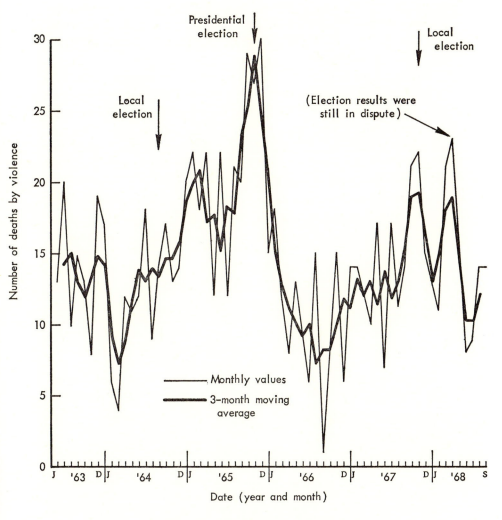

Fig. 14—Violence in Ilocos Sur

We believed that we had some knowledge of how crime should vary by city.[15] But we also knew that again there might be a simultaneity problem in any process of statistical estimation. We therefore postulated two alternative city crime models for comparison. These models are shown in diagrammatic form in Figure 15. The first one is a recursive model where crime rate depends upon socioeconomic variables and upon the arrest rate. Arrest rate in turn depends upon police per thousand and median police pay. The second model is similar to the first except that crime rates and arrest rates are now interdependent.

The fitted models for the homicide rate are shown in Table 53.[16] In both models the dummy variables representing the Manila area and fraction Muslims are significant. The arrest rate is at the margin of significance in both models. The homicide arrest rate in turn is negatively related to the homicide rate. That is, the higher the homicide rate the lower the arrest rate. Arrest rate is not related to police per thousand or median pay.

In both of these models the homicide rate is determined principally by ethnic factors and proximity to Manila. The concomitants of urbanization—population density and population growth—have little or equivocal effect. Police outputs as measured by the arrest rate have some impact on reducing the level of violence, but the arrest rate is not related to any police inputs we could discover. Thus these models suggest that it will be difficult to reduce the level of violence in Philippine society.

[15] The large amount of literature on crime in American cities cannot be cited here; but see, for example, Bernard Lander, *Towards an Understanding of Juvenile Delinquency*, Columbia University Press, New York, 1954. Lander's work consists of a cross-sectional analysis of Baltimore census tracts, but the methods lend themselves to any kind of cross-section data. See also Marshall B. Clinard, *Sociology of Deviant Behavior*, Holt, Rinehart and Winston, Inc., New York, 1966, especially the chapter on urbanization.

[16] As in the United States, murder may be a "private" act of passion where deterrence by the police and the arrest rate play little role. For analyses of U.S. criminal homicide, see Marvin E. Wolfgang, *Patterns in Criminal Homicide*, Science Edition, John Wiley & Sons, Inc., New York, 1958, p. 214: "... the more excessive degrees of violence during a stabbing or shooting occur in the home rather than outside the home and ... severe degrees of violence in which more than five acts are involved are most likely to use a home for the scene." Models fitted to the murder rate alone show that only "fraction of Muslims" is a significant explanatory variable.

126

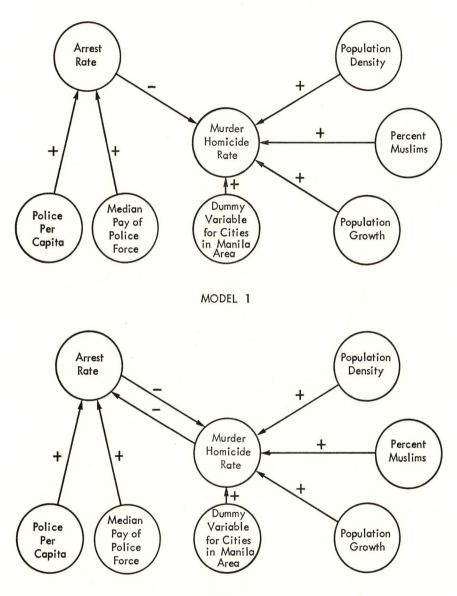

MODEL 1

MODEL 2

Fig. 15—Alternative models of city crime

TABLE 53

FITTED MODELS FOR CITY MURDER/HOMICIDE RATES
(observations weighted by population)

Model 1 $\text{HOM RT}_{67} = 25.3 + .50 \text{ PCT MUS} + 2.7 \text{ POP DEN} + 10.9 \text{ POP GRO}$
                (17.7) (.21)   (1.4)   (6.4)
                    $+ 45.0 \text{ CT MAN} - .28 \text{ MARST} - .14 \text{ ILOC}$
                     (14.4)   (.15)   (.24)
                     $R^2 = .73, F = 19.7 \text{ with } 6,44 \text{ D.F.}$

    MARST $= 94.1 - 12.0 \text{ POL THOUS} - .040 \text{ MED PAY}$
                    (6.5)   (.12)
                $R^2 = .08, F = 2.0 \text{ with } 2,48 \text{ D.F.}$

Model 2 $\text{HOM RT}_{67} = 122 - 1.36 \text{ MARST} + .46 \text{ PCT MUS} + 1.24 \text{ POP DEN}$
                (71) (.78)   (.18)   (1.6)
                     $+ 3.21 \text{ POP GRO} + 39.9 \text{ CT MAN} - .57 \text{ ILOC}$
                     (7.7)   (12.7)   (.36)
                     $F^a = 35.9 \text{ with } 6,1 \text{ D.F.}$

    MARST $= 76.4 - .27 \text{ HOM RT}_{67} - 6.8 \text{ POL THOUS} - .078 \text{ MED PAY}$
                    (22)   (.10)   (6.2)   (.12)
                    $F^a = 4.5 \text{ with } 3,4 \text{ D.F.}$

NOTES:
HOM RT_{67} = Joint murder/homicide rate in cities 1967.
PCT MUS   = Percent of city population that is Muslim.
POP DEN   = Population density, 1000 persons per km².
POP GRO   = 1960 population/1948 population.
CT MAN   = Dummy variable for cities in Manila area.
MARST   = Murder/homicide arrest rate.
ILOC   = Percentage in city with Ilocano as mother tongue, 1960 Census.
POL THOUS = Police per 1000 persons.
MED PAY   = Median police pay, pesos per month.
[a] Phoebus Dhrymes' F. Dhrymes, "Alternative Asymptotic Tests."

Individual Analysis

The conclusions we draw from the preceding aggregate models can be checked by referring once again to our survey data. Table 54 shows an individual's own evaluation of the chance that he will

TABLE 54

INDIVIDUAL ESTIMATE OF CHANCE OF BEING KILLED

    $\text{CBK} = .98 + .55 \text{ CT MAN} - .24 \text{ ILOC} + .40 \text{ MUS} - .13 \text{ SES}$
             (.08)   (.06)   (.09)   (.03)
    $R^2 = .07, F = 21.4 \text{ with } 5,1545 \text{ D.F.}$

NOTE:
CBK   = Individual's estimate on chance of being killed (0, very low; 3 very high).
CT MAN = Resident of Manila.
ILOC   = Ilocano individual.
MUS   = Muslim individual.
SES   = Individual's socioeconomic status (0, highest, 3, lowest).

be killed as a function of several socioeconomic variables. The results are consistent with the importance of ethnicity that emerged from the city and province models. Muslims, Manilans, and individuals of high socioeconomic status show greater fear of being killed; Ilocanos are less concerned. Since aggregate violence rates are very high in Ilocos, we believe that the explanations stressing organized but selective political violence are again supported.[17] Most of the population is not endangered by the feuding among political factions.

Individual "tastes" for violence can be explored in another way by considering responses to Pegasus question 26, concerning conditions under which it is morally permissible to take a life. Table 55 shows several equations relating different conditions under

TABLE 55

MORALLY PERMISSIBLE CONDITIONS FOR TAKING A LIFE

(1) $KRJ = .28 + .05\,CT\,MAN - .07\,ILOC + .49\,MUS - .008\,SES,$
$\qquad\qquad\quad (.05) \qquad\quad (.05) \qquad\quad (.06) \qquad\quad (.02)$
$\qquad R^2 = .04, F = 16.8$ with 4,1545 D.F.

(2) $KIH = .48 + .07\,CT\,MAN + .06\,ILOC + .31\,MUS - .04\,SES,$
$\qquad\qquad\quad (.06) \qquad\quad (.05) \qquad\quad (.08) \qquad\quad (.03)$
$\qquad R^2 = .01, F = 4.7$ with 4,1545 D.F.

(3) $KF\ \ = .15 - .04\,CT\,MAN + .06\,ILOC + .15\,MUS - .02\,SES,$
$\qquad\qquad\quad (.04) \qquad\quad (.02) \qquad\quad (.04) \qquad\quad (.01)$
$\qquad R^2 = .01, F = 4.9$ with 4,1545 D.F.

NOTE: Same notations as in Table 54 except:

KRJ = Kill to retaliate for injury (0, never, to 3, always).
KIH = Kill for insult to honor (0, never, to 3, always).
KF   = Kill in political feud (0, never, to 3, always).

which killing is permissible to the ethnic and socioeconomic characteristics of the respondents. Muslims answer more frequently that killing is permissible in retaliation for injury or insult to honor. They are joined, however, by Ilocanos and individuals of high socioeconomic status when the situation shifts to a political feud. This is yet another confirmation of the earlier suggestion that a good deal of the violence we observe in the Philippines appears to be related to politics.

[17] Individuals who live in dissident areas feel that their chances of being killed are also relatively lower. The explanation may be the same as for the Ilocanos. Aggregate crime rates in Huklandia are relatively low, but we know that the HMB controls the reporting system.

Crime Rate and Policy

Philippine society *is* relatively violent, but our analysis suggests that the crime problem has been overstated as a general nationwide crisis. "Mounting crime" is largely the result of arithmetic error. Furthermore, perceptions of crisis seem to be limited to the area surrounding Manila, where violence rates are, in fact, higher than in the rest of the country.

Violence does not appear to be related to factors that could be manipulated by government policy. In the regression models at both province and city level, crime rates depended most strongly on ethnic factors. The survey data further support the role of ethnic differences, since they show the permissibility of taking a life as highly variable across ethnic groups. The one policy variable that appeared in the models, the arrest rate, appeared to depress the level of crime somewhat but was not itself related to any of the characteristics of police forces.[18]

In one sense, however, the crime rate may be related to policy. As we saw in the models and in the survey responses, Manilans are much more violent and afraid of violence than the rest of the country. It can be argued reasonably that the high level of homicide we find in Manila is symptomatic of the social disorganization attending urban growth. The rapid growth of Manila was encouraged by the disequilibrium foreign exchange policy pursued in the fifties. This policy shifted income from the export sector—spread across the country—to import substituting industries—concentrated in Manila. The mechanism of exchange allocation, by requiring would-be importers to bargain with the bureaucracy for foreign exchange, further favored growth near the capital at the expense of the rest of the country. Thus, although direct links between law enforcement policy and crime are undetectable, there may be important and unsuspected links between economic policy and violence.

[18] We have questionable data on 350 Philippine municipalities as well as on cities. We were unable to relate the crime rates in these municipalities to any socioeconomic factors with either simultaneous equation or recursive models.

Dissidence Within the System

7

THE PHILIPPINES has a long history of dissident movements forming, becoming active, and then declining. Since 1900 the nation has experienced no successful revolution, although many believe that the Hukbalahap uprising of 1949-1953 came close to success.[1] Some, impressed by analogies to Vietnam, believe that the contemporary organization called the HMB or Huk poses a similar revolutionary threat.

The view that the current organization may be a threat of some consequence rests on the resurgence of the HMB since 1961. In 1961 it would have been fair to say that the dissidence in Central Luzon had been reduced to a few HMB regulars and their families.[2] By 1968 there were about 300 reported "regulars" throughout the Philippines and 150 reported in Central Luzon. (The count of regulars included some persons who had been active in the 1949-1953 insurgency but were no longer active. These account for much of the HMB strength reported outside Luzon.) There was a reported "mass base" of about 9,000 in 1961 and 32,000 in 1968, along with a reported 3,600 combat support.[3]

---

[1] See A. H. Peterson, G. C. Reinhardt, and E. E. Conger, eds., *Symposium on the Role of Air Power in Counterinsurgency and Unconventional Warfare: The Philippine Huk Campaign*, The Rand Corporation, RM-3652-PR, June 1963. This work shows HMB "control" extending throughout Central and Southern Luzon, with bases existing in Northern Luzon. Activity was also reported in the southern islands of the archipelago. For a history of the HMB, see Renze L. Hoeksema, "Communism in the Philippines," Ph.D. dissertation, Harvard University, 1956.

[2] Constabulary files distinguish four types of Huks: (1) regulars—persons who conduct insurgent activities on a full-time basis, (2) combat support—"die-hard" followers who are *part-time* fighters, (3) service support—collectors, messengers, persons who work for the Huks but within the laws of the republic, and (4) mass base—persons who voluntarily extend sympathetic assistance and cooperation. Source: Constabulary reports, 1st Zone (Central Luzon). Collating reports across the entire country gives 122 regulars in 1961. Although these reports represent the raw material for estimates of Huk strength and control, the underlying intelligence process remains unclear. For example, incentives for agents to deliver true and false information are unknown to us.

[3] In practice, mass base means the total number of people who live in the area that the Constabulary defines as controlled by the HMB.

Such numbers should not be taken too seriously. For example, between June 1966 and June 1968 the number of reported combat support and mass base tripled with no apparent increase in the number of regulars and no explanation of why each regular had suddenly become so much more efficient a manager of men and resources. In Central Luzon, the reported mass base quintupled from 5,000 to roughly 25,000 between 1965 and 1966, again with no increase in full-time regular HMB. These data are even more ambiguous than the other types of data we have discussed.

Whatever their numbers, the area over which the HMB operates and the incidence of HMB killings and kidnappings appear to have increased significantly since 1961. Figure 16 plots the areas within which HMB incidents—primarily killings and kidnappings—occurred in three time periods. The pattern is akin to an expanding doughnut with a decreasing level of activity in the center and an increasing rate of liquidations and kidnappings on the periphery. The number of incidents per year has also increased sharply. These data appear to be reliable. Attribution of killings and kidnappings to the HMB usually rests on definite intelligence information or physical evidence; for example, people killed with Armalites or AK-47s can safely be attributed to the HMB. By this criterion alone, without reference to the estimates of HMB numbers, the organization would have to be judged a growing problem.

The Philippine government seems to believe that its problem is partly social and partly a problem for the Constabulary and the army. Given either interpretation or both, the dissidence problem often seems intractable. If dissidence arises because of a bad land-tenure system, there is little prospect for eliminating it by carrying out massive land reform. In the Philippines land reform has long been a topic for oratory, but little has ever been accomplished in the face of public apathy and powerful opposition. If dissidence is a straightforward police and military problem, it will be hard to eliminate because of the constraints imposed by political considerations. The HMB operate under the protection of local politicians and even campaign for their candidates.[4] A zealous Constabulary officer who violates the implicit *modus vivendi* will quickly find

---

[4] The effectiveness of such campaigning is questionable. Statistical models relating HMB campaigning to votes received by HMB candidates show no relation. For

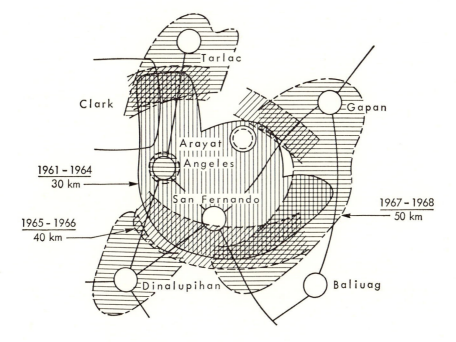

Number of HMB incidents

1961-64	141
1965-66	142
1967-68	177

Fig. 16— Pattern of HMB incidents

himself in trouble. For example, Constabulary officers complain that although they know where wanted Huks live and when they are at home, if troopers enter the barrio to apprehend them, the troopers will be charged with false arrest or other procedural infractions. Since such court cases frequently drag on for two years—during which time the defendants must go on leave without pay—the Constabulary has had no incentive to round up the Huks.

Our first question in this chapter, as in earlier ones, is "What do Filipinos think? In particular, what do the people of Central Luzon think of the HMB? Do their attitudes reflect discontent?" Second, "What factors account for the ability of the HMB to operate in Central Luzon? Does its survival reflect wide popular support, particularly from tenant farmers, or does it rest upon the organization's own activities—its terror and coercion?"

Filipino Attitudes Toward the HMB

Nearly half of all Filipinos think the Huks are bandits. Tables 56 and 57 show attitudes across the entire country.[5] Classified by SES, about two-thirds of all groups (and relatively more in the

---

example, the 1967 gubernatorial election in Pampanga yields the following equation:

$$\text{PCT LP VOTE} = 50.8 - 6.1 \text{ HMB CAMP} + .30 \text{ HC} - .36 \text{ OWN}$$
$$\phantom{\text{PCT LP VOTE} = 50.8} (6.5) \phantom{\text{ HMB CAMP} +} (.14) (.18)$$
$$+ 4.6 \text{ N MAY} + .205 \text{ SGR}$$
$$ (5.7) \phantom{\text{ N MAY} +} (.19)$$
$$R^2 = .27, \text{ F} = 3.8 \text{ with } 5,51 \text{ D.F.}$$

where PCT LP VOTE is the percentage vote received in a municipio by the LP candidate (who was supposedly supported by the HMB), HMB CAMP is a dummy variable equal to 1 for municipios in which the Constabulary reported the HMB campaigned, HC is HMB controlled barrios as a percentage of all barrios in the municipio. N MAY is a dummy equal to 1 if the municipal mayor was NP, and SGR is the percentage of municipio land planted to sugar.

[5] Widespread appeal would be important to rapid expansion. Survey data must be interpreted cautiously, particularly when it comes from areas where insurgents and the government are in conflict. The problems, however, do not appear to be insurmountable. We asked the respondents factual questions about the nature of HMB activities in their area. Responses to these questions corresponded closely to our other information on HMB activities by area. The correspondence on these questions increases our confidence in the validity of the responses to the attitudinal questions. It should be noted, however, that the proportion of nonresponses to the HMB questions was higher in Central Luzon than elsewhere, about half compared with one-third nationwide.

TABLE 56

ATTITUDES TOWARD HMB, BY SES
(percent)

	Not Applicable (0)	Partly Descriptive (1)	Descriptive (2)	Mean Response	SSR
1. *HMB as the hope of the tenant*					
High SES	36	53	11	.75	126
Medium SES	56	28	16	.60	298
Low SES	57	26	17	.60	386
$\chi^2_1 = 34.14$ with 4 D.F., $\chi^2 = 23.83$ with 4 D.F.					
2. *HMB as men of justice*					
High SES	64	26	10	.46	135
Medium SES	67	28	5	.38	315
Low SES	61	24	16	.56	398
$\chi^2_1 = 31.25$ with 4 D.F., $\chi^2 = 18.20$ with 4 D.F.					
3. *HMB as brutal*					
High SES	19	40	41	1.22	129
Medium SES	15	28	57	1.42	317
Low SES	14	31	55	1.41	432
$\chi^2_1 = 3.99$ with 4 D.F., $\chi^2 = 6.62$ with 4 D.F.					

NOTE: Weighted percentages.

TABLE 57

ATTITUDES TOWARD HMB, BY TENANCY CLASS
(percent)

	Not Applicable (0)	Partly Descriptive (1)	Descriptive (2)	Mean Response	SSR
1. *HMB as the hope of the tenant*					
Farmers—non-tenants	50	17	33	.83	79
Tenants	46	48	6	.60	47
Nonfarmers	58	28	14	.56	692
$\chi^2_1 = 17.8$ with 4 D.F., $\chi^2 = 55.2$ with 4 D.F.					
2. *HMB as men of justice*					
Farmers—non-tenants	59	20	21	.62	82
Tenants	48	36	16	.68	50
Nonfarmers	66	25	9	.43	728
$\chi^2_1 = 24.51$ with 4 D.F., $\chi^2 = 26.4$ with 4 D.F.					
3. *HMB as brutal*					
Farmers—non-tenants	11	23	67	1.56	84
Tenants	18	47	36	1.18	53
Nonfarmers	15	30	55	1.40	754
$\chi^2_1 = 19.1$ with 4 D.F., $\chi^2 = 26.0$ with 4 D.F.					

NOTE: Weighted percentages.

lower SES groups) think the HMB are not men of justice. Tenants seem to have a slightly more favorable view than the rest of the population, but the differences are small.

Table 58 shows the responses by mother tongue for the Central

TABLE 58

ATTITUDES TOWARD HMB, BY MOTHER TONGUE
(percent)

	Not Applicable (0)	Partly Descriptive (1)	Descriptive (2)	Mean Response	SSR
1. HMB as the hope of the tenant					
Pampangan	40	33	27	.87	23
Pangasinan and					
Tagalog	36	45	19	.83	190
$\chi^2 = .2$ with 1 D.F.					
2. HMB as men of justice					
Pampangan	33	60	7	.74	27
Pangasinan and					
Tagalog	43	48	9	.66	191
$\chi^2 = .09$ with 1 D.F.					
3. HMB as brutal					
Pampangan	47	42	12	.66	30
Pangasinan and					
Tagalog	26	46	29	1.04	196
$\chi^2 = 2.2$ with 1 D.F.					

NOTE: Weighted percentages. Bhapkar χ^2_1 statistic is not appropriate here, since the observations are classified roughly by stratum. Chi squares were done combining partly descriptive and descriptive responses.

Luzon area. Individuals who speak these languages have a relatively more favorable view of the HMB than do most other language groups. Pampangans hold about the same views as other language groups in Central Luzon—not particularly favorable. And Pampangans are relatively optimistic concerning their current and future welfare, as indicated in Pegasus question No. 2 concerning life status.

Table 59 presents a breakdown of responses on welfare by proximity to HMB-controlled areas. Respondents in the HMB areas do not appear to be different in their responses. Nor do they appear to view the government in any worse light than other groups (Table 60). Constabulary and the police rate about equally, slight-

TABLE 59

MEDIAN RESPONSES ON WELFARE, BY PROXIMITY TO HMB

Area	Life Present[a]	Rank	Life Future[a]	Rank
HMB[b]	4.36	3	7.39	2
Near HMB[b]	3.30	2	6.14	3
Laguna	2.92	5	5.42	4
Pangasinan	4.57	2	5.48	3
Greater Manila	4.95	1	7.35	1
Ilocos	3.09	4	5.28	5
Bicol	2.75	6	4.40	6
National median	3.13		5.52	

NOTES:

[a] The scale runs from 1-10, the ladder question in Pegasus (No. 2). Medians based on weighted percentages.

[b] "HMB" refers to municipios containing some barrios listed as controlled. "Near HMB" refers to other municipios in Central Luzon.

TABLE 60

VIEWS ON GOVERNMENT, BY PROXIMITY TO HMB

	Mean Response[a] on			
	Constabulary	Local Politicians	Local Police	SSR
1. Honesty of government representatives				
HMB	1.25	1.09	1.32	179
Near HMB	1.34	1.05	1.27	67
Laguna	1.38	1.05	1.31	54
Pangasinan	1.37	1.08	1.30	6
Greater Manila	1.23	.96	.98	97
Ilocos	1.64	1.46	1.67	129
Bicol	1.28	.97	1.35	94

NOTE:

[a] Scale is 0, corrupt; 1, half and half; 2, honest. Mean responses based on weighted percentages.

	Percent Responses			
	Not Prevalent (0)	Prevalent Not a Major Problem (1)	Prevalent Major Problem (2)	SSR
2. Graft and corruption				
HMB	4	13	82	195
Near HMB	0	21	79	65
Greater Manila	10	9	80	148
Laguna	12	28	60	64
Pangasinan	2	12	86	65
Ilocos	47	7	47	197
Bicol	12	25	63	133

NOTE: Weighted percentages.

137

ly above the middle ranking, with politicians falling at the middle. Areas close to Manila react more strongly to the graft and corruption issue, but this may reflect only greater exposure to the mass media, particularly the press. Overall these data suggest the government's image is no worse in the HMB areas than it is in other regions.[6]

If there is no evidence of strong social unrest correlated with HMB presence, then why do they persist in Central Luzon and only in Central Luzon? Historical and organizational factors provide an alternative explanation to theories of social unrest. We argue here that Philippine dissidence exists largely because of a self-perpetuating organization. Perhaps the original reasons for its geographic location were social and economic,[7] but, given a moderately cohesive organization, we believe that coercion and terror, not social unrest, account for HMB presence and control.

The subject of the process of "control" and its relation to organizational behavior and social and economic factors is a controversial one.[8] Control is really control over people. But statistical arguments have raged over the role of aggregate variables—for example, fraction of tenants in a municipality or fraction of Pampangans—as related to control.[9] The problem of making inferences about individual behavior or attitudes from aggregate data has been explored

[6] Responses on other questions concerning the government were tabulated, but these results are typical.

[7] David Sternberg (oral communication), argues that the prosperity of Pampangan sugar planters in the early twentieth century led them to send their sons to Europe where they learned Marxism. When they came home to Pampanga, they tried to spread these ideas.

[8] Anyone familiar with the history of the insurgency in Vietnam knows the difficulty of defining control. As used here a *controlled* barrio means that the barrio is one where full time HMB are reported frequently and where they are willing to sleep. An *influenced* barrio is one where regular HMBs are seen frequently but where they do not sleep.

[9] See E. J. Mitchell, *The Huk Rebellion in the Philippines: An Econometric Study*, The Rand Corporation, RM-5757-ARPA, January 1969. This study argues that control of municipalities is related to "contiguity," the proximity of other controlled municipalities, and area devoted to sugar and fraction tenants. The author argues that the presence of Pampangans is "necessary" for control.

Mitchell did not have access to any data on HMB operations. In his work coercive operations are reflected indirectly through the "contiguity" of municipalities. But controlled barrios are not necessarily contiguous. H. A. Averch and J. E. Koehler, *The Huk Rebellion in the Philippines: Quantitative Approaches*, The Rand Corporation, RM-6254-ARPA, August 1970.

for a long time. No satisfactory way exists to make these infer-ences;[10] in this case we had direct access to individuals in "con-trolled" areas, and they did not seem very different from other Filipinos.

This evidence on attitudes in Central Luzon should certainly not be taken as conclusive. However, it is not consistent with the con-tention that insurgency persists here and not elsewhere in the Philippines because of greater dissatisfaction with government per-formance and a much more favorable view of the HMB. Other considerations must be invoked to explain the presence of the HMB.

Alternative Models of Control for Municipios and Barrios

If the population of Central Luzon does not appear to differ markedly from the rest of the country in its views of the govern-ment and the HMB, then we must look at the actual operations of the HMB to see if these can explain the pattern of control we observe. From the Philippine Constabulary we were able to get data on HMB terror and liquidations over time by barrio as well as a list of controlled barrios. These data underlie the alternative models that follow.

Figure 17 shows two alternative models for Huk control at the municipal level.[11] The first is a simultaneous equation model where current Huk control is related to current incidents, to 1960 land ownership, to the fraction of land in the municipality devoted to sugar, and to the fraction of Pampangans reported in 1938.[12] We have related incidents to current control and to distance from Mt. Arayat, which is allegedly the main center for Huk logistics and command and control. The second model is a dynamic one. We

[10] For a discussion, see M. Dogan and S. Rokkan, *Quantitative Ecological Analysis in the Social Sciences*, MIT Press, Cambridge, 1969.

[11] By control at the municipal level we mean the fraction of barrios in each municipality listed as "controlled" by the Philippine Constabulary. The denominator of the fraction is the total number of barrios in 1960. In some municipios new barrios have been created since 1960, but it is impossible to obtain an authoritative list for any year. We did experiment with a list of 1968 barrios obtained from the Bureau of the Census and Statistics. The regression coefficients were changed only slightly.

[12] Percent Pampangans by municipio was not reported in the 1960 census. We were able to obtain an estimate of the 1960 percentage for 46 out of 57 municipios through the courtesy of Dr. Mercedes Concepcion of the University of the Philippines who gave us access to a ½ percent sample of the 1960 census. The correlation between percent Pampangans in 1939 and 1960 for the 46 municipios is .92.

139

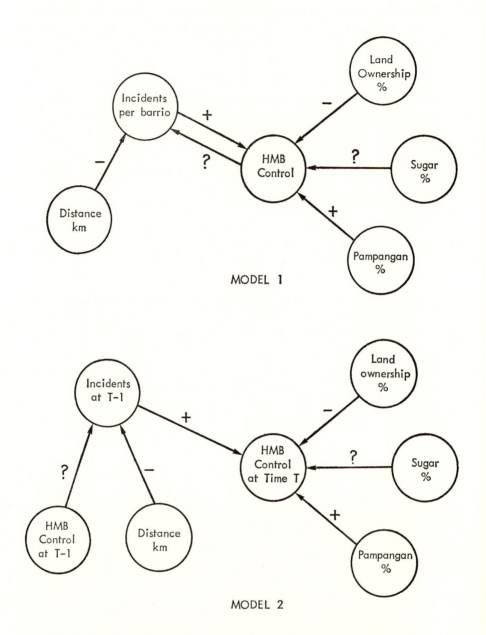

MODEL 1

MODEL 2

Note: HMB Control means fraction of barrios in municipality listed as controlled by constabulary. The expected signs of the coefficients are shown on the arrows.

Fig. 17—Alternative models of HMB control—municipalities

relate Huk control in 1968 (time T) to past incidents and to the same social and economic factors as in Model 1. Past incidents, say at time T-1, depend on distance and on control at time T-1.[13]

Both models were fitted weighting municipios by their adult population. Larger municipios therefore have more effect on the regression coefficients. The results are shown in Table 61.[14] In the first model the only variable that appears as significant in both weighted and unweighted versions is incidents per barrio, which is in turn related to control and distance. In the second model, incidents per barrio at time T-1 are again the major determinant of control, and we are able to explain incidents per barrio at time T-1 only as a function of control at time T-1. This model suggests that terror, as created by liquidations and assassinations, is a major contributor to control. Pampangans and owners are never significant.[15] The weighted models show control as even more strongly related to incidents than the unweighted versions.

The analysis of control at municipal level is somewhat misleading, for if we plot municipalities with some degree of control, Central Luzon appears solidly controlled by the HMB. However, if we plot barrios, controlled barrios exist right next to uncontrolled ones. Figure 18 shows three alternative models for barrio control in Central Luzon.[16] They represent different assumptions about

[13] Here the T refers to 1968 and T-1 to 1965. The Constabulary did not to our knowledge keep lists of "critical" barrios in 1965, since there was not much insurgency. All lists of critical barrios are derived from the basic Constabulary intelligence documents. The Constabulary intelligence officers in the first zone used the 1965 documents to construct a list of critical barrios for that year.

[14] In Table 61 the first model was estimated by two-stage least squares. The second model, since it is formally recursive, was estimated by ordinary least squares. Since there is little relation between HC_T and HC_{T-1}, when we fitted Model 2 using two-stage least squares and treating HC_{T-1} as jointly determined, no variables were significant.

[15] In Model 2, percent Pampangans is not significant even using a two-tailed test. A two-tailed test is appropriate since the survey data suggest that individually Pampangans do not particularly favor the HMB. So we should not expect a positive ecological correlation. Fraction Pampangans is collinear with sugar and tenancy. The models do not change very much when Pampangans, tenancy, and sugar are put into the equations by themselves. Incidents per barrio remain the major determinant of municipal control.

[16] By barrio control we mean a binary variable: (0) if the barrio is listed as uncontrolled, (1) if the barrio is listed as controlled. Data on barrios are much more difficult to obtain than data on municipalities. The manuscript census for 1960 was burned, and it was the only source from which detailed data on barrios could have

141

TABLE 61

ALTERNATIVE MODELS OF MUNICIPAL CONTROL
(standard errors in parentheses)

Model 1 $HC_T = .03 + 1.70$ INCIDENTS PER $BARRIO_T - .002$ OWN
        (.06) (.45)   (.0017)
        $- .0003$ SGR $+ .0008$ PAMPANGAN,
        (.002)   (.0009)
        $F = .8$ with 4, 1 D.F.

    INCIDENTS PER $BARRIO_T = - .19 + .55$ $HC_T + .005$ DISTANCE,
                      (.07) (.10)   (.002)
        $F = 38$ with 2, 3 D.F.

Model 1   (Observations weighted by adult population)
    $HC_T = .038 + 1.65$ INCIDENTS PER $BARRIO_T - .0021$ OWN
        (.058) (.38)   (.0017)
        $- .0016$ SGR $+ .00096$ PAMPANGAN,
        (.0014)   (.00075)
        $F = 1.7$ with 4, 1 D.F.

    INCIDENTS PER $BARRIO_T = - .12 + .52$ $HC_T + .003$ DISTANCE,
                      (.05) (.08)   (.001)
        $F = 55$ with 2, 3 D.F.

Model 2 $HC_T = .05 + 1.10$ INCIDENTS PER $BARRIO_{T-1} - .0014$ OWN
        (.06) (.26)   (.0016)
        $- .0011$ SGR $+ .0014$ PAMPANGAN,
        (.0018)   (.0008)
        $R^2 = .49$, $F = 12$ with 4, 52 D.F.

    INCIDENTS PER $BARRIO_{T-1} = .02 + .0065$ $HC_{T-1} - .0006$ DISTANCE,
                       (.04) (.0009)   (.0009)
        $R^2 = .53$, $F = 30$ with 2, 54 D.F.

Model 2   (Observations weighted by adult population)
    $HC_T = - .06 + 1.20$ INCIDENTS PER $BARRIO_{T-1} + .0019$ OWN
        (.05) (.25)   (.0016)
        $+ .0004$ SGR $- .001$ PAMPANGAN,
        (.001)   (.0007)
        $R^2 = .52$, $F = 14$ with 4, 52 D.F.

    INCIDENTS PER $BARRIO_{T-1} = .02 + .006$ $HC_{T-1} - .0005$ DISTANCE,
                     (.03) (.0008)   (.0008)
        $R^2 = .55$, $F = 33$ with 2, 54 D.F.

NOTE: Time "T" refers to 1968 and "T-1" to 1965-1966. Incidents per $barrio_{T-1}$ included as an instrument in the two-stage estimates.

been obtained. The barrios considered all lie within 50 kilometers of Angeles City. This includes all barrios listed as controlled in February 1968 and a random sample of uncontrolled barrios, giving 305 total barrios. Published census data on mother tongue, tenancy, and labor force in sugar were available at municipio level but not

142

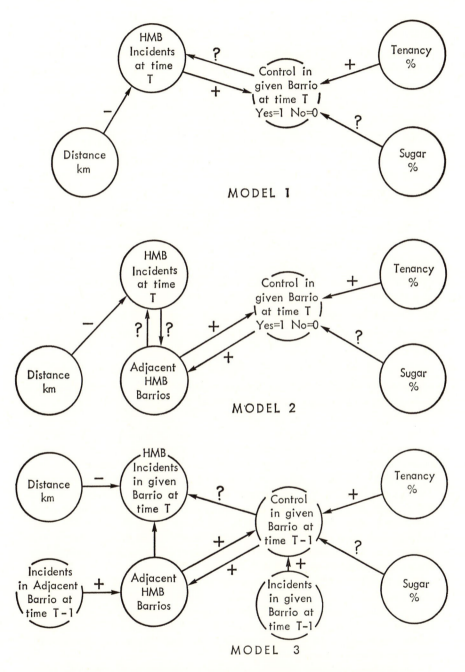

Fig. 18 —Alternative models of HMB control—barrios

Note: The expected signs of the coefficients are shown on the arrows

how control is achieved. Model 1 assumes that it occurs directly through incidents and terror in a given barrio. Model 2 assumes that control in a given barrio occurs by demonstration, by controlling and targeting adjacent barrios. Metaphorically, in Model 1 the dissidents shoot the mayor. In Model 2 they shoot the mayor in the barrio next door and say, "See what happened to him." Model 3 tries to relate current control to past incidents in adjacent controlled barrios, and socioeconomic variables. In turn current incidents are related to current control in a given barrio and its adjacent barrios as well as logistics factors. Model 3 also tries to explain the number of adjacent controlled barrios next to or contiguous to controlled barrios.

The results of fitting these three models are shown in Table 62. In all cases, the observations have been weighted by the adult population. The results of the three models together suggest again that HMB control and terror interact with each other, and socioeconomic variables play a lesser role. Proportion Pampangan is not a significant variable in any of the models except in Model 1. In all the models tenancy and sugar tend to offset each other. Barrios that devote a large fraction of their land to growing sugar have a lower probability of being controlled than other barrios[17] and conversely with respect to tenants. Model 1 is less satisfactory than the other two; only two of its six coefficients are significant. We do not attempt to choose between Models 2 and 3.

---

for barrios. This would create only a minor problem in estimation if the within-municipio variance were small relative to the between-municipio variance. It has been shown by David M. Grether that when independent variables are serially correlated very highly, interpolation of missing values may result in substantial gains in the efficiency of estimation. We would expect that barrios in one municipio would not differ greatly in percent Pampangan, tenancy, and sugar. Thus, the efficiency of estimation would be increased by using the municipio values, which are themselves weighted averages of the barrio values. See Grether, "Notes on Missing Observations in Regression Models with Serially Correlated Independent Variables," unpublished Cowles Foundation Paper, September 18, 1969.

If we express the difference between the municipio value and the true barrio value for which it is substituted as p_{ij} where i indexes variables and j barrios, the expected values of elements in the moment matrix are unchanged if (a) $E(p_{ij}x_{ji})$ $= 0$ and (b) $E(p_{ij}p_{ji}) = 0$. Using data for the 17 barrios that can be found both in our sample and in the ½ percent sample of the 1960 Census, (a) appears to be true. Condition (b) cannot be tested.

[17] At the municipal level sugar was not significant. Mitchell, *The Huk Rebellion*, finds a positive relation between sugar and control.

144

TABLE 62

BARRIO CONTROL MODELS, TWO-STAGE WEIGHTED ESTIMATES
(standard errors in parentheses)

Model 1	CONTROL = −.21 + .91 INBT + .00099 TEN − .028 SUGR + .52 PAMP
	(.06) (.0011) (.0020) (.045)
	INBT = −.021 + 1.49 CONTROL + .0049 DISTANCE, F = .4 with 2,2 D.F.
	(1.40) (1.26) (.038)
Model 2	CONTROL = −.20 + .076 ADJBA + .0034 TEN − .0047 SUGR + .10 PAMP
	(.0086) (.0017) (.0012) (.075)
	ADJBA = −.71 + 9.44 CONTROL + 1.84 INBT, F = 47 with 2,2 D.F.
	(.70) (.28)
	INBT = −3.66 − 1.42 CONTROL + .53 ADJBA + .11 DISTANCE,
	(1.09) (.07) (.03)
	F = 26 with 3,2 D.F.
Model 3	CONTROL = − .23 + .080 ADJBA − .082 INBTM + .40 TEN − .0044 SUGR
	(.009) (.036) (.17) (.0012)
	+ .12 PAMP, F = 88 with 5,1 D.F.
	(.08)
	ADJBA = − .59 + 10.57 CONTROL + .32 INATM, F = 15 with 2,4 D.F.
	(.94) (.11)
	INBT = − 3.0 − 1.60 CONTROL + .49 ADJBA + .092 DISTANCE,
	(.98) (.05) (.022)
	F = 96 with 3,3 D.F.

NOTE:

CONTROL = 1968 HMB control of the barrio, 1 = yes, 0 = no.
INBT = Number of HMB incidents within 2 kilometers, 1967-1968.
TEN = Tenancy rate for municipio.
SUGR = Percent of farmland in municipio planted to sugar.
PAMP = Fraction of the population speaking Pampangan in municipio.
DISTANCE = Distance of barrio from base of Mt. Arayat.
INBTM = Number of HMB incidents within 2 kilometers, 1965-1966.
INATM = Number of HMB incidents 2 to 6 kilometers distant, 1965-1966.
ADJBA = Number of HMB-controlled barrios within 2 kilometers, 1968.
F is P. J. Dhrymes' F. See footnote a, Table 61.

At both barrio and municipio level, the statistical results consistently emphasize the importance of operational considerations in
determining the pattern of HMB control. In all of the models HMB
incidents play a powerful role in the control equations. Socioeconomic variables are more ambiguous and weaker in effect, although they appear significant in some specifications.[18]

[18] Fitted without weighting, these models are substantively the same, although
as we would expect, levels of significance are lower.

The HMB in Laguna

Since 1965 there has been increasing HMB activity in the Tagalog province of Laguna, at least as measured by sightings (agent reports). Although terror and violence have not been used as techniques to gain control of barrios, some one hundred barrios are listed as controlled or influenced. The status of the HMB is even more ambiguous in Laguna than in Central Luzon. There have been reports of very large numbers of armed men circulating in Laguna or of several hundred HMB holding a conference in a barrio. We are skeptical of such reports. The data on HMB movements do suggest that some southward movement began in 1965 skirting the mountains east of Manila. This movement has been explained by either increased pressure from the Philippine Constabulary or alternatively the establishment of centers for rest and recreation. In any case the reported scale of activities seems inconsistent with the reported size of the HMB and its logistics capability.

Notes on the HMB Organization

For policy purposes we need to understand not only the determinants of insurgent control but the reasons the insurgents are "in business" at all. Terror and violence have many purposes. What is the purpose of the modern HMB? In particular, do they have the same revolutionary motives as the 1949-1953 HMB or are they more like the Mafia, made up of individuals motivated by personal gain? Continuity of motivation is at least a necessary condition for identifying the modern HMB with the historical organization.

Large amounts of detailed evidence on the structure and procedures of the Huk organization are hard to acquire. In 1969 we were able, through the Constabulary, to gain access to interviews with 12 Huk prisoners having recent service.[19] During their service

---

[19] The subjects interviewed range in age from 21 to 46; most are in their twenties. Six of them had three or fewer years of education, three had five years, and two had some high school; the education of one is unknown. Seven are from Pampangan-speaking families, three are Tagalogs, one is an Ilocano, and one a Cebuano. Thus, a cross-section of major Philippine ethnic groups is represented. All but one of them had experience in the HMB during 1968 or later; their views should be quite contemporary. However, none had a long period of service; the most experienced spent four years in the HMB. Six were captured by the PC and six surrendered.

146

the Huks apparently were split in two major factions, ideological and criminal. Since that time the organization has continued to evolve. There are now alleged to be three major factions: a Maoist group whose principal leader was trained in Peking, a smaller Moscow-oriented group, and the old criminal faction.[20] Our discussion here will be limited to the 1969 period where we have some direct primary evidence.

All but three of the respondents came from the area nominally under the control of Commander Freddie.[21] This area includes southwest Pampanga, northern Bataan, and the Olongapo-Subic complex. Nine of the interviewees were privates in armed groups. There was also a commander and a vice commander from the military arm of the HMB, and one low-level cadre.

All but one of the nine interviewees from Freddie's area, when asked about the training they had received, mentioned political indoctrination. Most of them held the same political views. Typical quotations from four of the subjects are given below.

We have group meetings and in said meetings, we were lectured to by the commander. We were told that the Philippine Government is not bad, and it is only the administrators of said government that ought to be changed. Change could be effected either by elections or violence if need be.

China and Russia were the only countries mentioned to us in lectures and in group talks by our leaders. It is said that those two countries are the only ones that are now led by the true sons of the motherland, that see to it that the people are served and not the people serving the officials in the government. They said that the HMB movement aims to attain what had happened in those countries, China and Russia.

. . . the main enemies of the HMBs are, first: the local exploiters who suck the blood of the common *tao* so as to enrich themselves; the people in the government who commit graft and corruption and all sorts of anomalies just to entrench themselves in power; those people who serve as stool-pigeons

[20] See R. Evans and R. Novak, "Philippine Guerrillas Active," *Los Angeles Times*, May 18, 1970; a UPI report on June 3 reports that the young Maoists have been trying to grab power from the older Maoists (*Los Angeles Times*, June 3, 1970).

[21] Until he was killed in an engagement with the PC early in 1969.

for the above-mentioned personalities, and secondly, those foreigners who drain our rich natural resources, export it to other countries and bring it back as finished products and sell it beyond the reach of the common people. Most of these aliens are the Americans. These were what we called American imperialists.

They told us that they wanted to establish a New Democracy that will give justice to everybody, and that there will be no more poor and no more rich, but everybody will be equal. "How?" By establishing a government that is really after the welfare of the working man, a government for the Filipinos not dictated by foreigners.

These statements resemble those in early Viet Cong documents. Perhaps of some interest and unlike Vietnam is the lack of an attack on the government as an institution. Only the people in the institution are attacked.

As for the alleged ideological split between Sumulong, the chief of the HMB at that time, and Freddie and the other commanders, five subjects were aware of some split.[22] Two others described Sumulong as loyal to the HMB's political motivation. The strongest criticism of Sumulong ran as follows: "I think the leaders of the HMB are in the organization in order to guide the movement of the HMB and their ardent desire is to champion the cause it is fighting for. I do not know any of the persons you mentioned [personally]. All I know is that the group of Commander Caviteño is out to get Commander Sumulong because this Sumulong has already turned traitor to the cause of the HMB."

The one interviewee from Sumulong's group—the Angeles-Clark faction—stated that Sumulong himself was a "die-hard Communist." However, this person was extremely vague on the goals and purposes of the organization. He could not cite any specific political indoctrination.

One other subject whom we could not specifically place in the organization, although he was apparently not in Sumulong's or Freddie's group, said he knew Sumulong personally and spoke

[22] Sumulong was supposed to control the area around Clark and Angeles. It is argued that Sumulong and his men were interested in personal gain while other branches are ideological. The factionalism has erupted into violence. Sumulong was captured by the PC in September 1970.

about him in knowledgeable terms. Again, unfortunately, his information was less useful than it might have been, since he was the only person without very recent experience in the HMB. He left the organization in December 1966. However, he did have personal experience of Sumulong's teaching the standard line, and he also called Sumulong a "die-hard Communist."

The interviews suggest that the group under Freddie received regular political training. That training is similar to that used by Communist dissident organizations around the world. Freddie's group seems to have been generally aware of a power struggle going on in the organization. The signals were much less clear about whether this power struggle was over ideology or its betrayal. In 1969 the evidence suggests that the Huks were split, with the Angeles-Clark faction primarily interested in personal gain.

Clearly, we should not rely very heavily on these 12 interviews to establish the nature of the HMB—although 12 is not a trivial fraction of all reported HMB regulars. It may be significant that five are not ethnic Pampangans; this is inconsistent with the proposition that a Pampangan-speaking population is a necessary condition for HMB control in a properly specified model. These interview data confirm the reports that the HMB organization is torn by power struggles and underscores the complex nature of the process by which the organization succeeds or fails. Although operational variables are as important in determining the pattern of control as variables relating to social unrest, it is still possible that members of the HMB themselves—particularly at lower levels—may be motivated in large part by idealistic visions of transforming society.

Policy Toward the HMB

It is important not to apply the metaphor of other insurgent groups—for example, the Viet Cong or the Cuban 26 July Movement —to the HMB. The current Philippine insurgency bears little resemblance to either. Actions based on an alleged similarity are likely to be unproductive. When we speak, for example, of HMB "control" of a barrio it should be clear that the government has not been denied access to the barrio and that its social structure has not been rebuilt by the insurgents, as was the case in Vietnam. The HMB themselves often live fairly ordinary lives with their families, quite unlike Castro's followers. Compared with the early Viet

149

Cong and the Cubans, the HMB appear to be rather indolent and poorly organized.[23] The organization is apparently split over the division of funds and over long-range goals. This rebellion does not fit the models of a classical insurgency.

Although it may not be a typical insurgency, the HMB is still a nuisance for the Philippine government. The common view of politicians and the press is that the HMB draws its power from popular discontent with social conditions—particularly land-tenure arrangements—and dissatisfaction with the performance of the government. If this is true, the HMB may be a serious threat. Areas of tenancy extend beyond the current area of HMB operations providing, according to this view, promising areas for HMB expansion. By the same token, it would be difficult to reduce the level of HMB control because it is hard for the government to accomplish significant changes in the social conditions alleged to underlie HMB support among the people.

The models presented here carry a mixed message for policy. The success of the HMB rests in large measure on what they do rather than on the condition of Philippine society; the roles of social variables are equivocal. This suggests that if the insurgents were astute and ambitious, the area they control might be substantially extended. It might also be possible for the government to compress that area by moves designed to checkmate HMB operations. The outcome in these models depends largely on the relative effectiveness of the Constabulary and the insurgents and the relative costs they incur. Of course the relative effectiveness of the Constabulary depends in part on political factors outside its control.

In our estimate, the HMB are likely to remain a major nuisance. They are not currently a great threat to the government. On the other hand, they have shown some resiliency and they do have access to a considerable flow of resources. Yet even if there were signals of widespread discontent that we have not picked up and this were a precondition of insurgency, the HMB do not now appear to be an organization that could mobilize and exploit that unrest.

---

[23] For example, the timing of HMB incidents indicates that the HMB seem to follow the customs of *merienda*—the Filipino coffee break—and *siesta*.

The Uses of Quantitative Analysis

FOR THE LAST FIVE CHAPTERS we have been trying to follow our own prescription—that is, to be quantitative, to get inside the information systems, to use multiple tests and measures—for analyzing the problems of LDCs. Application of this prescription to the Philippines has produced an image with the following characteristics:

+ The political system appears to be stable and generally responsive to the desires of most people. The stability rests on a rural sector voting along traditional lines with politicians responding primarily to rural demands. The only group we found that is relatively less oriented to traditional political behavior is the emerging modern labor force. It is growing fast and appears somewhat discontented with the current political system, but it is not yet an important political force.
+ The economy appears to have been performing better than commonly thought. Official figures have probably understated the rate of growth of GNP, and the emphasis on macroeconomic indicators has masked the substantial geographic dispersion of growth that has occurred since 1961.
+ The periodic lurching of the economy and the balance-of-payments crises which attract the attention of foreign observers are deeply rooted in the behavior of the political system and should not be seen as manifestations of any "fundamental disequilibrium" in the usual economic sense.
+ Crime is not a nationwide problem; violence and fear of violence are concentrated in a few areas. But, although crime is a less serious problem than usually thought, it also appears unaffected by the current instruments of government policy.
+ The HMB are not a serious threat to the government. The organization persists more by the application of terror and coercion than by satisfying any demand for social and economic reform. Even if there were deep dissatisfaction with government performance, the HMB are so ineffective that it seems an unlikely group to execute a successful uprising.

The general image of the Philippines needs to be changed. The change is important for the United States. The image of a country —though it often exists at a fairly high level of abstraction—serves as the context within which U.S. policies toward the country are viewed, evaluated, and formulated. If we see a country as tottering on the brink of disaster, our behavior is likely to be different than if we see the country as basically stable. In particular, wrongly viewing a country as unstable may lead the United States to over-react to ephemeral manifestations of political unrest. For Filipinos, too, the change is important. Political conduct and rhetoric center around general proclamations of crisis. These proclamations use up scarce resources—the time and attention of the public and policy-makers. They provide little guidance for creating new alternatives or clarifying social priorities, since no specific policies or programs are ever offered.

We found again and again that it is misleading to view the Philippines as an aggregate. The country is so diverse, with regions varying sharply on many dimensions, that its characteristics cannot be meaningfully summed up in a few aggregate indicators or collective impressions. Most Philippine government policies and many U.S. policies affect particular regions, or industries, or groups rather than the country as a whole. Aggregate indicators alone fail to show where resources should be allocated. For example, knowledge that Ilocos Sur is violent while Albay is peaceful provides specific guidance for the allocation of government and AID resources, but the overall murder rate does not.

Assessing the validity of any country's image requires in part gathering the right kinds of data, in part understanding reporting procedure, but fundamentally it requires doing more sophisticated analysis. Most of the information on which this study is based has always been available either in published documents or in the files of Philippine government agencies. Earlier surveys contained many of the data necessary to test our propositions about political behavior. Even though most of the data were available, however, little rigorous quantitative analysis had ever been done. The key element, therefore, was really the style of analysis rather than new data.

The availability of information in the Philippines made quantitative analysis easier than it might be in many other countries. We suspect, however, that there are many other countries where our experience in the Philippines could be a guide. Most developing countries build their statistical systems around the need to report various national aggregates to U.N. agencies or model their procedures after those of the United States or European countries. Wherever this is the case, the kinds of data that underlie this study can probably be obtained, wholly or in part.

Day-to-day operational reporting is properly characteristic of most U.S. agencies. However, the interpretations rest on general perceptions. From time to time the images should be reexamined systematically. Otherwise, both overall policy and day-to-day reporting may turn out to be poorly adapted to the needs of policymakers.

Pegasus Sample Design and Questionnaire

THIS APPENDIX describes the design and implementation of the Pegasus survey, which was conducted by the Asia Research Organization (ARO) of Manila with the permission of the Philippine government. The interviewing was done largely between January 9 and February 12, 1969. The questions covered attitudes toward the Philippine government and toward social, economic, and political conditions in the Philippines; attitudes toward and knowledge of dissidents and exposure to crime; and attitudes toward violence. The questionnaire was made up almost exclusively of closed, multiple-response questions.

Sample Design

One purpose of the Pegasus survey was to provide data at the individual level against which to check ecological relationships that had already appeared in our analysis. Also, in some areas of interest there were no existing data. It was logical to attempt to obtain information by surveying. Pegasus thus provided a means for filling in some gaps in our knowledge.

Since ethnic differences appear in a number of the ecological analyses, we decided that the sample should be stratified by language to insure coverage of the smaller ethnic groups. Since we were interested particularly in voting behavior, we restricted the sample to those between the ages of 21 and 65.

The population was broken into 11 strata: the 10 major language groups, accounting in 1960 for nearly 90 percent of the population, plus one stratum for Greater Manila. Since the stratification was by language groups rather than by areas there was some arbitrariness in the choice of areas to sample. In some cases, language groups nearly correspond to provinces. Most native speakers of the Pampangan and Pangasinan dialects, for example, are found in the provinces of Pampanga and Pangasinan, dictating the choice of these two provinces as sample areas. Other language groups, particularly the Ilocanos, are spread more broadly across the country. In these cases the most homogeneous provinces were chosen, so that the actual interviewing in any area could be conducted in only one language. Since only 75 interviews were conducted in any single province,[1]

[1] Except in Greater Manila, where 150 interviews were conducted, and Sulu, which was sampled as an add-on of 50 interviews.

two to four provinces were sampled for each of the five major language groups. (See Figure A-1 for sampling areas.) Table A-1 shows

TABLE A-1

STRATUM PROPORTIONS AND INTERVIEWS OBTAINED

Stratum	Proportion of Universe in Stratum[a]	Number of Provinces Sampled	Number of Interviews Obtained
Greater Manila	.072	1	150
Ilocano	.133	3	225
Tagalog	.191	3	225
Bicol	.082	2	150
Pampanga	.035	1	75
Pangasinan	.026	1	75
Ilongo	.122	2	150
Samar-Leyte	.061	1	75
Cebuano	.259	4	300
Magindanao	.014	1	75
Tausog	.004	1	50
	1.000	20	1550

NOTE:

[a] Based on tabulations of the .5 percent sample of the 1960 Census of Population.

the proportion of the adult population in each stratum, the number of provinces sampled, and the number of interviews obtained.

Within each province the major city—usually the provincial capital—was chosen as an interview area. In addition, one municipal *poblacion* and one rural barrio were chosen at random. The 75 interviews allocated to each province were divided equally among these three sample areas; thus, in each province 25 interviews come from the principal city, 25 come from some other urban area, and 25 come from a rural place.[2]

Sampling Procedures

URBAN SAMPLING

For all cities, except Greater Manila, and for all municipal *poblaciones* the area of the city proper was divided into a number of regions consisting of 50 to 100 houses. One of these subunits was randomly selected as an interview area. In Greater Manila the subdivisions corresponded to voting precincts of which 30 were selected on a random basis as interview areas.

[2] In Sulu the interviews were conducted in the city of Jolo and the *poblacion* of Taglibi.

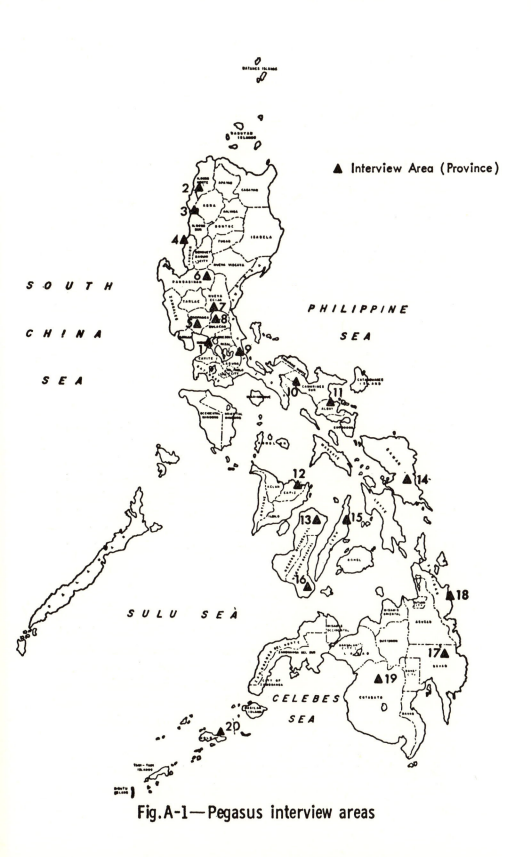

▲ Interview Area (Province)

Fig.A-1—Pegasus interview areas

RURAL SAMPLING

One rural barrio was selected on a random basis for each province. The rural interview area was the entire barrio.

SAMPLING WITHIN THE INTERVIEW AREA

Each interviewer was provided with a map of his interview area marked with a specified starting point. The dwelling unit on or nearest to the indicated starting point was the first dwelling unit the interviewer sampled, and the household living in that unit was the first sample household. The route or direction of coverage was also indicated, and every other house was visited along the route until the quota of 5 per area in the Greater Manila area and 25 per area elsewhere was met. The interviewer was instructed to alternate interviewing males and females and to interview only persons of the given mother tongue (except in Manila where mother tongue was not a sampling criterion). Only Philippine citizens were interviewed.

SAMPLING WITHIN A HOUSEHOLD

At each household the interviewer had a specified sex and mother tongue for the prospective subject. All eligible subjects in the household were listed, and with the aid of a random number table one was selected. If the indicated subject was not at home the interviewer was instructed to return twice. If the desired subject could not be reached after the return calls, another household was substituted by continuing along the specified route. If no eligible persons lived in the substituted household, a second household was substituted. Household help, boarders, and visitors were not considered to be household members.

SOCIOECONOMIC STATUS

The sampling procedures outlined above were expected to result in a lower coverage of higher income households than desired. Particularly in the more rural areas, very few higher income households would be found. Thus, the interviewers were instructed that if they had not covered three households from the higher income categories after 22 interviews, they were to stop their regular sampling procedure and attempt to find three such households.

Recheck of Interviewing

At the end of each interviewing day, field supervisors of ARO collected the completed questionnaires from each interviewer and retraced the interviewer's path, verifying that the interviews had actually been executed. In addition to this recheck, we personally observed about 25 interviews in various parts of the country.

After all of the interviewing was completed, we sent Filipino members of our staff to nine interview areas. In each area two subjects were partly reinterviewed and the sample area was checked to verify that the indicated respondents had actually been interviewed. Thus, we were satisfied that ARO's field work had been carried out as planned.

To check reproducibility, we compared the partial interviews carried out by our staff with the original interviews of the same subjects. If we consider responses that differed by no more than one point on a three or more point scale as identical, about 85 percent of the responses on the reinterview matched those obtained in the original interview. Adopting the more rigorous criterion of *exact* correspondence between the two interviews, but ignoring questions to which the respondent made no response or answered "Don't know" on only one occasion, the reproducibility is about 63 percent. The proportion of exactly corresponding answers, including "Don't know," was 55 percent.

Data Processing

WEIGHTING

Because interviews had to be conducted in blocks of 25, the number of subjects drawn in each stratum is not exactly proportional to the stratum size. Thus, it was necessary to weight the responses to obtain estimates of total population proportions. Similarly, within each province the proportion of interviews in the principal city, in a *poblacion*, and in rural barrios did not correspond to the proportion of the population residing in these three types of places. The total was calculated as the product of these two corrections, that is:

$$\text{Total Weight} = \frac{I_s}{P_s} \times \frac{I_p}{P_p}$$

Where I_s = Interviews in stratum/total interviews.
P_s = Population in stratum/total universe.
I_p = Interviews in type of place in province/population in type of place in province.
P_p = Population in type of place in province/total population in province.

TESTS OF SIGNIFICANCE

Many of the tables in the text present two tests of homogeneity, χ^2 and χ_1^2. The ordinary χ^2 requires no explanation; it was calculated on sums across strata using the standard correction for continuity when small cells were encountered. The χ_1^2 is presented because χ^2 is, strictly speaking, not an appropriate test for a *stratified* random sample such as Pegasus. The χ_1^2 statistic, unlike χ^2, considers the distribution of responses stratum by stratum.[3] The computational algorithm is as follows:

Consider a contingency table with r rows, s columns, and t strata. Defining:

(1) P_k = The population of stratum k as a proportion of the total universe.

(2) N_k = The number of observations in the sample drawn from stratum k.

(3) n_{ijk} = The number of elements in the i, j, k cell of the contingency table.

(4) $\hat{p}_{ijk} = n_{ijk} \dfrac{P_k}{N_k}$

The χ_1^2 statistic $= \underline{c}\, G^{-1} \underline{c}'$

where $\underline{c} = (c_{11}, c_{12}, \ldots c_{(r\text{-}1)(s\text{-}1)})$
and

$$
G = \begin{bmatrix}
g_{1111} & g_{2111} \cdots \cdots & g_{(r\text{-}1)(s\text{-}1)11} \\
g_{1121} & g_{2121} \cdots \cdots & g_{(r\text{-}1)(s\text{-}1)21} \\
\cdot & \cdot & \cdot \\
\cdot & \cdot & \cdot \\
\cdot & \cdot & \cdot \\
g_{11(r\text{-}1)1} & g_{21(r\text{-}1)1} \cdots \cdots & g_{(r\text{-}1)(s\text{-}1)(r\text{-}1)1} \\
\cdot & \cdot & \\
\cdot & \cdot & \\
\cdot & \cdot & \\
g_{11(r\text{-}1)(s\text{-}1)} & g_{21(r\text{-}1)(s\text{-}1)} \cdots & g_{(r\text{-}1)(s\text{-}1)(r\text{-}1)(s\text{-}1)}
\end{bmatrix}
$$

G is an (r-1) (s-1) $\times$ (r-1) (s-1) matrix.

[3] The general derivation of Bhapkar's statistic may be found in V. P. Bhapkar, "Some Tests for Categorical Data," *Annals of Mathematical Statistics*, 32 (March 1961), pp. 72-83. The computational algorithm follows Gad Nathan, "Tests of Independence in Contingency Tables from Stratified Samples," in Norman L. Johnson and Harry Smith, Jr., eds., *New Developments in Survey Sampling*, New York, John Wiley & Sons, Inc., 1969, pp. 578-600.

(5) $c_{ij} = \hat{p}_{ij}. - \hat{p}_i.. \hat{p}.._j.$

(6) $g_{ijIJ} = \sum_k' \frac{P_k}{N_k} \sum_{x,y} \left(\frac{f_{ijxyk} - b_{ijk}}{P_k}\right) \left(\frac{f_{IJxyk} - b_{IJk}}{P_k}\right) \hat{p}_{xyk}$

(7) $b_{ijk} = \sum_{x,y}' \frac{f_{ijxyk}}{P_k} \hat{p}_{xyk}$

(8) $f_{ijxyk} = P_k(\delta_i^x \delta_j^y - \delta_i^x \hat{p}._j. - \delta_j^y \hat{p}_i.)$

where δ is the Kronecker delta and $(i,I = 1, \ldots, r-1; j,J = 1, \ldots, s-1; \chi = 1, \ldots, r; y = 1, \ldots, s; k = 1, \ldots, t)$. Under the null hypothesis of homogeneity, χ_1^2 is asymptotically distributed as χ^2 with $(r-1)(s-1)$ D.F.

Although χ_1^2 is the appropriate test statistic, its small sample properties are unknown. These are especially important since working with 11 strata we frequently encounter cells in contingency tables that are empty or nearly empty. Since this happens most frequently in small strata, which are given only small weight in the calculation of χ_1^2, the problem is reduced. Nonetheless, we decided it would be desirable to require relations that emerged in contingency tables to pass both the χ_1^2 and χ^2 criteria of significance.

The Questionnaire

The English version of the Pegasus questionnaire is reproduced below. Although it appears first in the questionnaire, the block of questions on personal characteristics of the respondent was administered at the end of the interview.

Classification Data

	Card 1
	Column

Map No. _____

Date of Interview: _____, 1969.   1 - 2

Respondent's Name: _____

Address-Hse. No. Street: _____

   —Province   : _____   3 - 4

   —Municipality/City : _____   5 - 6

   —Barrio/Poblacion : _____   7 - 8

Sex: 0 ( ) Male   1 ( ) Female   - 9

Education: No. of years in school: _____   10 - 11

            (If 0): Reads-writes?   1 ( ) No   2 ( ) Yes   - 12

Civil Status: 0 ( ) Single   2 ( ) Divorced/Separated   - 13

            1 ( ) Married   3 ( ) Widowed

Religion   : 0 ( ) Catholic   3 ( ) Muslim   - 14

            1 ( ) Iglesia ni Kristo   4 ( ) Other _____

            2 ( ) Aglipayan   5 ( ) None   Specify

Age   : _____   15 - 16

Position in Household: 0 ( ) Male Head   2 ( ) Other, related   - 17

                    1 ( ) Chief Female   3 ( ) Other, not related

Are Parents Alive? — Mother: 0 ( ) No   1 ( ) Yes   9 ( ) DK   - 18

                  — Father : 0 ( ) No   1 ( ) Yes   9 ( ) DK   - 19

(*If Dead*:) Respondent's age at time of — Mother's death: _____   20 - 21

                              — Father's death: _____   22 - 23

Number of persons living in the household: _____   24 - 25

Number of living children of respondent : _____   26 - 27

Household Socioeconomic Status: 0 ( ) A   2 ( ) C   - 28

                          1 ( ) B   3 ( ) D

Migration: Number of years in present barrio/city: _____   29 - 30

(*In Urban Areas*): Did respondent spend childhood in rural area?

                    0 ( ) N   1 ( ) Y   - 31

Occupation : Respondent   : _____   32 - 33

            Household Head : _____   34 - 35

Employment: Is respondent regularly employed?   0 ( ) No   1 ( ) Yes   - 36

            Is hh. head regularly employed?   0 ( ) No   1 ( ) Yes   - 37

            No. of persons in hh. willing to work but jobless: _____   38 - 39

            No. of persons in hh. with jobs: _____   40 - 41

162

Tenancy Status: Owns the house?	0 ( ) No	1 ( ) Yes	-42
Owns the lot?	0 ( ) No	1 ( ) Yes	-43
(*If not own hse*): Pays rent?	0 ( ) No	1 ( ) Yes	-44

(*If farmer*): 0 ( ) Owns land 1 ( ) Tenant 2 ( ) Lessee 3 ( ) Comb. -45

Language : 1st language the respondent learned? _____ -46

Language of father _____ -47

Language of mother _____ -48

Compadre Status: How many compadres does respondent have? _____ 49-50

Ownership of Appliances: Radio	0 ( ) No	1 ( ) Yes	-51
TV	0 ( ) No	1 ( ) Yes	-52
Refrig.	0 ( ) No	1 ( ) Yes	-53

Persons Present During Interview: -54

Respondent only   0 ( )   Family & Others 2 ( )

Family members   1 ( )   Others   3 ( )

Spontaneity of answer: -55

Reluctant to answer 0 ( ) No   1 ( ) Yes

++

I CERTIFY THAT THE FOREGOING IS A TRUE AND HONEST INTERVIEW.

Supervised by : _____ Date: _____ _____

Spotchecked by : _____ Date: _____ Interviewer

Edited by   : _____ Date: _____

Questionnaire

1. I will read to you some problems facing our country. For each problem I read will you please tell me if you think it is not important . . . of some importance . . . or very important to the welfare of our country:

	Not Imp.	Some Imp.	Very Imp.	DK/No Op.	Card 1 Column
a) Raising taxes	0 ( )	1 ( )	2 ( )	9 ( )	58
b) Increasing exports	0 ( )	1 ( )	2 ( )	9 ( )	59
c) High cost of living	0 ( )	1 ( )	2 ( )	9 ( )	60
d) High crime rate	0 ( )	1 ( )	2 ( )	9 ( )	61
e) Rapid population growth	0 ( )	1 ( )	2 ( )	9 ( )	62
f) Widespread graft & corruption	0 ( )	1 ( )	2 ( )	9 ( )	63

163

g) Dissidence or the Huk
problem   0 ( )   1 ( )   2 ( )   9 ( )   64

h) Treatment of minority
groups   0 ( )   1 ( )   2 ( )   9 ( )   65

2. Here is a ladder with 10 steps (SHOW LADDER). Let us say that the highest step (POINT) represents the best life you can imagine. The lower the steps in the ladder (TRACE STEPS DOWNWARD) the worse the kind of life—so that the bottom step (POINT) represents the *worst* kind of life you can imagine. Now—

Code: STEP NO.
(No response = 0)   *Column*

a) What step on the ladder were you on 3 years ago? _____   66 - 67

b) What step are you on today? _____   68 - 69

c) What step do you expect to be on 3 years from now? _____   70 - 71

d) (If DK on Q. 2c): Ask "well do you expect life to be . . ." _____   72

0 ( ) Worse   1 ( ) Same   2 ( ) Better   9 ( ) DK

NOTE: For Keypunch Code Number   75 - 78

Card Number (1)   80

3. If you had an extra P1000 would you spend none of it . . . some of it . . . or most if not all of the P1000 on (*item*)? How about (*item*)? etc.

	None	*Some*	*Most/ All*	*DK/No Op.*	*Card 2 Column*
a) Invest in a business	0 ( )	1 ( )	2 ( )	9 ( )	1
b) Buy a TV set or other household appliances	0 ( )	1 ( )	2 ( )	9 ( )	2
c) Partial payment for house or land	0 ( )	1 ( )	2 ( )	9 ( )	3
d) Education for your children	0 ( )	1 ( )	2 ( )	9 ( )	4
e) Save it	0 ( )	1 ( )	2 ( )	9 ( )	5

4. From your impressions of politicians, is the word I will read to you descriptive of none or very few politicians . . . some of them . . . or most of them?

	None/ Few	*Some*	*Most*	*DK/No Op.*	*Column*
a) Greedy	0 ( )	1 ( )	2 ( )	9 ( )	6
b) Honest	0 ( )	1 ( )	2 ( )	9 ( )	7
c) Hard-working	0 ( )	1 ( )	2 ( )	9 ( )	8
d) Corrupt	0 ( )	1 ( )	2 ( )	9 ( )	9
e) Nationalistic	0 ( )	1 ( )	2 ( )	9 ( )	10
f) An example to follow	0 ( )	1 ( )	2 ( )	9 ( )	11

5. How important are the following characteristics in determining whether a person is good or not? Let us start off with (*characteristic*): is this not very important . . . of some importance . . . or very important? How about (*characteristic*)? Etc.

	Not Imp.	Some Imp.	Very Imp.	DK/No Op.	Column
a) Honesty	0 ( )	1 ( )	2 ( )	9 ( )	12
b) Pride	0 ( )	1 ( )	2 ( )	9 ( )	13
c) Industriousness	0 ( )	1 ( )	2 ( )	9 ( )	14
d) Loyalty	0 ( )	1 ( )	2 ( )	9 ( )	15
e) Courage	0 ( )	1 ( )	2 ( )	9 ( )	16
f) Compassion	0 ( )	1 ( )	2 ( )	9 ( )	17
g) Aggressiveness	0 ( )	1 ( )	2 ( )	9 ( )	18
h) Competitiveness	0 ( )	1 ( )	2 ( )	9 ( )	19
i) Courtesy	0 ( )	1 ( )	2 ( )	9 ( )	20
j) Helpfulness	0 ( )	1 ( )	2 ( )	9 ( )	21

6. I will read to you some factors that people take into account when selecting a candidate for the presidency of our country. In your own case, do you consider this factor not important . . . somewhat important . . . or very important?

	Not Imp.	Some Imp.	Very Imp.	DK/No Op.	Column
a) Candidate comes from your area or speaks your dialect	0 ( )	1 ( )	2 ( )	9 ( )	22
b) Honesty of candidate	0 ( )	1 ( )	2 ( )	9 ( )	23
c) General policy of the candidate	0 ( )	1 ( )	2 ( )	9 ( )	24
d) Your close friend's or compadre's attitude towards the candidate	0 ( )	1 ( )	2 ( )	9 ( )	25
e) Help given to your area in the past	0 ( )	1 ( )	2 ( )	9 ( )	26
f) Promise of help to your area	0 ( )	1 ( )	2 ( )	9 ( )	27
g) Party of the candidate	0 ( )	1 ( )	2 ( )	9 ( )	28

7a. Do you believe that elections for President in our country are . . .   29

    0 ( ) Seldom if ever honest . . .   2 ( ) Always honest?

    1 ( ) Usually honest . . . or   9 ( ) DK—No opinion

7b. Do you believe that elections for Mayor in our country are . . .   30

    0 ( ) Seldom if ever honest . . .   2 ( ) Always honest?

    1 ( ) Usually honest . . . or   9 ( ) DK—No opinion

8. Did you vote for the Nacionalista candidate . . . the Liberal candidate . . . the Progressive Party candidate . . . or some other candidate for (*position*) in the (*year*) election?

	Nac.	Lib.	Prog.	Oth.	None	Not Vote	DK	Column
a) President, 1961 Garcia NP Macapagal LP	0 ( )	1 ( )	2 ( )	3 ( )	4 ( )	5 ( )	9 ( )	31
b) President, 1965 Marcos NP Macapagal LP Manglapus PPP	0 ( )	1 ( )	2 ( )	3 ( )	4 ( )	5 ( )	9 ( )	32
c) Mayor, 1967	0 ( )	1 ( )	2 ( )	3 ( )	4 ( )	5 ( )	9 ( )	33

INTERVIEWER: Do not ask Q. 9 if respondent did not vote in 1967.

9. In the 1967 election, which of the following factors which I will read most influenced you to register:

	Column 34	Column 35	Column
Civic duty	0 ( )	0 ( )	34 - 35
Platform of the party	1 ( )	1 ( )	
Contact by party worker	2 ( )	2 ( )	
Persuasion by friend, compadres	3 ( )	3 ( )	
Concern with outcome of the election	4 ( )	4 ( )	
The candidate	5 ( )	5 ( )	

10. Here are some activities of our government. (SHOW LIST) Which of these do you feel is the most important to you and your family? Which is the next one? And after that?

	Lowest	Next Lowest	Second Highest	Highest	Column
Building school	0 ( )	1 ( )	2 ( )	3 ( )	36
Building roads	0 ( )	1 ( )	2 ( )	3 ( )	37
Building markets or hospital	0 ( )	1 ( )	2 ( )	3 ( )	38
Providing employment	0 ( )	1 ( )	2 ( )	3 ( )	39
DK	0 ( )	1 ( )	2 ( )	3 ( )	40

11. I will read to you again those factors that people take into account when selecting a candidate. This time please tell me how important the factor is in your selection of a candidate for mayor.

	Not Imp.	Some Imp.	Very Imp.	DK/No Op.	Column
a) Candidate comes from your area or speaks your dialect	0 ( )	1 ( )	2 ( )	9 ( )	41

b) Honesty of the
   candidate   0 ( )   1 ( )   2 ( )   9 ( )   42

c) General policy of the
   candidate   0 ( )   1 ( )   2 ( )   9 ( )   43

d) Your close friend's or
   compadre's attitude
   towards the candidate   0 ( )   1 ( )   2 ( )   9 ( )   44

e) Help given to your area
   in the past   0 ( )   1 ( )   2 ( )   9 ( )   45

f) Promise of help to
   your area   0 ( )   1 ( )   2 ( )   9 ( )   46

g) Party of the candidate   0 ( )   1 ( )   2 ( )   9 ( )   47

12a. Have you ever been offered money to vote for a particular candidate?

     0 ( ) No   1 ( ) Yes   9 ( ) No Response   48

12b. (IF YES): How much?

     (IF IN KIND CONVERT TO PESO VALUE) Code: 49

                   Peso Value

13. Here is a different type of question. What are the things you are most proud of as a Filipino citizen?

     _____

     _____   50-51

     _____

14. If you had a problem which needed action from the government, do you feel . . . as a general rule . . . that you could get such action?

     0 ( ) No   1 ( ) Yes   9 ( ) DK   52

15. On the whole do the activities of our national government tend to have any influence on your day-to-day life?

     0 ( ) No   1 ( ) Yes   9 ( ) DK   53

16. Do you think your life would be worse . . . just the same . . . or better without these government activities?

     0 ( ) Worse   2 ( ) Better

     1 ( ) Just the same   9 ( ) DK—No opinion   54

17. Suppose there was some question that you had to take to a government office . . . for example, a tax question or a housing regulation. Do you think you would be treated as well as anyone?

     0 ( ) No   1 ( ) Yes   9 ( ) DK   55

18. From your impressions of government employees, is the word I will read descriptive of none or very few of them ... some of them ... or most of them?

	None/Few	Some	Most	DK/No Op.	Column
a) Courteous	0 ( )	1 ( )	2 ( )	9 ( )	56
b) Arrogant	0 ( )	1 ( )	2 ( )	9 ( )	57
c) Efficient	0 ( )	1 ( )	2 ( )	9 ( )	58
d) Responsive	0 ( )	1 ( )	2 ( )	9 ( )	59
e) Corrupt	0 ( )	1 ( )	2 ( )	9 ( )	60
f) Helpful	0 ( )	1 ( )	2 ( )	9 ( )	61
g) Indifferent	0 ( )	1 ( )	2 ( )	9 ( )	62

19a. For this next question we would like to know how safe or unsafe you feel in your own neighborhood. What do you think your chances are of being killed in your neighborhood: Would you say the chances are very low ... low ... moderate ... or high?

19b. And would you say that the possibility of your being robbed in your neighborhood is very low ... low ... moderate ... or high?

	Very Low	Low	Moderate	High	DK/No Op.	Column
a) Being killed	0 ( )	1 ( )	2 ( )	3 ( )	9 ( )	63
b) Being robbed	0 ( )	1 ( )	2 ( )	3 ( )	9 ( )	64

20a. Have you ever been involved in a court case?

0 ( ) No
9 ( ) No response } PROCEED TO Q. 21   1 ( ) Yes   65

20b. As the complainant ... or the defendant?

0 ( ) Complainant   1 ( ) Defendant   2 ( ) Witness   66

20c. In your opinion was your case settled quickly ... in a reasonable time ... or did it take a long time?

0 ( ) Took a long time   2 ( ) Settled quickly

1 ( ) Reasonable time   9 ( ) DK—Not yet settled   67

20d. What did you think of the court proceedings: Was it unfair ... or fair?
0 ( ) Unfair   1 ( ) Fair   9 ( ) DK—Not yet settled   68

21. Do you think our courts are generally honest and efficient?
0 ( ) No   1 ( ) Yes   9 ( ) DK—No opinion   69

168

22. Putting it another way, do you think our courts convict the guilty only sometimes . . . most of the time . . . or all of the time?

0 ( ) Only sometimes   2 ( ) All of the time

70

1 ( ) Most of the time   9 ( ) DK—No opinion

23. What is your opinion of justice in our country?

_____

_____   71 - 72

_____

NOTE: For Keypunch Code Number   75 - 78
Card Number (2)   80

24. What is your opinion of the following persons or officials with regard to their honesty or corruption: Would you say most of them are generally honest . . . partly honest and partly corrupt . . . or generally corrupt?

	Corrupt	Half-half	Honest	DK/No Op.	Card 3 Column
a) Your policeman	0 ( )	1 ( )	2 ( )	9 ( )	1
b) The local PC	0 ( )	1 ( )	2 ( )	9 ( )	2
c) The fiscals here	0 ( )	1 ( )	2 ( )	9 (·)	3
d) The lawyers here	0 ( )	1 ( )	2 ( )	9 ( )	4
e) The judges here	0 ( )	1 ( )	2 ( )	9 ( )	5
f) The politician here	0 ( )	1 ( )	2 ( )	9 ( )	6

25a. During the last two years was there any serious crime committed against yourself, your family or close relatives, or to any of your close friends?

0 ( ) No   1 ( ) Yes   2 ( ) DK   7

25b. (IF YES): What was the nature of the crime? Who was the victim? How many times did this happen to the victim? Any other incidents? (PROBE)

	Personal	Col.	Fam/Rel	Col.	Friends	Col.
Homicide/Murder	_____	8	_____	13	_____	18
Physical injuries	_____	9	_____	14	_____	19
Theft/Robbery	_____	10	_____	15	_____	20
Crime vs. Chastity	_____	11	_____	16	_____	21
Others	_____	12	_____	17	_____	22

169

26. In your opinion, is taking the life of a person never morally permissible . . . permissible in special cases . . . mostly permissible . . . or always permissible (SHOW CARD) under the following conditions:

	Never	Special Cases	Mostly	Always	DK/No Op.	Column
a) Self-defense	0 ( )	1 ( )	2 ( )	3 ( )	9 ( )	23
b) Retaliation for injuries to a relative or close friend	0 ( )	1 ( )	2 ( )	3 ( )	9 ( )	24
c) Retaliation for an insult to one's honor	0 ( )	1 ( )	2 ( )	3 ( )	9 ( )	25
d) Rape of a close relative	0 ( )	1 ( )	2 ( )	3 ( )	9 ( )	26
e) Political or other feuds	0 ( )	1 ( )	2 ( )	3 ( )	9 ( )	27

27a. Have you ever been asked for money by a government official or employee in order to expedite a service you needed?

0 ( ) No   1 ( ) Yes   9 ( ) No response   28

27b. (IF YES): How often has this been done to you: once or twice . . . a few times . . . or frequently?

0 ( ) Once or twice   2 ( ) Frequently

1 ( ) A few times   9 ( ) Can't recall—No response   29

28a. Have you ever been forced into a situation where you had to offer money to a government employee or official in order to avoid complications?

Column

0 ( ) No   1 ( ) Yes   9 ( ) No response   30

28b. (IF YES): How often did you have to do this: once or twice . . . a few times . . . or frequently?

0 ( ) Once or twice   2 ( ) Frequently

1 ( ) A few times   9 ( ) Can't recall—No response   31

29. If a friend of yours needed some help from a government office, would you advise him to . . .

0 ( ) Go there by himself and seek the help he needs through channels . . .

1 ( ) Bring someone with right connections . . . or   32

2 ( ) Try to give "lagay" or "put" to the right persons in that office?

9 ( ) DK—No opinion

30. How much would you expect to pay to get a minor paper expedited?

0 ( ) None   3 ( ) P11 to P20   9 ( ) DK—No

1 ( ) P1 to P5   4 ( ) P21 to P50   opinion   33

2 ( ) P6 to P10   5 ( ) More than P50

31. How do you feel about graft and corruption in the national government, do you think it is not prevalent at all . . . prevalent but not a major problem . . . or that it is prevalent and is a major problem?

0 ( ) Not prevalent   2 ( ) Prevalent, major problem

1 ( ) Prevalent, not major problem   9 ( ) DK—No opinion   34

32. How about in the local government, is graft and corruption not prevalent at all . . . prevalent but not a major problem . . . or that it is prevalent and is a major problem?

0 ( ) Not prevalent   2 ( ) Prevalent, major problem

1 ( ) Prevalent, not major problem   9 ( ) DK—No opinion   35

33. Do you think the common man in the Philippines who lies and steals does so because of . . .

	No	Partly	Yes	DK/ No Op.	Column
a) Little or no schooling	0 ( )	1 ( )	2 ( )	9 ( )	36
b) Bad example set by leaders	0 ( )	1 ( )	2 ( )	9 ( )	37
c) Lack of religion	0 ( )	1 ( )	2 ( )	9 ( )	38
d) Poverty	0 ( )	1 ( )	2 ( )	9 ( )	39
e) Inherent nature	0 ( )	1 ( )	2 ( )	9 ( )	40

34a. Ever since our country became a republic, a lot of things have been said about the Huks. Different people have different opinions about them. You have heard about the Huks, haven't you?

34b. Would you prefer not to talk about them?   41

0 ( ) No   2 ( ) Prefers not to talk: PROCEED TO Q. 40.

1 ( ) Yes

35. To your knowledge, how well does each of the following descriptions apply to the Huks: is the term I will read not applicable to them . . . partly true . . . or descriptive of them?

	Not App.	Partly	Descrip.	DK/ No Op.	Column
a) Nationalistic	0 ( )	1 ( )	2 ( )	9 ( )	42
b) Bandits	0 ( )	1 ( )	2 ( )	9 ( )	43

171

c) Misguided men	0 ( )	1 ( )	2 ( )	9 ( )	44
d) Brutal	0 ( )	1 ( )	2 ( )	9 ( )	45
e) Hope of the tenant	0 ( )	1 ( )	2 ( )	9 ( )	46
f) Tools of Red China	0 ( )	1 ( )	2 ( )	9 ( )	47
g) Men of justice	0 ( )	1 ( )	2 ( )	9 ( )	48
h) Enemies of the rich or the landlords	0 ( )	1 ( )	2 ( )	9 ( )	49

36. Have you ever heard about the Huks being seen in your area? 50

    0 ( ) No   1 ( ) Yes

    9 ( ) DK—No response   } PROCEED TO Q. 40

37. From what people here say, which of the following activities have happened in your surrounding area?

	No	Yes	DK	Column
a) Occasionally seen	0 ( )	1 ( )	9 ( )	51
b) Work with politicians	0 ( )	1 ( )	9 ( )	52
c) Has influence over local politicians	0 ( )	1 ( )	9 ( )	53
d) Tax people	0 ( )	1 ( )	9 ( )	54
e) Enforce the laws	0 ( )	1 ( )	9 ( )	55

38. Again from what you have heard, what kind of persons most strongly support and help the Huks?

39. And what kind of persons tend to join the Huks? Are they the . . .

	38. Support				39. Join			
	No	Yes	DK	Column	No	Yes	DK	Column
a) Young	0 ( )	1 ( )	2 ( )	56	0 ( )	1 ( )	2 ( )	62
b) Landless	0 ( )	1 ( )	2 ( )	57	0 ( )	1 ( )	2 ( )	63
c) Poor	0 ( )	1 ( )	2 ( )	58	0 ( )	1 ( )	2 ( )	64
d) Criminals	0 ( )	1 ( )	2 ( )	59	0 ( )	1 ( )	2 ( )	65
e) Jobless	0 ( )	1 ( )	2 ( )	60	0 ( )	1 ( )	2 ( )	66
f) Landlords	0 ( )	1 ( )	2 ( )	61	0 ( )	1 ( )	2 ( )	67

40. Do you now have less, the same, or more money to spend than you had three (3) years ago?

                                                                              Column

    0 ( ) Less   1 ( ) Same   2 ( ) More   9 ( ) DK   68

41a. Which of the following occupations would you most like your son to follow?

Priest	1 ( )	69 - 70
Doctor	2 ( )	
Lawyer	3 ( )	
Teacher	4 ( )	
Manager of a firm	5 ( )	
Engineer	6 ( )	
Gov. official	7 ( )	
Architect	8 ( )	
Artist	9 ( )	
Politician	x ( )	
AFP official	y ( )	

41b. Why?

_____

_____   71 - 72

_____

NOTE: For Keypunch Code Number   75 - 78

Card Number (3)   80

APPENDIX B

Factor Analysis Data Base

IN THIS APPENDIX we describe the variables that went into the factor analysis and sketch the logic behind the decision to include certain general classes of variables. In addition to the substantive variables, which represent activities or conditions in Philippine society, we felt that certain basic structural characteristics of the Philippine islands were of importance in understanding the way social systems interact and interlock. The Philippines is a nation still heavily dependent on agriculture.[1] Obviously, the typhoon and "dry-season" rainfall pattern in the area is an important physical component in Philippine agriculture. Typhoons tend to inhibit the growth of certain crops and make the growth of any crop a risky affair. The dry season in some areas is so pronounced that growth of a productive crop is severely inhibited. Consequently, variables representing the likelihood of typhoons in each province and the amount of dry-season rainfall are included as structural variables designed to aid in understanding the spatial distribution of agriculture.

In terms of social behavior our other analyses indicated considerable differences in tastes and behavior among some of the ethnic (language) groups in the Philippines. In Philippine folklore the Ilocanos are noted for their industriousness and their thriftiness, and, to some extent, for the violence of their electoral process. To account for these differences, we included variables such as the percent of the population living in the province of a given ethnic type. Since Philippine provinces tend to be homogeneous along ethnic lines, there is a strong tendency for the values on these variables to be near 0 or 100.

Specifically, the data relate to:

Agriculture. Much of the population is still engaged in agriculture, and agricultural exports are the major source of foreign exchange. Moreover, change in the agricultural sector is postulated to be a major cause of dissidence. Much of the infrastructure program is oriented toward integrating the rural areas into the modern sector. A number of variables are included to represent some aspects of the rural-farming sector.

Tenancy rates for 1938 and 1960 are included, since tenancy has

[1] See McKendry et al., *The Psychological Impact of Social Change*, pp. 1-27.

174

allegedly been a major source of rural dissidence. The presence of sugar production has also been associated with dissidence as well as with high rates of nonpolitical violence.

Sugar and coconuts are major foreign exchange earners for the Philippines. Percentages of farmland planted to sugar and coconut in 1938 and 1960 are variables included to represent the importance of these crops in the province.

Transportation and Communication. Indicators of the density of the road network per unit of area and number of telegraph messages in and out per capita (domestic only) are included to represent the degree to which the area is tied into the modern sector.

Ethnic. There are important differences in behavior and beliefs for the different language groups in the Philippines. The Ilocanos show violent behavior in the crime statistics but express a strong distaste for violence in interview data. At the same time Ilocanos show the greatest degree of sophistication politically, vote as a bloc, and express considerable confidence in the integrity and efficiency of their local governmental structure. In the composite factor analysis the percentages of the population giving Ilocano and Cebuano as their mother tongue are included as variables to see how ethnic type correlates with the political and social structure. Also the percent of the province population of the Muslim religion is included since Muslims are obviously different from the majority of the population.

Crime Rates. Indicators of violence and crime against property are included. Most of the data on crime that we have been able to locate are no older than 1962 and thus the crime data do not cover our three basic time frames. We were able to find one rough index of province crime rates for the 1930s, and these data are included. A major goal in including these data was to determine the degree of relation between spatial economics and crime.

Politics. Percent of votes for the winner in each of the presidential elections of 1957, 1961, and 1965 are included as separate variables. Indicators of vote dispersion between different national offices are included, as are indicators—"mayor"—of the extent to which one party controlled local political offices. An index of deviance from national averages is included to represent bloc voting tendencies, since groups that can deliver a block of votes have a much better political bargaining position than do groups who split their votes. Also included in the politics area are the public works appropriations by province. These public works data are economic in nature, but they are partially connected with political promises or reward. We have public works appropriations per capita for 1960 and 1963-1965.

Population. Population rates of change and in-migration and out-migration statistics were of interest for their own sake. However, it appears that a high influx of population is associated with crime and that a high rate of economic growth ought to be associated with a subsequent high rate of in-migration. Stagnant areas should show high out-migration rates. Thus a number of variables on population, population density, population growth rate, and in- and out-migration rates are included.

Economics. Of particular interest in our research was the inter-relation between economic structure and the other social facets of the country as well as factors causing economic growth in general. A number of economic indicators are included. Unfortunately, the data are not as good nor as contemporary as we would like them to be. Modernization is indicated by the percent of labor force in the "modern" sector. Such data are available for the 1930s, 1940s, and early 1960s. Percent of labor force unemployed is also included. Number of business establishments and the rate of change of these establishments are included as indicators of economic development and change.

Since the data go back to the 1930s when there were fewer provinces in the Philippines than today, the latest province list could not be used. Rather, the 1939 province list of 49 provinces was used to define the units of observation. Data for provinces that were later divided were added together in order to obtain a value for the province as it was in 1939.

Composite Factor Analysis

List of Variables	Title and Source
1 DSDN40*[2]	Dissidence index 1925-1940 taken from a variety of sources on pre-war dissidence. Provinces ranked on a scale of 0-9

[2] One asterisk indicates that a variable was included in the separate 1938 factor analysis. Two asterisks indicate that a variable was included in the 1960 factor analysis. The 1960 factor analysis includes a few more ethnic variables than the composite one and a few more economic variables. The 1938 and 1960 factor analyses include a few variables not in the composite one, because of the difficulty of obtaining representation of an activity for a given year. For example, for 1938 we have to use percent of population under 10 as a proxy for migration.

List of Variables	*Title and Source*
2 TENC38*	Percent of farms operated by other than full owners, 1938 *Census of Agriculture* 1938, Table 2
3 TENC60**	Percent of farms operated by other than full owners, 1960 *Census of Agriculture* 1960, Table 8-a
4 SUG38*	Percent of farmland planted to sugar, 1938 *Census of Agriculture* 1938, Table 29
5 SUG60**	Percent of farmland planted to sugar, 1960 *Census of Agriculture* 1960, Table 23
6 COCO38*	Percent of farmland planted to coconut, 1938 *Census of Agriculture* 1938, Tables 4 and 37
7 COCO60**	Percent of farmland planted to coconut, 1960 *Census of Agriculture* 1960, Table 3
8 WFRM38*	Percent of all workers in farming or fishing, 1938 *Census of Population* 1938, by provinces, Table 15
9 ROAD32	Kilometers of roads per 1000 hectares, 1932 *Statistical Handbook of the Philippines* 1932, p. 247
10 ROAD62**	Kilometers of roads per 1000 hectares, 1962 *Philippine Economic Atlas* 1962, p. 90

11 COMM61** Number of received and transmitted domestic telegraph messages per hundred, 1961
Yearbook of Philippine Statistics Table 42, p. 172

Abra set	= 04	Antique set	= 11
Batanes set	= 02	Romblon set	= 11
Cavite set	= 02	Sulu set	= 17
Marinduque set	= 07	Agusan set	= 15

12 IRRG38*	Percent of land irrigated, 1938 Batanes set = 0 *Census of Agriculture* 1938, Table 4
13 IRRG60**	Percent of land irrigated, 1960 Batanes = 0 *Census of Agriculture* 1960, Table 67
14 CLTV38*	Ratio of farmland to total land, 1938 *Census of Agriculture* 1938
15 CLTV60**	Ratio of farmland to total land, 1960 *Census of Agriculture* 1960, Table 2
16 RAIN	Average rainfall in inches per month in 4 driest months
17 TYPHON	Percent exposure to typhoons *The Philippine Economic Atlas*, 2nd edition, 1965, p. 18
18 ILOCOS**	Percent population with Ilocos as mother tongue 1960 Summary Report, *Census of the Philippines* 1960
19 MUSLIM**	Percent population of Muslim religion, 1960 Summary Report, *Census of the Philippines* 1960

177

List of Variables	Title and Source
20 CEBUANO**	Percent population with Cebuano mother tongue, 1960 Batanes set = 0 Summary, *Census of the Philippines* 1960
21 M-HM62**	Murders and homicide per 100,000 population 1962 NBI statistics
22 ROB62**	Robberies per 100,000 population 1962 Rizal set = 80.0 was 195.2 Bukidnon set = 7.0 NBI statistics
23 DSTNCE	Miles from provincial capital to Manila or Cotabato City whichever is shorter *Map of the Philippines* 1968 edition
24 URBN60**	BCS percent population in urban areas, 1960 Batanes set = 6 *Statistical Handbook*, Table 7, 1965
25 VOTD65	1965 party vote dispersion $\|\%\text{NPP} - \%\text{NPVP}\| + \|\%\text{NPP} - \%\text{NPSN}\|$ $+ \|\%\text{NPVP} - \%\text{NPSN}\|$ Commission on Elections (COMELEC) $\%\text{NPP} = \%$ for NP President, $\%\text{NPVP} = \%$ for NP Vice President, $\%\text{NPSN} = \%$ for all NP Senators
26 VOTD57**	1957 party vote dispersion $\|\%\text{NPP} - \%\text{NPVP}\| + \|\%\text{NPP} - \%\text{NPSN}\|$ $+ \|\%\text{NPVP} - \%\text{NPSN}\|$ COMELEC
27 WIN65	Percent vote for presidential winner 1965 COMELEC
28 WIN57	Percent vote for presidential winner 1957 COMELEC
29 LMAY63	Percent Liberal mayors in province 1963
30 NMAY55	Percent Nacionalista mayors 1955 Mt. Province set = 50 COMELEC
31 SIGMAV	$\|\%\text{NPP}_{65} - \%\text{NPP}_{53-65}\| + \|\%\text{NPP}_{61} - \%\text{NPP}_{53-65}\| +$ $\|\%\text{NPP}_{57} - \%\text{NPP}_{53-65}\| + \|\%\text{NPP}_{53} - \%\text{NPP}_{53-65}\|$ $\%\text{NPP}_{65} = \%$ for NP president 1965; $\%\text{NPP}_{53-65} = $ Average $\%$ NP president 1953 thru 1965 elections
32 PUBW60	Total public works appropriations in pesos per capita, 1959 *Republic Act 2093*
33 PUBW65	Total public works expenditures for public buildings in pesos per capita, 1963-1965 *Public Works Statistics*
34 PGRO60**	1960 population ÷ 1948 population Summary, *Census of the Philippines* 1960, Table 2

List of Variables	*Title and Source*
35 PGRO48	1948 population ÷ 1938 population
	Summary, *Census of the Philippines* 1960, Table 2
36 PGRO38*	1938 population ÷ 1918 population
	Summary, *Census of the Philippines* 1960, Table 2
37 RGRO65	Provincial revenues, 1965 ÷ provincial revenues, 1961
	Report of Auditor General
38 RGRO60**	Provincial revenues, 1961 ÷ provincial revenues, 1955
	Reports of GAO
39 OMIG60**	Percent persons born in province not living in province
	Migration Statistics, *Census of the Philippines* 1960
40 IMIG60**	Percent persons living in province not born in province
	Migration Statistics, *Census of the Philippines* 1960
41 GMIG60**	IMIG 1960 ÷ OMIG 1960
42 UNEMP65	Percent of work force unemployed, 1965. Provinces with missing values set as follows: $7 = 2.0$; $31 = 7.0$; $48 = 6.0$; $49 = 6.0$
	BCS Reports
43 UNEMP38*	Percent of work force unemployed, 1938
	Census of Population 1938, by provinces, Table 22
44 MORN61**	Percent of work force in modern sector, 1961
	Rizal set = 15.0, was 26.8
	Economic Census 1961
45 MORN38*	Percent of work force in modern sector, 1938
	Census of Population 1938, by provinces, Table 15
46 RADO60**	Percent households with radios
	Rizal set = 30, was 51
	Census of Housing 1960; Table 6
47 TRAN60**	Percent of population ≧ 20 years of age in transportation, 1960
	Handbook of Philippine Statistics 1960
48 TRAN48	Percent of population ≧ 20 years of age in transportation, 1948
	Batanes set = 0.5
	Palawan set = 0.3
	Masbate set = 0.2
	Economic Census Report 1948, Table 22
49 TRAN38*	Percent of population ≧ 20 years of age in transportation, 1938
	Batanes set = 0.5
	Isabela set = Cagayan set = 0.2
	N. Vizcaya set = 0.1
	Bukidnon set = 0.1
	Economic Census Report 1938
50 TRANGROWTH60	Percent of population ≧ 20 years old working in transportation in 1960 ÷ percent of population ≧ 20 years old working in transportation in 1948
	Provinces Nos. 02, 09, 21, 32, 48, 50, set = 9.00

179

List of Variables	Title and Source

51 ESTB61** — Number of establishments per 1000 capita in 1961
Economic Census 1961

52 VOTD65 — |% NP President 65 — average % NP President 65|
COMELEC

53 VOTD57 — |% NP President 57 — average % NP President 57|
COMELEC

54 CRME34* — Number of criminal cases filed per 1000 capita, 1934
(1938 population base)
   Batanes set = 1.55
From *Governor General's Annual Report* for 1934

55 WIN61** — Percent of vote for presidential winner, 1961
COMELEC

Additional Variables Included in 1960 Factor Analysis

56 FVAL60 — Value of farm product in pesos per capita, 1960
Census of Agriculture 1960

57 WFRM60 — Ratio of farm population to total population
Census of Agriculture 1960, Table 73

58 PDEN60 — Population per hectare of farm land, 1960
Population Census 1960

59 TAGALOG — Percent population with Tagalog mother tongue, 1960
Summary Report, Population Census of the Philippines 1960

60 BICOL — Percent population with Bicol mother tongue, 1960
Summary Report, Population Census of the Philippines 1960

61 ILONGO — Percent population with Ilongo mother tongue, 1960
Summary Report, Population Census of the Philippines 1960

62 WARAY — Percent population with Waray mother tongue, 1960
Summary Report, Population Census of the Philippines 1960

63 FGRO60 — Growth in value of farm product (value of farm product 1960/value of farm product 1948) *Census of Agriculture* 1960
Facts and Figures About the Economic and Social Conditions of the Philippines 1948-49

64 YNGP60 — Percent of population less than or equal to 10 years old
Census of the Philippines 1960

65 EGRO61 — Growth in establishments (Establishments 1961 ÷ Establishments 1948)

66 MNGR61 — Growth in manufacturing establishments (Manufacturing Establishments 1961 ÷ Manufacturing establishments 1948)

180

APPENDIX C

Congressional Questionnaire

Respondent # _____   Date of Interview _____

Interviewee _____   Interviewer _____

	Card #	Column

I. IDENTIFICATION

	Card #	Column
Position held: 0 Senator 1 Congressman	1	1
Age: _____	1	2 - 3
Party affiliation:	1	4

    0 LP   2 Independent

    1 NP   3 Other: _____

	Card #	Column
Province represented: _____	1	5 - 6
Province where childhood was spent _____	1	7 - 8
Mother tongue:	1	9

    0 Iloco   5 Waray-waray

    1 Pangasinan   6 Cebuano

    2 Pampanga   7 Hiligaynon

    3 Tagalog   8 Magindanao

    4 Bikol   9 Other including Tausog

	Card #	Column
Religion:	1	10

    0 Catholic   4 Moslem

    1 Protestant   5 Buddhist

    2 Aglipay   6 Others

    3 Iglesia ni Kristo

	Card #	Column
Profession: _____	1	11 - 12
Age when first held public office: _____	1	13 - 14
Father's occupation: _____	1	15 - 16

II.

1. What do you think is the most serious problem facing the Philippines
today? _____   1   17

_____

_____

_____

2. What factors do you think determine the vote of your people? _____   1   18

_____

_____

_____

3. How much should the government control private industry?   1   19

    _____ (5) much more   _____ (2) less

    _____ (4) more   _____ (1) much less

    _____ (3) the same as now   _____ (0) don't know;

                                                        no answer

4. What policies do you think would best advance the social and
economic development of the Philippines? _____   1   20

_____

_____

4a. Do you have any specific economic policy in mind?   1   21
_____ (0) None

_____

_____

4b. If so, under what circumstances would you initiate such   1   22
measures? _____

_____

5. Why do you think politicians enter politics?   1   23

_____

_____

5a. Do you personally and actually enjoy politics?   1   24
_____ (2) Yes
_____ (1) No
_____ (0) don't know; no answer

5b. Why/Why not? _____   1   25

_____

6. If given a choice, do you think most congressmen would prefer to
engage in another profession?   1   26
_____ (2) Yes
_____ (1) No
_____ (0) don't know; no answer

6a. (IF YES) What profession? _____   1   27-28

7. Generally speaking, how many among the members of Congress are
more interested in specific programs than in achieving status? 1   29
_____ (3) most
_____ (2) some
_____ (1) few
_____ (0) don't know; no answer

7a. How many would you say are more interested in achieving
status than in specific programs?   1   30
_____ (3) most
_____ (2) some
_____ (1) few
_____ (0) don't know; no answer

Card #   *Column*

8. What do you think of the present conditions in Congress?   1   31

_____
_____
_____
_____

    8a. What improvements can be made?   1   32

    _____
    _____
    _____
    _____

9. The press has often charged that politics is too prevalent in the
government's budget decisions. What is your reaction to this charge?   1   33

_____
_____
_____
_____
_____

REMARKS:

183

APPENDIX D

Estimates of National Income

Introduction

IN CHAPTER 5 we argued that estimates of Philippine national income and product are quite uncertain. Yet these estimates underlie evaluations of the performance of the economy, especially the evaluations of foreigners. It is important, then, to have some idea of the sources of the uncertainty and some estimates of the actual range of the uncertainty that surrounds the official numbers.

We will begin by examining the history of national income accounting in the Philippines. This is essential because the national accounts as they stand today represent the outcome of years of controversy, of criticism and adjustments to criticism. Following the discussion of the history that has shaped the present estimates, we will try to construct an estimate of the range within which Philippine GNP, *if it could be measured precisely*, would probably lie. Finally, we will examine national accounting procedures in general and argue that estimates of national income, particularly in an LDC, are inherently uncertain.[1]

The precursors of the present national income estimates were prepared in 1952 by William I. Abraham of the United Nations in collaboration with the Department of Economic Research of the Central Bank.[2] The underlying data were drawn basically from the 1948 Census of Population, which gathered detailed information on wages and self-employment income by industry.

The economic portions of the Census contained some serious flaws.[3] Because of confusion over the interpretation of a heading on the census form, only monthly rather than monthly *and* annual income was obtained from some households and had to be extrapolated

[1] For an analysis of problems inherent in the interpretation of even perfectly estimated national income figures see Daniel Usher, *The Price Mechanism and the Meaning of National Income Statistics*, Clarendon Press, Oxford, 1968.

[2] William I. Abraham, *The National Income of the Philippines and Its Distribution*, United Nations Technical Assistance Program, New York, 1952. This paper was also presented as a doctoral dissertation to Columbia University in 1953.

[3] See Clarence L. Barber, "National Income Estimates in the Philippines," *The Philippine Economic Journal*, 4, no. 1 (1965), pp. 66-77. This section draws heavily on Barber's article.

184

to an annual figure. Also, all unpaid family workers were arbitrarily assigned a wage income of P1.50 per day, and income in kind was lumped with cash incomes, so it is impossible to determine how completely this last item was measured. These errors would probably cause some overstatement of the wage and salary component of national income. The Census did not gather information on all types of income, so adjustments and imputations had to be made for the unreported value of food consumed by farm workers and farm families, income in kind received by domestic servants, and the rental value of owner-occupied homes. There was little outside information on which to base these imputations.

In addition to the problems inherent in the Census data, Abraham committed several major errors, which resulted in the near total omission of dividend and property income from the national income totals.[4] Also, he deducted transfer payments and foreign donations from the Census income totals, although they were not included in the information gathered by the Census.

Thus, the Abraham estimates for 1946-1951 should have been treated with considerable reserve. Instead, they served as the benchmarks from which the succeeding Central Bank estimates were extrapolated.

In 1957, responsibility for national income estimation was transferred to the NEC. The methods used, however, remained essentially the same.

As late as 1964, although there had been a substantial increase in the quantity and quality of basic data available, Emmanuel Levy found that the NEC accounts were, for most sectors, simply extrapolations of Abraham's 1948 data, and were, therefore, very likely misleading.

> In practically all sectors value added is obtained, explicitly or implicitly, as the difference between the value of gross output and non-factor operating expenses. The estimates of gross output (other than agricultural output) are themselves very rough. At the same time, non-factor operating expenses are not estimated directly but are assumed to constitute fixed percentages of the value of gross output in the various branches. The percentages employed are in almost all branches the same as those determined for 1948 by W. I. Abraham.

[4] *Ibid.*, pp. 73-74.

In view of the deepening of production and the technological changes in production processes that have occurred since 1948, as also the differing trends of input and output prices during the same period, there is every reason to believe that the use of the 1948 percentages must seriously distort the picture obtained of the absolute level of the total national income and value added by branch, as also of the year to year changes and development over time. This is in addition, moreover, to the wide margin of error implicit in the gross output figures to which the fixed cost ratios are applied.[5]

Public and private criticism of the national accounts became quite sharp in the late 1950s and early 1960s. Ruben F. Trinidad, a statistician with the NEC, demonstrated in a 1958 M.A. thesis and a 1960 *Statistical Reporter* article that the gross domestic investment component of GNP had been underestimated by about 40 percent.[6] Shortly thereafter, a critique of the national accounts by Clarence L. Barber, Senior Advisor on National Income Statistics at the Statistical Center, UP, was circulated informally among government offices.[7] The modifications suggested by Trinidad and Barber, together with their criticisms, evidently provided the basis for unsatisfactory negotiations over estimation procedures between the Program Implementation Agency (PIA), BCS, and NEC starting in 1963.

In 1963 and 1964 David Cole and Richard Hooley published studies that supported Trinidad's position on investment estimates.[8] These studies presented independent measures (based in part on survey and financial data) that showed savings and investment to have been higher than NEC had been saying they were. Also, an article

[5] Emmanuel Levy, *Review of Economic Statistics in the Philippines*, Interim Report-B, World Bank Resident Mission, Manila, May 1964, pp. 10-11 (mimeo). See also Ramon B. Cardenas, "A Re-estimation of the Philippine National Accounts, CY 1953-1966," pp. 5-10 and Chapter II.

[6] Ruben F. Trinidad, "An Inquiry into the Sources and Methods of National Income Accounting in the Philippines," M.A. thesis, University of the Philippines, 1958; and "Some Proposed Improvements in the Estimation of Capital Formation in the Philippines," *The Statistical Reporter*, 4 (April 1960), 28-40.

[7] This is the same paper that was reprinted in *The Philippine Economic Journal* in 1965 cited above.

[8] David Cole, *Growth and Financing of Manufacturing in the Philippines*; R. W. Hooley, "A Critique of Capital Formation Estimates in Asia with Special Reference to the Philippines," *The Philippine Economic Journal*, 3, no. 2 (1964), 114-129. See also Hooley, *Saving in the Philippines, 1951-1960*.

by G. P. Sicat argued that the consumption function and incremental capital output ratios implicit in the NEC data were implausible.[9] The severest blow of all fell when Emmanuel Levy's report was submitted to the Government of the Philippines.[10] Levy had been charged with assisting "in an examination of the adequacy of existing economic statistics in various agencies of government in order to advise on and assist in the preparation and introduction of statistics necessary to serve as measures of economic performance and as guides for policy and planning."[11] His report was, in fact, a quasi-official and highly prestigious evaluation of most major Philippine statistical series. The national accounting branch of NEC came off badly.[12] Levy judged the accounts to be so inaccurate (both in level and annual changes) as to be useless "for most purposes of analysis and projection."[13]

NEC did finally undertake revisions, which were released in June 1967 accompanied by an explanation that the new series "incorporate improvements in sources and methods of estimation covering more than half of the total of national income."[14] In view of the claim that this was a substantially new series, the results are quite remarkable: as Table D-1 shows, there were very large shifts in some components of GNP, but the *totals* shifted only trivially in the new accounts. Either this is great good luck or the old GNP figure was used as a control total to which the new components were adjusted. If the old figure *was* used as a control, then the new *totals* are no more reliable than the previous estimates. (Table D-1 presents only the comparison for 1962. The result is the same for subsequent years.) In fact, the revisions did fail to satisfy critics. *Business Day* reported "A controversy of sorts, in fact, appears to loom over the revised GNP estimates. There still remains some amount of professional

[9] Gerardo P. Sicat, "On the Accuracy of the Philippine National Accounts," *Philippine Review of Business and Economics*, October 1964.

[10] Levy, *Review of Economic Statistics in the Philippines*; this was for private circulation only, but quickly made its way into citations in articles by Philippine economists. Parts of Levy's report were later summarized in "The Usefulness of Existing National Accounts for the Analysis of the Philippine Economy," *The Philippine Economic Journal*, 5, no. 1 (1966), 134-135.

[11] *Ibid.*, p. 1.

[12] Cf. the quotation on pp. 185-186.

[13] Levy, *Review of Economic Statistics in the Philippines*, p. 7.

[14] "Technical Notes to the 1966 Overall Revision of the National Accounts of the Philippines, CY 1962-1966," *The Statistical Reporter*, 11 (April-June 1967), 34-36.

187

dissatisfaction with the present methods of computing the national income and Presidential Economic Staff Deputy Director General Cesar Virata has been quoted as saying that GNP figures, even now, may still be understated by as much as 10 percent."[15]

TABLE D-1

COMPARISON OF OLD AND NEW (1967 REVISIONS) NEC
NATIONAL ACCOUNTS FOR 1962

	Old	New	New/Old
A. National Income			
Compensation of employees ⎫ Property income of persons ⎬	12,410	11,956	.96
General government income from property	84[a]	84	
Corporate income	458	678	1.48
a. Corporate tax	211	215	1.02
b. Corporate savings	247	463	1.87
Sum: NNP at factor cost	13,043	12,718	.98
Indirect taxes less subsidies	1,166	1,282	1.10
Capital consumption allowance	817	1,094	1.34
Sum: GNP at market prices	15,026	15,094	1.004
B. Net Domestic Product and National Income at Factor Cost			
Agriculture	4,285[b]	4,120[c]	.96
Mining[d]	261	175	
Manufacturing[d]	2,383	2,435	
Construction	414	448	1.08
Transportation, etc.	451	590	1.31
Commerce	1,533	1,937	1.26
Services	3,632	3,798	
NDP		12,798	
National income	12,959	12,718	.98
C. Expenditure Shares			
Consumption	11,681[e]	12,181	1.04
Government	1,420	1,380	.97
a. Salaries	961		
b. Others	459		
Gross investment	1,965	2,883	1.47
Exports	3,088	1,982	
Imports	3,050	3,115	
Net investment income	−78	−218[f]	
GNP	15,026	15,094	1.004

NOTES:

[a] This item was accidentally omitted in earlier accounts. See Levy, *Review of Economic Statistics in the Philippines*, p. 11.

[b] The figures in this column are national income.

[c] The figures in this column are NDP.

[d] Part of the changes in mining and manufacturing can be accounted for by shifting of cement production from mining to manufacturing. The six large cement factories produced a gross value added of P37 million in 1961.

[e] Profit income of government added to old series.

[f] Includes statistical discrepancy.

[15] *Business Day*, 1, no. 18 (June 26, 1967) 6.

As it turned out, all this was only a prelude to a bitter and open battle between BCS and NEC over the two agencies' input-output tables. In October 1967, NEC released a preprinting edition of its input-output table for 1961.[16] In view of the criticisms of the national accounts that had been accumulating—most of which suggested that the estimates were on the low side—the GNP implicit in the table was quite startling. It showed 1961 GNP as only P12,726 million, more than 5 percent *below* the previous official figure for that year. In March 1968 a joint UP-BCS group, which had been concurrently preparing another 1961 table, released *their* findings.[17] This input-output table showed a 1961 GNP of P16,846 million, 25 percent *above* the national income accounts and more than 32 percent above the NEC input-output table. Furthermore, the UP-BCS table showed a very different distribution of output by industry and by expenditure shares (see Table D-2).

TABLE D-2

COMPARISON OF BCS INPUT-OUTPUT TABLE WITH NATIONAL
ACCOUNTS AND NEC INPUT-OUTPUT TABLE

	BCS I-O	NEC[a] National Accounts	NEC I-O[b]
Agriculture	1,943	3,858	3,683
Mining	80	209	125
Manufacturing	3,984	2,090	2,288
Construction	102	432	365
Trade, finance, real estate	5,337	1,410	2,203
Transport, communication	1,032	418	1,966
National income (at factor cost)	14,590	11,737	10,958
Private consumption	12,048	10,811	11,129
Government current expenditure	1,529	1,223	1,088
Gross domestic investment	3,594	1,800	2,623
Exports	1,332	2,347	1,176
Less imports	1,657	2,749[c]	3,290
Gross national expenditure	16,846	13,432	12,726

NOTES:

[a] This is the *first* version of the NEC table.

[b] The national accounts *before* the 1968 revisions.

[c] Includes net investment income.

[16] Statistical Research and Development Project, OSCAS, NEC, *1961 Philippine Interindustry Relations (Input-Output) Table*, Manila, October 1967, mimeo.

[17] University of the Philippines School of Economics, and Bureau of the Census and Statistics, *Inter-industry Relations Study of the Philippine Economy—Partial Report*, Manila, March 1968, mimeo. The table was later reprinted in *The Journal of Philippine Statistics*, 19 (January-March 1968).

Bernardo G. Bantegui, Director of the Office of Statistical Coordination and Standards (OSCAS), reacted sharply with an article in the *Philippines Herald*.[18] Bantegui argued that (1) the size of the UP-BCS agricultural sector and the proportion of GNP going to investment were inconsistent with the country's level of development; (2) the size of the service sector and the rate of profit in the financial sector shown in the BCS matrix were probably due to double counting; and (3) the UP-BCS treatment of competitive imports might lead to unstable coefficients. The business press, too, entered the controversy.[19]

In August, Tito A. Mijares, Director of the UP-BCS project, counterattacked in a seminar given at the University of the Philippines and in an accompanying discussion paper.[20] Mijares argued that, because NEC had used purchasers' rather than producers' prices, a good deal of activity that should have been in transport and trade had been allocated to other sectors.[21] Furthermore, this pricing scheme is likely to yield unstable coefficients and is, therefore, not used by other countries. As a rebuttal to Bantegui's *Philippines Herald* articles, Mijares and Valdapeñas presented lists of developing countries with low proportions of GNP generated in agriculture and high rates of capital formation, then attacked NEC for introducing *both* an "unallocated" sector and a "statistical discrepancy" and for building a table with 60 percent of the cells blank. Finally, they noted that the NEC "input-output table and GNP accounts have remarkably the same distribution of the origin of national income," and argued that "there remains the possibility that the NEC statisticians were 'influenced' congenitally by the figures they have been building into their GNP accounts since 1957,"[22] in other words, the NEC table was not a new, independent estimate and therefore did not offer an improved estimate of GNP.

[18] June 19, 1968, p. 20. See also above, p. 81.

[19] See p. 82 above.

[20] Tito A. Mijares and Vicente B. Valdapeñas, Jr., *An Inter-Industry Study of the 1961 Philippine Economy*, University of the Philippines Institute of Economic Development and Research, Quezon City, August 1968, Discussion paper No. 68-25, pp. 100-103. See Hollis B. Chenery and Paul G. Clark, *Interindustry Economics*, John Wiley & Sons, Inc., New York, 1959, p. 141, for an explanation of the difference between the two pricing schemes.

[21] Mijares and Valdapeñas, *An Inter-Industry Study of the 1961 Philippine Economy*, pp. 113-115.

[22] *Ibid.*, pp. 104, 108.

190

But Mijares and Valdapeñas were aiming at a moving target. In September, NEC released the final version of their table, both in producers' and purchasers' prices.[23] Although the accompanying article makes no mention of the fact, NEC had eliminated two serious errors and made a number of minor adjustments to the first version of the table. The two serious mistakes corrected were the previous omission of value added to imports by the domestic trade sector (P600 million) and failure to enter P80 million or so of exports of services.[24] Minor adjustments were made to nearly all sectors. The net effect of these changes raised the implicit GNP to P13,248 million, a figure almost identical to the old estimate of GNP for 1961, P13,432 million.

The article accompanying the table did not mention the UP-BCS versus OSCAS controversy. However, OSCAS did release a paper by Bantegui, comparing the two tables and pointing out several errors in the UP-BCS version.[25] This paper consists mainly of an elaboration of points made in Bantegui's earlier statements to the *Philippines Herald*. There is, however, one good new point: The UP-BCS table is fundamentally flawed because the numbers in the investment column do not represent *outputs* of investment goods by the row industry but rather each industry's *investment*, that is to say, the cell in the investment column, food manufacturing row, corresponds to new canneries, say, rather than to canned fruit marching off into fixed capital formation. Thus the UP-BCS matrix does not represent the usual set of balance equations for each industry, and a fortiori, its inverse can *not* be used to solve for interindustry demands corresponding to some level of output. In the seminar mentioned earlier, Mijares admitted that this was so, but argued that with the data available it would have been impossible to allocate investment in the conventional way. (How did NEC do it?) He

---

[23] "The 1961 Interindustry (Input-Output) Accounts of the Philippines," *The Statistical Reporter*, 12 (July-September 1968), 1-16.

[24] We think these two errors were due to the peculiarities of accounting in purchasers' prices. In a purchasers' price system, imports would be valued at the prices actually paid by final users. If the import sector were to be treated like any other sector, the trade and transport markups would have to be entered as purchases by the import sector from the trade and transport sector. But there is no cell corresponding to such a transaction since the import sector is not assigned a row. Since there was no obvious place to put the number, it was forgotten. Much the same thing happened to exports of finance and insurance services.

[25] B. G. Bantegui, "A Comparison between the NEC and UP-BCS Input-Output Tables" (mimeo).

pointed out, however, and quite rightly, that this allocation problem should have had no effect on the *total* GNP estimate.

These events would seem to have clarified the GNP problem considerably. NEC produced an input-output table, containing no obvious errors, and consistent with the GNP series. Perhaps the errors for which OSCAS was flayed really *had* cancelled in the past, yielding a GNP very close to the true level. Perhaps NEC was right all along.

Not so. After basking in this triumph for only a few weeks, NEC released yet another overall revision of the national accounts.[26] In this newest set of accounts, 1961 GNP is given as P14,209 million, nearly P1 billion above the input-output estimate. Comparable changes are made for other years. Examination of the detailed tables, however, indicates that most of the changes in total GNP come from *very* large changes in private consumption, offset somewhat by increases in the statistical discrepancy. (See Table D-3.)

THE RANGE OF PLAUSIBLE GNP ESTIMATES

By now it should be obvious that the best we can do is to define some range within which Philippine GNP, if it *could* be measured precisely, would probably lie. We will define this range by first trying to define the plausible maximum and minimum for a base year (in this case 1961), then extrapolating that range at the maximum and minimum defensible rates.

The two input-output tables for 1961 bracket the current range of national income estimates for that year. They lie more than P3.5 billion apart, though. Is it possible to narrow this range? Table D-4 suggests that the differences between the two input-output matrixes are not as marked as the differences in implicit GNPs would indicate. If fixed capital formation and government current expenditures are combined, the totals are nearly identical in the two tables. This indicates that the differences in the components may be due to problems in allocating government expenditures to current or capital account.

Inventory change is very different in the two tables. This is due to both understatement by NEC and a definitional error in the UP-BCS table. The NEC figure is clearly low. A survey of 250 mining

[26] *The National Accounts of the Philippines with Supporting and Analysis Tables, CY 1946 to 1967*, Office of Statistical Coordination and Standards, National Economic Council, August 30, 1968, mimeo.

TABLE D-3

COMPARISON OF NATIONAL ACCOUNTS STATISTICS

	1962	1963	1964	1965	1966	1967
Personal						
consumption	11,898	12,814	13,444	–	–	–
	12,181	12,973	13,810	14,694	15,632	–
	12,286	13,737	15,525	16,582	18,080	19,802
Government						
consumption	1,427	1,677	1,934	–	–	–
	1,380	1,637	1,829	1,986	2,163	–
	1,380	1,637	1,829	1,974	2,189	2,414
Gross domestic						
capital forma-	1,888	2,272	3,073	–	–	–
tion	2,884	3,501	4,303	4,474	4,562	–
	3,082	3,767	4,426	4,658	5,005	5,514
Exports	2,641	3,437	3,947	–	–	–
	1,982	2,894	3,073	3,691	4,768	–
	1,982	2,894	3,073	3,691	4,584	4,506
Imports	2,817	2,987	3,637	–	–	–
	3,115	2,987	3,651	3,902	4,171	–
	3,115	2,987	3,651	3,902	4,161	5,216
Gross domestic						
product[a]	–	–	–	–	–	–
	15,312	18,018	19,364	20,943	22,954	–
	15,615	19,048	21,202	23,003	25,697	27,020
Net factor income						
from abroad and	−65	−68	−60	–	–	–
statistical	−218	−546	−489	−498	−616	–
discrepancies	+106	−913	−1,743	−1,933	−2,451	−1,595
Gross national						
product	14,972	17,145	18,701	–	–	–
	15,094	17,472	18,875	20,445	22,338	–
	15,721	18,135	19,459	21,070	23,246	25,425

NOTES: In each group of three figures, the top number is the NEC estimate of June 1965; the middle number is from the June 1967 overall revision; the bottom number is from the August 1968 overall revision.

[a] GDP not presented in earliest series.

and manufacturing corporations showed their expenditures on inventories to be P421 million in 1961.[27] The 1961 Economic Census showed an additional P83 million in other sectors. This would give a total of around P500 million if the net inventory accumulation of the rest of the economy were zero. The UP-BCS table, on the other hand, shows P749 million of inventory accumulation from agriculture, 20 percent of this sector's total output. When challenged on

[27] See Hooley, "A Critique of Capital Formation Estimates in Asia with Special Reference to the Philippines," p. 118.

TABLE D-4

COMPARISON OF UP-BCS AND NEC INPUT-OUTPUT TABLES
(P millions)

	UP-BCS	NEC	NEC/UP-BCS
Output Shares			
Private consumption	12,048	11,110	.92
Fixed capital formation	1,831	2,290 ⎱	1.00
Government current expenditures	1,529	1,082 ⎰	
Inventory change	1,763	172	.10
Exports	1,332	1,213	.91
Imports	1,657	2,618	1.58
Intermediate inputs	6,397	7,463	1.17
Total supply	26,557	25,948	.98
Factor Shares			
Depreciation allowances	1,308	658	.50
Wages and salaries	3,675	5,648	1.54
Profits	10,914	5,917	.54
Indirect taxes less subsidies	1,308	709	.54

this improbable magnitude, Mijares answered in a fashion that indicated that what had been measured was the *level* rather than the change of agricultural inventories so this may be a spurious number.

The last major difference on the output side is in the level of imports and exports. Here the difference is one of valuation. In 1961 the Philippines was in the middle of devaluing and decontrolling foreign exchange transactions. Because of changing regulations at least eight separate rates, ranging from P2.00 to P3.45 per dollar, prevailed during 1961.[28] It appears that BCS used a unitary rate of P2.00 per dollar—the rate implicit in the statistical procedures of the foreign trade branch of the Bureau. The NEC, on the other hand, must have applied the prevailing split rates, which means valuing imports at around P3.00 per dollar, exports at about P2.00.[29]

The impact on GNP of using the split rather than the unitary rate can be quite substantial and there are no established conventions for dealing with the problem. Using the real rates for imports and exports as they are split, drift upward at different times, and are then reunified at a higher level will cause GNP to move erratically and

[28] See the account of decontrol in Robert F. Emery, "The Successful Philippine Decontrol and Devaluation," *Asian Survey*, 3 (June 1963), 274-284.

[29] Oddly enough, this obvious point has never been mentioned in the NEC-BCS controversy.

will imply the addition of a fictitious net capital inflow or outflow to the national accounts which does not correspond to any magnitude in the *dollar* balance of payments. This difference in exchange rate conventions accounts for about P745 million of the gap between the two tables.

Looking only at the output side, we can make the minimum adjustments suggested by the preceding discussion (see Table D-5).

TABLE D-5

A PARTIAL RECONCILIATION OF THE 1961
INPUT-OUTPUT TABLES

	NEC	UP-BCS
Original GNP	13,248	16,845
Correction for inventories	+328	−749
	13,576	16,096
Change to split exchange rate	0	−745
	13,576	15,351

These two adjustments reduce the GNP gap substantially. But in order to fully justify thus reducing the UP-BCS *output* estimate, we have to find a doubtful number in one of their factor payment rows. There are two obvious candidates: depreciation and indirect taxes less subsidies. The UP-BCS depreciation figure seems thoroughly implausible, especially so since half of the total (P661 million) is attributed to the transport services sector, implying enormous disinvestment. This number remains a mystery, but it seems safe to argue that it is too large. The same is true of indirect taxes less subsidies. If we could get access to the raw data and estimating procedures these two items could probably be reduced nearly enough to restore equality between output and factor payments at a lower level of GNP.

Figure D-1 shows our candidate for the likely range of GNP estimates. The range we have just derived for 1961 is used as the base. The lowest curve projects this level year by year at the growth rate shown in the latest official set of GNP accounts. The highest curve is based on the 1961 and 1965 Surveys of Family Income and Expenditure, taken in conjunction with the labor force surveys of May of those years. The surveys showed an average annual rate of growth of 13 percent for family income. In principle, we would expect family income to be a *declining* fraction of national income in the

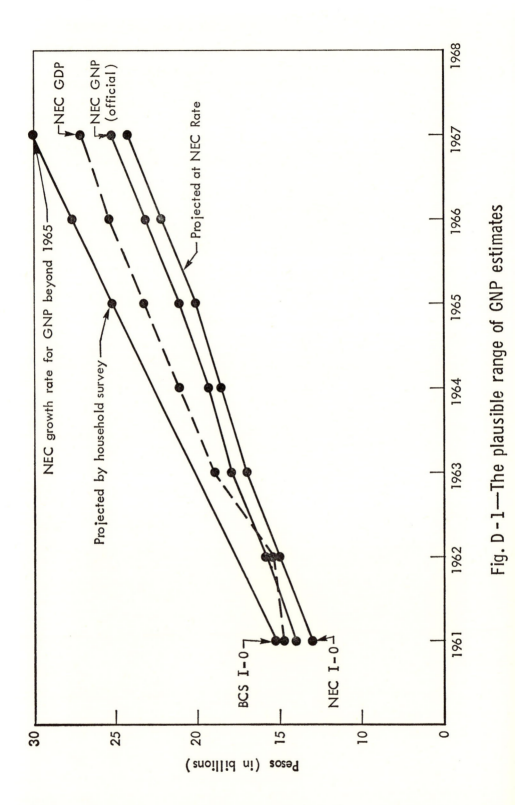

Fig. D-1—The plausible range of GNP estimates

course of development since it effectively excludes income from interest and dividends. So we can argue that projecting at this rate is conservative. The two internal lines are taken from the current official statistics; Gross Domestic Product *includes* the statistical discrepancy. Since there is no reason to suppose that estimates from the output side are more accurate than estimates from the expenditure side, NEC's conventional treatment of this item as error in the expenditure side is simply arbitrary.

The Random Character of GNP Estimates

Is there any lesson to be drawn from the history of Philippine national accounts? Some of the disagreements can be resolved or their range narrowed, as we have seen. With more time and effort, perhaps the ranges could be narrowed a bit further. But the controversies appear to grow around hard, irreducible kernels, which are products of the very nature of national accounting in the Philippines.

National income is, because of the way it must be measured, a random variable. That is to be taken in the strictest sense: Repeated independent "trials" by different but equally "competent" groups, working with the same data, would produce a distribution of estimates with some nontrivial variance. These "trials" can be viewed as branching trees with many nodes. Each node represents some arguable decision; reasonable men could disagree over the proper value to choose or the best method to adopt.

An example will clarify this notion. Figure D-2 shows, in outline, how one small part of Philippine GNP was estimated ca. 1964, in this case NDP in production of palay (rough rice). The basic data come from the Crop and Livestock Surveys of the Bureau of Agricultural Economics. Naturally, these contain some sampling error. Also, since the Bureau samples only *farms*, some output on plots that do not qualify as farms is omitted. There is, of course, also some danger that the sampling and calculations are not done properly. How much shall we inflate the sample estimate to correct for these errors? The circle, "percent undercoverage in sample," represents that decision.

The undercoverage adjustment yields a value of gross output. How much of this should be attributed to non-factor costs? There is no current information, only the ratio found in the 1948 Census

197

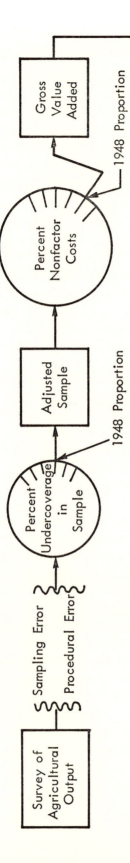

Survey of Agricultural Output

Sampling Error
Procedural Error

Percent Undercoverage in Sample

1948 Proportion

Adjusted Sample

Percent Nonfactor Costs

1948 Proportion

Gross Value Added

Net Value Added

1948 Proportion

Percent Depreciation

Fig. D-2—Estimating NDP in production of Palay

of Agriculture. But obviously this proportion will be affected by the weather, by changing technology and cropping patterns, and so on. How much?

Given that we have made some decision on non-factor costs, we still have to subtract depreciation on farm buildings and equipment to get net value added. Depreciation of farm capital has never been measured; the last time the stock of capital was evaluated was in the 1948 Census. Some extrapolation to the present may be available, but it must be rather chancy. And what percentage of it should be taken as depreciation?

At each of these nodes, some choice other than the 1948 proportion was possible. And a complete set of national income accounts must contain thousands of such nodes.[30] If there is no uniquely "best" path on which everyone could agree unambiguously, then GNP must be a random variable in the sense described.

The quality and quantity of basic data available define the range of choices that can be deemed reasonable at each node. The less complete the data, the more errors they contain; the older they are, the greater the scope for differing opinions and treatment. Only a fraction of the data required for GNP estimates are gathered in any one year in the Philippines, even in census years. The variance of independent "trials" on Philippine GNP should be correspondingly large. Even worse, many relevant magnitudes have never been measured at all: a comparison of Economic Census data with labor force survey data will demonstrate this.

Table D-6 shows employment by industry for 1960 and 1961 reported from three separate sources: The Population Census of 1960, the Economic Census of 1961, and the PSSH of May 1961. The differences are striking. They are also fairly easy to explore: The PSSH and Population Census are both built around the *household* as the unit of enumeration and sampling. Thus, they capture the entire non-institutional population. The Economic Census draws from the universe of business *establishments*. The Economic Census is thus likely to overlook activities that are not associated with particular, fixed locations, that do not require municipal licenses, do not pay business taxes, and the like. Obviously a great deal of economic activity is carried on outside census establishments. Obviously, too, there are some less serious inconsistencies between the PSSH

[30] As do, in turn, the survey and census data underlying the accounts.

TABLE D-6

EMPLOYMENT, BY INDUSTRY

(thousands)

Industry	Survey	Population Census	Economic Census	Omitted by Economic Census
	(1)	(2)	(3)	(4)
Forestry and logging[a]		83	28	
Fishing[a]		422	65	
Mining and quarrying	34	24	25	9
Manufacturing	1113	838	359	754
Construction	251	117	21	230
Utilities	22	13	13	9
Commerce	896	506	341	555
Transport and communication	319	201	138	181
Services			105	

SOURCES: Column (1) is from the May 1961 sample survey of the labor force (PSSH) reported in *Yearbook of Philippine Statistics, 1966*, p. 87. Column (2) is from *Census of the Philippines 1960, Fertility and Labor Force Characteristics (Special Report)*, pp. 2-3, and is based on the one in ten sample of households taken in conjunction with the total enumeration. Column (3) is from various volumes of the 1961 Economic Census. Column (4) = Column (1) minus Column (3).

NOTE:

[a] Forestry, logging, and fishing are combined with agriculture in the PSSH.

and the Population Census, although we must make some allowance for sampling error in the survey.

How much do these "omitted" workers contribute to value added? It has never really been measured.[31] The only really frank account of output in "unorganized" manufacturing has been imputed in a set of Philippine national accounts in Cardenas' thesis.[32] The assumptions required are, of course, heroic. And the GNP total is quite sensitive to small differences in the value added per worker that we happen to assume, since nearly 2 million workers fall in this unmeasured group.

Annual Changes in GNP

Granting that the absolute *level* of GNP may be very uncertain, it is still possible that year-to-year changes in the official accounts may mirror changes in the economy rather faithfully. If so, this may be sufficient for policymaking. What we want, after all, is just

[31] Except for "household industries."

[32] See Cardenas, *A Re-estimation of the Philippine National Accounts*, pp. 47-54.

some check—a crude check will do—on whether things are going well or badly overall.

The argument that year-to-year changes might be sufficiently accurate becomes a little clearer when viewed in terms of the branching tree. Successive estimates in a consistent series move down the same path through the tree, repeating the same choices. Since economic time series tend to be highly correlated and to move rather sluggishly on the whole, we may get a better estimate of annual changes by telling our statistician, "Do the same things you did last year, even the things you suspect might have been mistakes" rather than, "Here are the data. Forget everything that's ever been done before. Just give me the best possible estimate of GNP."

Do these arguments apply to the Philippine accounts? Probably so, but with three reservations: (1) the use of constant value added ratios in agriculture damps out some of the impact of very good or very bad crop years; (2) NEC's treatment of the split exchange rate introduces some noise into annual changes between 1961 and 1965; (3) movements of the statistical discrepancy are truly awesome in recent years. If we watch out for these quirks, we probably will not be misled into saying a good year was very bad and vice versa.

Can we expect better accounts? Undoubtedly some scope remains for improving the national income accounts, but not a great deal. It is unlikely that the data on which Philippine GNP estimates must be based are any more accurate than the data Kuznets used in his early estimates of U.S. national accounts. Combining expert opinion on the possible errors in the U.S. data, Kuznets produced a range of ± 20 percent in GNP, which he then reduced to "an average margin of error" of ± 10 percent or so on the assumption that some of the errors would be offsetting.[33] The band we have shown in Figure D-1 corresponds to a range of about ± 11 percent in 1967. Can we expect to improve much on that? It would be easy and cheap to give the *appearance* of much greater precision by persuading the statisticians to agree on their assumptions, but that is not the same as resolving the underlying uncertainties. National income accounts are just inherently uncertain.

[33] Simon Kuznets, *National Income and Its Composition*, National Bureau of Economic Research, vol. II, ch. 12, 1942.

APPENDIX E

Interviews of Economists

A SHORT, closed-form interview was administered to 18 economists, bankers, and businessmen in May 1968. The questionnaire was aimed at three points: (1) How those interviewed think the economy would respond to the manipulation of various instruments of government policy; (2) What information they use now and would like to have; (3) Whether or not their view of major problems facing the Philippines is similar to the views of the Pegasus respondents.

The sample was broken into three groups: (1) High-level policy-makers; (2) senior advisors; and (3) staff. We tried to draw five respondents from each category. The respondents were selected by asking several Philippine officials, "Who do you think is most influential in such-and-such institution?" Thus, the sample is non-random, but it should reflect the opinions of those who are most influential in the making of Philippine economic policy. Of the original 19 interviews, two were terminated by the respondents on the first question and one respondent refused to answer the questions on the impact of devaluation.

The text of the questionnaire follows, with the number of responses to each question inserted.

Biographical Data

Interview   Date, Time
Interviewer   Length
Interviewee

    Age
    Mother Tongue
    Education—# of years completed
            Highest degree
            Field of concentration

    When began to work for gov't. (or present employer)
    Years in present position
    Have worked full time for private/public institutions

Questionnaire

As part of a program of research on the Philippine economy, we are interested in what policymakers and their advisors think about the probable response of the economy to various policy measures. You have been selected as a person knowledgeable on the economy. I will present several hypothetical situations and ask you what you think the probable outcome would be. Of course, all answers will be used only for statistical tabulations; you will not be identified. I also want to make it clear that this is not an "examination." The issues we are interested in are so complex that there is no "right" answer; economists and other experts disagree. All we want to know is what *you* think.

A. If the government were able to raise the realized rate of tax collection substantially in the next year, and nothing else were changed, what do you think would happen to:
    1. Exports
        11 rise significantly
        6 stay about the same
        0 fall significantly
    2. Imports
        5 rise significantly
        6 stay about the same
        6 fall significantly
    3. GNP in current prices
        12 rise significantly
        4 stay about the same
        0 fall significantly
    4. CPI (consumer price index)
        5 rise significantly
        9 stay about the same
        1 fall significantly

B. If the peso were devalued to, say P5.00 per dollar and nothing else were changed, what do you think would happen in the next year to:
    1. Imports
        1 rise significantly
        2 stay about the same
        11 fall significantly

2. Exports
   10 rise significantly
   4 stay about the same
   0 fall significantly
3. GNP in current prices
   10 rise significantly
   3 stay about the same
   1 fall significantly
4. CPI
   13 rise significantly
   1 stay about the same
   0 fall significantly

C. With respect to the impact of the devaluation, what do you think would be the effect over a *three-year* period on:
1. Imports
   5 rise significantly
   6 stay about the same
   3 fall significantly
2. Exports
   8 rise significantly
   5 stay about the same
   0 fall significantly
3. GNP in current prices
   10 rise significantly
   4 stay about the same
   0 fall significantly
4. CPI
   10 rise significantly
   4 stay about the same
   0 fall significantly

D. If government expenditures rose by, say, 15 percent next year, and nothing else were changed, what do you think would be the effect on:
1. Imports
   7 rise significantly
   4 stay about the same
   3 fall significantly
2. Exports
   2 rise significantly
   9 stay about the same
   3 **fall significantly**

3. GNP in current prices
   10 rise significantly
   2 stay about the same
   2 fall significantly
4. CPI
   8 rise significantly
   4 stay about the same
   2 fall significantly

E. If the ratio of reserves required on commercial bank demand deposits were raised from 16 to, say, 20 percent while all other policies stayed the same, what do you judge would happen to:
1. Imports
   1 rise significantly
   6 stay about the same
   8 fall significantly
2. Exports
   0 rise significantly
   11 stay about the same
   3 fall significantly
3. GNP in current prices
   3 rise significantly
   8 stay about the same
   4 fall significantly
4. CPI
   7 rise significantly
   7 stay about the same
   1 fall significantly

F. I will read to you some problems facing our country. For each problem I read will you please tell me if you think it is not important ... of some importance ... or very important to the welfare of our country.

	Not Imp.	Some Imp.	Very Imp.	DK/No Op.
a) Raising taxes	0	1	16	1
b) Increasing exports	0	0	17	1
c) High cost of living	7	2	8	1
d) High crime rate	3	2	12	1
e) Rapid population growth	2	2	13	1
f) Widespread graft and corruption	6	2	9	1

g) Dissidence or the Huk problem	8	1	8	1
h) Treatment of minority groups	7	8	2	1
i) Unemployment	4	0	13	1

G. How about the influence of political considerations in the making of economic policy. Do you think that in the making of economic policy decisions political considerations play a role that is:
1. too large   14
2. about right   3
3. too small   0

H. One last question. When you make decisions or give advice, you have to rely on information about what is happening in the economy. What information do you rely on most? What improvements in the data you now use or what new kinds of data that you do not have would most help you make better decisions?

A. now rely
B. want
} See Tables 37 and 38 for responses.

BIBLIOGRAPHY

Abello, Amelia B. *Patterns of Philippine Public Expenditure and Revenue, 1951-1960.* Institute of Economic Development and Research, University of the Philippines, Quezon City, 1964.

Abraham, William I. *The National Income of the Philippines and Its Distribution.* United National Technical Assistance Program, New York, 1952.

Abueva, Jose V. *Focus on the Barrio.* Institute of Public Administration, University of the Philippines, Manila, 1959.

———. "Social Backgounds and Recruitment of Legislators and Administrators in the Philippines." *Philippine Journal of Public Administration,* 9 (January 1965), 10-29.

Adleman, Irma and Cynthia Taft Morris. "A Quantitative Study of Social and Political Determinants of Fertility." *Economic Development and Cultural Change* (January 1966), 129-157.

———. "An Econometric Model of Development." *American Economic Review,* 58 (December 1968), 1184-1228.

———. *Society, Politics and Economic Development.* The Johns Hopkins Press, Baltimore, 1967.

Agoncillo, T. A. and A. M. Alfonso. *History of the Filipino People,* 2nd ed. Malaya Books, Quezon City, 1968.

Agpalo, Remigio E. "Interest Groups and Their Role in the Philippine Political System." *Philippine Journal of Public Administration,* 9 (April 1965), 87-106.

Allen, W. R. and R. E. Baldwin. "Market Structures and Misallocation. . . ." *Economia Internazionale,* 16 (November 1963), 655-661.

Almond, G. A. and S. Verba. *The Civic Culture.* Princeton University Press, Princeton, 1963.

American Factor Associates, Ltd. *Audit of the Philippine Sugar Industry, April 28-May 30, 1965.* Prepared for the Sugar Development Committee of the Philippines, Honolulu, Hawaii, August 1965.

Ashburn, Franklin G. *A Study of Differential Role Expectations of Police Patrolmen in the Manila Police Department, Republic of the Philippines.* Florida State University, Tallahassee, 1966.

Asian Social Institute. *Pattern for Rural Reform.* Solidaridad Publishing House, Manila, 1969.

Averch, H. A. and J. E. Koehler. *The Huk Rebellion in the Philippines.* The Rand Corporation, RM-6254-ARPA, August 1970.

Ayal, Eliezer B. *The Development of Philippine Manufacturing Since World War II.* Field Work Report No. 6, Center for Development Planning, National Planning Association, Washington, D.C., June 1966.

Ayal, Eliezer B. *The Philippine Cotton Textile Industry.* Field Work Report No. 24, Center for Development Planning, National Planning Association, Washington, D.C., January 1968.

——. *The Private Sector in Development Planning.* Field Work Report No. 16, Center for Development Planning, National Planning Association, Washington, D.C., April 1967.

Aytona, Dominador R. "Capital Formation in the Philippines." *Economic Research Journal* (Manila), 6 (March 1960), 216-224.

Baclagon, U. S. *Lessons from the Huk Campaign in the Philippines.* M. Colcol & Company, Manila, 1960.

Bacon, M. and H. Barry. "A Cross Cultural Study of Correlates of Crime." *Journal of Abnormal and Social Psychology,* 66 (1963), 291-300.

Balmaceda, Cornelio. "Commercial Policy and Economic Development." *Philippines Economy Bulletin* (Manila), 2 (September-October 1963), 14-17.

Banfield, Edwin C. and James Q. Wilson. *City Politics.* Harvard University Press, Cambridge, 1963.

——. *The Moral Basis of a Backward Society.* The Free Press, Glencoe, 1958.

Bantegui, B. G. "A Comparison Between the NEC and UP-BCS Input-Output Tables" (mimeo), n.d.

Barber, Clarence L. "National Income Estimates in the Philippines." *The Philippine Economic Journal,* 4, no. 1 (1965), 66-77.

Barber, James D. *The Law Makers.* Yale University Press, New Haven, 1965.

Bautista, A. M. *"The Hukbalahap Movement in the Philippines, 1942-1952."* M.A. thesis, University of California, Berkeley, 1954.

Bautista, Romeo M. *"Capital Coefficients in Philippine Manufacturing: An Analysis."* Discussion Paper No. 66-3, Institute of Economic Development and Research, School of Economics, University of the Philippines, Quezon City, July 29, 1966 (mimeo).

Belarmino, Isagani C. "The Statistical Anatomy of Our Perennial Rice Problem." *Philippine Statistician,* 12 (June and September 1963), 55-71.

Berelson, Bernard, Paul F. Lazarsfeld, and William McPhee. *Voting.* University of Chicago Press, Chicago, 1954.

Berry, Brian and Duane Marble, eds. *Spatial Analysis: A Reader in Statistical Geography.* Prentice-Hall, Englewood Cliffs, 1968.

Bhapkar, V. P. "Some Tests for Categorical Data." *Annals of Mathematical Statistics,* 32 (March 1961), 72-83.

Blalock, Hubert M., Jr. *Causal Inference in Non-Experimental Research.* University of North Carolina Press, Chapel Hill, 1964.

Block, Hubert. *Research Report in Homicide, Attempted Homicide, and Crimes of Violence.* Ceylon Police Report, Colombo, 1960.

Bohannon, Paul. *African Homicide and Suicide*. Princeton University Press, Princeton, 1960.

Braybrooke, David and Charles E. Lindblom. *A Strategy of Decision*. The Free Press, Glencoe, 1963.

Burdick, Eugene and Arthur J. Brodbeck. *American Voting Behavior*. The Free Press, Glencoe, 1959.

Campbell, Angus, Philip Converse, Warren Miller, and Donald Stokes. *The American Voter*. John Wiley & Sons, Inc., New York, 1960.

Cardenas, Ramon Bello. "A Re-estimation of the Philippine National Accounts, Calendar Years 1953-1963: A Description and Evaluation of the Alternative Estimating Methodology." M.A. thesis, Cornell University, Ithaca, June 1967.

Castillo, Andres V. "Directions of Monetary Policies of the Central Bank." *Philippine Economy Bulletin*, 2 (September-October 1963), 39-43.

————. "The Philippine Decontrol Program: The Government's Point of View." *Philippine Journal of Public Administration*, 5 (October 1961), 287-292.

Chenery, Hollis B. and Paul G. Clark. *Interindustry Economics*. John Wiley & Sons, Inc., New York, 1959.

Christ, Carl F. *Econometric Models and Methods*. John Wiley & Sons, Inc., New York, 1966.

Clark, Colin. *Population Growth and Land Use*. St. Martin's Press, New York, 1967.

Cloward, Richard A. "Illegitimate Means, Anomie, and Deviant Behavior." *American Sociological Review*, 24 (April 1959), 164-176.

Clinard, Marshall B. *Sociology of Deviant Behavior*. Holt, Rinehart and Winston, Inc., New York, 1966.

Coale, Ansley J. and Edgar M. Hoover. *Population Growth and Economic Development in Low Income Countries*. Princeton University Press, Princeton, 1958.

Cole, David. *Growth and Financing of Manufacturing in the Philippines*. University of the Philippines, Institute of Economic Development and Research, Quezon City, 1963.

————. "The Tools of Monetary Policy in the Philippines." *Philippine Economy Review* (December 1960), 16-35.

"Communism in Pampanga." *Philippine Free Press* (Manila), June 7, 14, and 21, 1939.

Corpuz, Onofre D. "The Cultural Foundations of Filipino Politics." *Philippine Journal of Public Administration*, 4 (October 1960), 297-310.

Croxton, Frederick E. *Elementary Statistics with Applications in Medicine and the Biological Sciences*. Dover Publishing Co., New York, 1959.

Currie, Lauchlin. *Accelerating Development: The Necessity and the Means*. McGraw-Hill, New York, 1966.

209

Cutwright, Philip. "National Political Development: Measurement and Analysis." *American Sociological Review*, 28 (April 1963), 253-264.

Dahl, Robert A. *A Preface to Democratic Theory*. University of Chicago Press, Chicago, 1956.

———, ed. *Political Opposition in Western Democracies*. Yale University Press, New Haven, 1966.

Dalisay, Amando M. et al. "The Level of Government Spending in the Philippines, 1947-1957." *Economic Research Journal* (Manila), 6 (December 1959), 128-151.

——— and Jose S. Gutierrez. "The Rice Crisis Revisited." *University of the East Business Review* (Manila), 6 (August 1964), 13-25.

Davis, James C. "Toward a Theory of Revolution." *American Sociological Review*, 27 (February 1962), 5-19.

Declaro, Conrado S. "The Conference Committee—Pivot in the Budget Process." *Philippine Journal of Public Administration*, 7 (April 1963), 113-121.

Deutsch, Karl W. "Social Mobilization and Political Development." *American Political Science Review*, 55 (September 1961), 493-514.

——— and W. Foltz, eds. *Nation-Building*. Prentice-Hall, New York, 1963.

Dia, Manuel A. "Filipino Farmer's Image of Government: A Neglected Area in Developmental Change." *The UP Research Digest*, 4 (April 1965), 7-24.

Dix, Robert H. *Colombia: The Political Dimensions of Change*. Yale University Press, New Haven, 1967.

Dogan, M. and Stein Rokkan. *Quantitative Ecological Analysis in the Social Sciences*. MIT Press, Cambridge, 1969.

Dorrance, G. S. "The Instruments of Monetary Control." International Monetary Fund, Staff Papers, 12 (July 1965), 272-279.

Downs, Anthony. "Why the Government Budget Is Too Small in a Democracy." *World Politics*, 12 (July 1960), 541-563.

Driver, Edwin D. "Interaction and Criminal Homicide in India." *Social Forces*, 40 (December 1961), 153-158.

Duncan, O. D. and B. Davis. "An Alternative to Ecological Correlation." *American Sociological Review*, 28 (December 1953), 665-666.

———, R. P. Cuzzart, and B. Duncan. *Statistical Geography*. The Free Press, Glencoe, 1961.

Durdin, Tillman. "Philippine Region Pursues Progress." *The New York Times*, January 19, 1969.

Eckhaus, R. S. "The Factor Proportions Problems in Underdeveloped Countries." *American Economic Review*, 45 (September 1955), 539-566.

The Economic Monitor, 1 and 2 (1966 through June 1969). Economic Publications, Inc., Manila.

210

Emery, Robert E. "The Successful Philippine Decontrol and Devaluation." *Asian Survey*, 3 (June 1963), 274-284.

Encarnacion, Jose, Jr. *On the Specification of Investment Functions.* Discussion Paper No. 67-16, School of Economics, University of the Philippines, Quezon City, November 8, 1967 (mimeo).

Estrella, C. F. "The Filipino Answer to Revolution." *Solidarity* (Manila), 4 (1969), 67-73.

Fabella, Armand V. *An Introduction to Economic Policy.* Philippines Executive Academy, College of Public Administration, University of the Philippines, Manila, 1968.

Farnsworth, C. H. "Defects, Uses, and Abuses of National Food Supply and Consumption Data." *Bulletin de l'Institut Internationale Statistique*, 39 (1962), 19-42.

Farrar, D. E. and R. R. Glauber. "Multicollinearity in Regression Analysis: The Problem Revisited." *Review of Economics and Statistics*, 49 (February 1967), 92-107.

Fei, John C. H. and Gustav Ranis. *Development of the Labor Surplus Economy: Theory and Policy.* Richard D. Irwin, Homewood, 1964.

Fitzgibbon, Russell H. "Pathology of Democracy in Latin America: A Political Scientist's Point of View." *American Political Science Review*, 54 (1950), 118.

Fleisher, Belton M. "The Effect of Income on Delinquency." *American Economic Review*, 56 (March 1966), 118-137.

Foster, George M. "Confradia and Compadrazgo in Spain and South America." *Southwestern Journal of Anthropology*, 9 (Spring 1953), 1-28.

Francisco, Gregorio A., Jr. *Higher Civil Servants in the Philippines.* University of the Philippines, College of Public Administration, Manila, 1960.

Garceau, Oliver. *Political Research and Political Theory.* Harvard University Press, Cambridge, 1968.

Glaser, Daniel and Kent Rice. "Crime, Age, and Unemployment." *American Sociological Review*, 24 (October 1959), 679-686.

Golay, Frank H. *Philippine American Relations, The Elements That Have Created Both Alliance and Antagonism.* Solidaridad Publishing House, Manila, 1966.

——. *The Philippines: Public Policy and National Economic Development.* Cornell University Press, Ithaca, 1963.

—— and Marvin E. Goodstein. *Rice and People in the 1990's. Philippine Rice Needs to 1990: Output and Input Requirements.* USAID Mission, Manila, 1967.

Gold, Martin. "Suicide, Homicide, and the Socialization of Aggression." *American Journal of Sociology*, 63 (May 1958), 651-661.

211

Goodman, L. A. "Ecological Regression and the Behavior of Individuals." *American Sociological Review*, 28 (December 1953), 663-664.

———. "Some Alternatives to Ecological Correlation." *American Journal of Sociology*, 64 (May 1959), 610-625.

———. "Statistical Methods for Analyzing Processes of Change." *American Journal of Sociology*, 68 (July 1962), 57-78.

Griliches, Z. and Y. Grunfeld. "Is Aggregation Necessarily Bad?" *Review of Economics and Statistics*, 42 (February 1960), 1-13.

Grossholtz, Jean. *Politics in the Philippines*. Little, Brown and Co., Inc., Boston, 1964.

Guthrie, George M. et al. *Modernization, Its Impact in the Philippines*. Ateneo de Manila University Press, Philippines, 1967.

Gutierrez, Jose S. "The Philippine Coconut Industry and the World Oil Market." *Economic Research Journal* (Manila), 6 (March 1960), 197-205.

Hansen, Bent. "Employment and Wages in Rural Egypt." *The American Economic Review*, 59 (June 1969), 298-313.

Harman, H. H. *Modern Factor Analysis*. 2nd ed. University of Chicago Press, Chicago, 1968.

Hartendorp, A. V. H. *History of Industry and Trade in the Philippines: The Magsaysay Administration, A Critical Assessment*. Philippine Education Company, Manila, 1961.

Hayden, J. R. *The Philippines: A Study in National Development*. The Macmillan Company, New York, 1942.

Henry, Andrew F. and James F. Short, Jr. *Suicide and Homicide: Some Economic, Sociological, and Psychological Aspects of Aggression*. The Free Press of Glencoe, New York, 1964.

Henson, M. A. *The Province of Pampanga and Its Towns*. Mariano A. Henson, Angeles City, Philippines, 1965.

Herrick, Bruce. *Urban Migration and Economic Development*. MIT Press, Cambridge, 1965.

———. *Urban Migration and Economic Development in Chile*. MIT Press, Cambridge, 1965.

Hester, Donald D., ed. *Financial Markets and Economic Activity*. John Wiley & Sons, Inc., New York, 1967.

Hicks, George L. *The Growing Import Dependence of Philippine Exports*. Field Work Report No. 22, Center for Development Planning, National Planning Association, Washington, D.C., November 1967.

———. *The Philippine Coconut Industry: Growth and Change, 1900-1965*. National Planning Association, Washington, D.C., June 1967.

———. *Philippine Foreign Trade, 1950-1965: Basic Data and Major Characteristics*. Field Work Report No. 10, Center for Development

Planning, National Planning Association, Washington, D.C., September 1966.

——. *Philippine Foreign Trade Statistics, Supplementary Data and Interpretations, 1954-1966.* Field Work Report No. 20, Center for Development Planning, National Planning Association, Washington, D.C., September 1967.

Hirshman, A. O. *Journeys Toward Progress: Studies of Economic Policymaking in Latin America.* Twentieth Century Fund, New York, 1963.

Hoeksema, R. L. "Communism in the Philippines." Ph.D. dissertation, Harvard University, Cambridge, 1956.

Hollensteiner, Mary. *The Dynamics of Power in a Philippine Municipality.* Community Development Research Council, University of the Philippines, Quezon City, 1963.

Hooley, Richard W. "A Critique of Capital Formation Estimates in Asia with Special Reference to the Philippines." *The Philippine Economic Journal,* 3, no. 2 (1964), 114-129.

——. *Savings in the Philippines, 1951-1960.* University of the Philippines, Institute of Economic Development and Research, Quezon City, 1963.

—— and Vernon W. Ruttan. *The Agricultural Development of the Philippines, 1902-1965.* Center for Development Planning, National Planning Association and Department of Agricultural Economics, University of Minnesota, February 1968 (mimeo).

Horst, P. *Factor Analysis of Data Matrices.* Holt, Rinehart and Winston, Inc., New York, 1965.

Huntington, S. P. "Political Development and Political Decay." *World Politics,* 17 (April 1965), 301-340.

——. *Political Order in Changing Societies.* Yale University Press, New Haven, 1968.

Hymer, Stephen and Stephen Resnick. "A Model of an Agrarian Economy with Nonagricultural Activities," *American Economic Review,* 59 (September 1969), 493-506.

IDLARS. International Data Library and Reference Service, Survey Research Center, University of California, Berkeley.

413-20-0001. Southeast Asia—Philippines: Attitudes Towards Domestic and Foreign Affairs. U.S. Information Agency, 1959.

416-59-0002. Southeast Asia—Philippines: National Political and Social Attitudes Index, Manila, 1963.

416-59-0008-10. Southeast Asia—Philippines: Attitudes Toward the Election in 1965, Donald Muntz, Robot, Manila, 1965.

Interpol. *International Crime Statistics, 1959-1960.* Geneva, 1961.

Jayewardene, C. H. S. "Criminal Homicide: A Study in Culture Conflict." Ph.D. dissertation, University of Pennsylvania, Philadelphia, 1960.

Jenkins, Shirley. *American Economic Policy Toward the Philippines.* Stanford University Press, Stanford, 1954.

De Jesus, Jose P. and Jose C. Benitez. *Sources of Social Unrest.* Citizenship and Research Foundation, Inc., Manila, 1970.

Johnson, Kenneth F. "Political Radicalism in Colombia: Electoral Dynamics of 1962 and 1964." *Journal of Inter-American Studies*, 7 (January 1965), 15-26.

Johnston, J. *Econometric Methods.* McGraw-Hill, New York, 1963.

Jureidini, P. A. et al. *Casebook on Insurgency and Revolutionary Warfare: 23 Summary Accounts.* The American University, Washington, D.C., 1962.

Kearns, Henry. "Philippines-U.S. Trade Relations." *Journal of the American Chamber of Commerce of the Philippines*, 36 (February 1960), 77-78.

Key, V. O., Jr. *The Responsible Electorate: Rationality in Presidential Voting, 1936-60.* Harvard University Press, Cambridge, 1966.

——. *Southern Politics in State and Nation.* Vintage Books, New York, 1949.

——. "A Theory of Critical Elections." *Journal of Politics*, 17 (February 1955), 3-18.

Koehler, John E. *Economic Policymaking with Limited Information: The Process of Macro-Control in Mexico.* The Rand Corporation, RM-5682-RC, August 1968.

Kornhauser, William. *The Politics of Mass Society.* The Free Press, Glencoe, 1959.

Krivine, David, ed. "Fiscal and Monetary Problems in Developing States." *Proceedings of the Third Rehovoth Conference.* Frederick A. Praeger, New York, 1967.

Kuznets, Simon. *National Income and Its Composition.* National Bureau of Economic Research, vol. II, ch. 12, 1942.

Landé, Carl H. *Leaders, Factions and Parties: The Structure of Philippine Politics.* Yale University Press, New Haven, 1965.

Lander, Bernard. *Towards an Understanding of Juvenile Delinquency.* Columbia University Press, New York, 1954.

Lambert, Richard D. and Bert Haselitz. *The Role of Savings and Wealth in Southern Asia and the West.* UNESCO, Paris, 1963.

Laquian, A. A. *Slums Are for People.* Bustamante Press, Manila, 1968.

Larkin, J. A. "The Evolution of Pampangan Society: A Case Study of Social and Economic Change in the Rural Philippines." Ph.D. dissertation, New York University, New York, 1966.

Lary, Hal B. *Imports of Manufactures from Less Developed Countries.* National Bureau of Economic Research, New York, 1968.

Lave, Lester. *Technological Change: Its Conception and Measurement.* Prentice-Hall, Englewood Cliffs, 1966.

Leff, Nathaniel. *Economic Policy-Making and Development in Brazil, 1947-1964.* John Wiley & Sons, Inc., New York, 1968.

Lev, Daniel S. "Political Parties in Indonesia." *Journal of Southeast Asian History,* 8 (March 1967), 52-68.

Levy, Emmanuel. *Review of Economic Statistics in the Philippines.* Interim Report-B, World Bank Resident Mission, Manila, May 1964 (mimeo).

————. "The Usefulness of Existing National Accounts for the Analysis of the Philippine Economy." *The Philippine Economic Journal,* 5 (1966), 134-135.

Lewis, W. A. "Unemployment in Developing Countries." *The World Today,* 23 (January 1967), 13-22.

Licaros, Gregorio S. "Development Bank of the Philippines; Highlights of 1958-1959 Operations." *Philippine Economy Review,* 7 (August 1960), 7-22.

Lieberman, V. "Why the Hukbalahap Movement Failed." *Solidarity* (Manila), 1 (1966), 22-31.

Lindblom, Charles E. *The Intelligence of Democracy.* The Free Press, Glencoe, 1965.

Lipman, Aaron and A. Eugene Havens. *The Colombian Violencia: An Ex Post Facto Experiment.* University of Wisconsin Land Tenure Center, Madison, 1965 (mimeo).

Lipset, S. M. *The First New Nation: The United States in Historical and Comparative Perspective.* Basic Books, New York, 1963.

————. *Political Man: The Social Basis of Politics.* Doubleday, Garden City, 1959.

————. "Some Social Requisites of Democracy: Economic Development and Political Legitimacy." *American Political Science Review,* 53 (March 1959), 69-105.

———— et al. "The Psychology of Voting: An Analysis of Political Behavior." In Gardner Lindsey, ed. *Handbook of Social Psychology,* vol. 2. Addison Wesley, Cambridge, 1954.

———— and S. Rokkan, eds. *Party Systems and Voter Alignments: Cross-National Perspectives.* The Free Press, New York, 1967.

Macapagal, Diosdado. *Five-Year Integrated Socio-Economic Program for the Philippines.* Address on the State of the Nation to the 5th Congress of the Republic of the Philippines, Manila, January 22, 1967.

————. *A Stone for the Edifice.* Mac Publishing House, Manila, 1968.

Madigan, Francis C. *The Farmer Said No.* Community Development Research Council, University of the Philippines, Quezon City, 1968.

Manglapus, Raul S. *Land of Bondage, Land of the Free.* Solidaridad Publishing House, Manila, 1967.

Marcos, Ferdinand E. "The Economic Policies of the Present Administration." *Commerce: The Voice of Philippine Business*, 63 (May 1966), 6-11.

———— and Miguel Cuaderno, Sr. "Is Politics a Necessary Factor to Economic Development?" *Economic Research Journal* (Manila), 7 (June 1960), 17-23.

Marlows, Martin. "Philippine Political Parties and the 1961 Election." *Pacific Affairs*, 35 (Fall 1962), 261-274.

Mason, Edward S. *Economic Planning in Underdeveloped Areas: Government and Business.* Fordham University Press, New York, 1958.

McKendry, James M., Margaret S. McKendry, and George M. Guthrie, *The Psychological Impact of Social Change in the Philippines.* Technical Report 857-R-2, HRB-Singer, Inc., State College, Pa., June 1967.

Mecklin, John M. "The Philippines: An Ailing and Resentful Ally." *Fortune*, 80 (July 1969), 119-123.

Mercado, Nestor J. "An Analysis of the Balance-of-Payments Problem of the Philippines." *Economic Research Journal* (Manila), 13 (June 1966), 4-16.

Merritt, R. L. and S. Rokkan, eds. *Comparing Nations, The Use of Quantitative Data in Cross National Research.* Yale University Press, New Haven, 1966.

Merton, Robert K. "Social Conformity, Deviation, and Opportunity Structures: A Comment on the Contribution of Dubin and Cloward." *American Sociological Review*, 24 (April 1959), 187.

Midlarsky, M. and R. Tanter. "Toward a Theory of Political Instability in Latin America." *Journal of Peace Research*, 3 (1963), 209-227.

Milne, R. S. "The New Administration and the New Economic Program in the Philippines." *Asian Survey*, 2 (September 1962), 36-42.

————. "Political Finance in Southeast Asia with Particular Reference to the Philippines and Malaysia." *Pacific Affairs*, 41 (Winter 1968-1969), 471-480.

————, ed. *Planning for Progress, The Administration of Economic Planning in the Philippines.* Studies in Public Administration No. 6, Institute of Public Administration and Institute of Economic Development and Research, University of the Philippines, Manila, 1960.

Mitchell, E. J. *The Huk Rebellion in the Philippines: An Econometric Study.* The Rand Corporation, RM-5757-ARPA, January 1969.

Montelibano, Alfredo. "Exchange Control." *Philippine Economy Review*, 6 (December 1959), 26-28, 44.

———. "Planning and Development: Lessons of Experience." *Philippine Economy Bulletin*, 4 (January-February 1966), 5-9.

Nathan, Gad. "Tests of Independence in Contingency Tables from Stratified Samples." In Norman L. Johnson and Harry Smith, Jr., eds. *New Developments in Survey Sampling*. New York, John Wiley & Sons, Inc., 1969, 579-600.

Nelson, Joan M. *Migrants, Urban Poverty and Instability in a Nation: Critique of a Myth*. Center for International Affairs, Harvard University, Cambridge, 1968.

Nelson, Richard R. "A 'Diffusion' Model of International Productivity Differences in Manufacturing Industry." *American Economic Review*, 58 (December 1968), 1219-1247.

———, T. Paul Schultz, and Robert L. Slighton. *Structural Change in a Developing Economy: Colombia's Problems and Prospects*. Princeton University Press, Princeton, 1971.

Nye, J. S. "Corruption and Political Development: A Cost Benefit Analysis." *American Political Science Review*, 61 (June 1967), 417-427.

Olson, Lawrence. "After Magsaysay, What?" *American Universities Field Staff Reports*. Southeast Asia Series, vol. 5, no. 16 (1957), 13.

———. "The Philippine Elections of 1957." *American Universities Field Staff Reports*. Southeast Asia Series, vol. 5, no. 18 (1957), 11.

Olson, Mancur. "Rapid Growth as a Destabilizing Force." *Journal of Economic History*, 23 (December 1963), 1529-1552.

Oñate, Burton T. *Estimation of Population and Labor Force in the Philippines*. International Rice Research Institute Journal Series no. 43 (revised 1966).

Pablo, Rizalino R. "Some Notions of Development Administration in the Philippines." *Philippine Economy Bulletin*, 3 (May-June 1965), 5-13.

Padgett, L. V. "Mexico's One Party System, A Re-evaluation." *American Political Science Review*, 51 (1957), 995-1008.

Paglin, Morton. "Surplus Agricultural Labor and Development: Facts and Theories." *American Economic Review*, 55 (September 1965), 815-834.

Parsons, Malcolm B. "Performance Budgeting in the Philippines." *Public Administration Review*, 17 (Summer 1957), 173-179.

Payne, James L. *Patterns of Conflict in Colombia*. Yale University Press, New Haven, 1968.

Peterson, A. H., G. C. Reinhardt, and E. E. Conger, eds. *Symposium on the Role of Air Power in Counterinsurgency and Unconventional Warfare: The Philippine Huk Campaign*. The Rand Corporation, RM-3652-PR, June 1963.

217

PHILIPPINES GOVERNMENT.

Annual Report of the Governor General of the Philippine Islands. Washington, D.C., 1923 through 1935.

Annual Report of the President of the Philippines to the President and Congress of the United States, Manila, 1935 through 1940.

Annual Report of the United States High Commissioner to the Philippine Islands, 1st through 7th reports, Washington, D.C. and Manila, 1935 through 1945.

Armed Forces of the Philippines. *The Role of the Military in Nation-Building. The Alternatives: Innovate or Stagnate* (n.d.).

Central Bank. *Annual Report,* various years.

Congress of the Philippines, Committee on National Defense and Security. *The Challenge of Central Luzon,* May 1967.

Department of Agriculture and Natural Resources, Bureau of Agricultural Economics. *Annual Report for 1967.*

Department of Commerce and Industry, Bureau of the Census and Statistics. *Annual Survey of Manufactures,* 1956-1962, 1965-1966.

———. *BCS Survey of Households Bulletin,* nos. 18-24.

———. *Philippines Statistical Survey of Households Bulletin,* nos. 1-17.

———. *Yearbook of Philippine Statistics,* 1966.

Department of Defense. *Handbook on the Philippine Communist Party,* 1961.

Department of Justice, National Bureau of Investigation. *Philippine Crime Report,* 1967.

Department of Public Works and Communications, Bureau of Public Highways. *Annual Report.* FY 1960-1967.

General Auditing Office. Digest of the 1967 Annual Report of the Auditor-General to the National Government. Philippines, 1967.

———. Report of the Auditor-General on Local Governments to the President, FY 1954-1966 (mimeo).

Manila Police Department. *Annual Report,* 1966-1967.

Marcos, Ferdinand E. *State of the Nation: A Message Delivered Before a Joint Session of Congress,* January 22, 1968.

National Economic Council. *National Accounts of the Philippines with Supporting and Analysis Tables,* 1946-1967 (mimeo).

———. *National Income of the Philippines for 1964 to 1966,* May 1967 (mimeo).

———. *1961 Philippine Interindustry Relations (Input-Output) Tables.* Preprinting issue, October 1967 (mimeo).

———. "1961 Interindustry (Input-Output) Accounts of the Philippines." *The Statistical Reporter,* 17 (July-September 1968).

"Technical Notes to the 1966 Overall Revision of the National Accounts of the Philippines, Calendar Year 1962-1966." *The Statistical Reporter,* 11, no. 2 (April-June 1967), 34-36.

218

"Philippine Rural Reconstruction Movement." *American Universities Field Staff Letter*, Pampanga, Central Luzon, May 1, 1955.

Pomeroy, W. J. *The Forest*. International Publishers, New York, 1963.

Pool, Ithiel de Sola, Robert P. Abelson, and Samuel L. Popkin. *Candidates, Issues and Strategies: A Computer Simulation of the 1960 and 1964 Presidential Elections*. MIT Press, Cambridge, 1964.

Quirino, Elise, ed. *NEPA: Objectives of Protectionism in the Philippines*. Bookman, Inc., Manila (n.d.).

Reischauer, E. O. "Transpacific Relations." In Kermit Gordon, ed. *Agenda for the Nation*. Brookings Institution, Washington, D.C., 1968.

Ridker, R. G. "Discontent and Economic Growth." *Economic Development and Cultural Change*, 11 (October 1962), 1-15.

———. "The Economic Determinants of Discontent: An Empirical Investigation." *Journal of Development Studies*, 4 (January 1968), 174-219.

Roxas, Gerardo M. "The Pork-Barrel System." *Philippine Journal of Public Administration*, 7 (October 1963), 254-257.

Roxas, Sixto K. "Decontrol: Preview of Progress and Definition of Future Imperatives." *Philippine Economy Bulletin*, 2 (January-February 1964), 29-36.

———. "Economic Planning: A Problem of Management." *Philippine Economy Bulletin*, 1 (March-April 1963), 5-9.

———. "Protectionism." *Philippine Economy Bulletin*, 1 (July-August 1963), 13-16.

———. "Statistical Requirements of Economic Planning." *The Philippine Statistician* (June-September 1963), 109-116.

Rummel, Rudolph. "Indicators of Cross-National and International Patterns." *American Political Science Review*, 63 (March 1969), 127-147.

———. "Understanding Factor Analysis." *Journal of Conflict Resolution*, 2 (December 1967), 444-481.

Ruprecht, Theodore K. "Philippine Labor Statistics: A Critique and Recomputation of PSSH Data." *The Philippine Statistician*, 15 (March-April 1966), 73-89.

Salas, Rafael. "Statistics and Decision-Making Process." *The Philippine Statistician*, 15 (March and June 1966), 61-64.

Salmon, J. D. "The Huk Rebellion." *Solidarity* (Manila), 3 (1968), 1-30.

Selvin, Hanan C. "Durkheim's *Suicide* and Problems of Empirical Research." *American Journal of Sociology*, 63 (May 1958), 607-619.

Shannon, Lyle W. "Is Level of Development Related to Capacity for Self-Government?" *American Journal of Economics and Sociology*, 17 (July 1958), 367-382.

———. "Socio-Economic Development and Demographic Variables as

219

Predictors of Political Change." *Sociological Quarterly*, 3 (January 1962), 27-43.

Sharkansky, Ira. "Economic and Political Correlates of State Government Expenditures." *Midwest Journal of Political Science*, 11 (May 1967), 173-192.

Shaw, C. R. *Delinquency Areas: A Study of the Geographic Distribution of School Truants, Juvenile Delinquents, and Adult Offenders in Chicago.* University of Chicago Press, Chicago, 1929.

—— and Henry D. McKay. *Juvenile Delinquency and Urban Areas.* University of Chicago Press, Chicago, 1942.

Shaw, H. J. "A Study of a Communist War of Liberation." M.A. thesis, University of Virginia, Charlottesville, 1962.

Sicat, Gerardo P. "On the Accuracy of the Philippine National Accounts." *Philippine Review of Business and Economics*, 1 (October 1964), 1-6.

——. *Regional Economic Growth in the Philippines, 1948-1966, Part I: Dimensions of Regional Growth.* University of the Philippines, March 19, 1968 (unpublished).

——. *The Philippine Economy in the 1960's.* Institute of Economic Development and Research, University of the Philippines, Quezon City, 1964.

Siegel, S. *Nonparametric Statistics.* McGraw-Hill, New York, 1956.

Sirkin, Gerald. *The Visible Hand: The Fundamentals of Economic Planning.* McGraw-Hill, New York, 1968.

Soares, Glaucio and Robert L. Hamblin. "Socio-Economic Variables and Voting for the Radical Left: Chile, 1952." *American Political Science Review*, 61 (December 1967), 1053-1065.

Soberano, Jose D. and H. Odell Waldby. *Philippine Public Fiscal Administration.* Graduate School of Public Administration, University of the Philippines, Manila, 1965.

Soja, E. J. *The Geography of Modernization.* Syracuse University Press, Syracuse, 1968.

Soliven, M. V. "Lessons for the Viet Cong from the Huk Debacle." *Solidarity* (Manila), 1 (1966), 31-53.

Spengler, J. J. "Economic Development: Political Preconditions and Political Consequences." *Journal of Politics*, 22 (August 1960), 387-415.

——. "Public Bureaucracy, Resource Structure, and Economic Development: A Note." *Kyklos*, 11, fasc. 4 (1958), 460-486.

Starner, Frances Lucille, *Magsaysay and the Philippine Peasantry: The Agrarian Impact on Philippine Politics.* University of California Publications in Political Science, vol. 10, University of California Press, Los Angeles, 1961.

Stockwin, Harvey. "Where Democracy Flourishes but Progress is Slow." *The Financial Times*, August 29, 1968.

Stokes, Donald E. "Spatial Models of Party Competition." *American Political Science Review*, 57 (June 1963), 368-377.

——, A. Campbell, and W. Miller. "Components of Electoral Decision." *American Political Science Review*, 52 (June 1958), 367-397.

Straus, J. H. and M. A. Straus. "Suicide, Homicide and Social Structure in Ceylon." *American Journal of Sociology*, 58 (March 1953), 461-469.

Strout, A. M. "AID Performance, Self Help, and Need." USAID, Policy Planning and Coordination (draft), 1968.

Stubbs, R. M. "Philippine Radicalism: The Central Luzon Uprisings, 1925-35." Ph.D. dissertation, University of California, Berkeley, 1951.

Sturtevant, D. R. "No Uprising Fails—Each One Is a Step in the Right Direction." *Solidarity* (Manila), 1 (1966), 11-21.

——. "Philippine Social Structure and Its Relations to Agrarian Unrest." Ph.D. dissertation, Stanford University, Stanford, 1968.

Sycip, Gorres, Velayo and Co., Research Division. *An Interim Study of Commercial Banks in the Philippines at September 30, 1968*. Manila, 1968.

"The System of Local Government in the Philippines." *Philippine Journal of Public Administration*, 3 (January 1959), 1-10.

Tanter, Raymond. "Dimensions of Conflict Behavior Within and Between Nations, 1958-1960." *Journal of Conflict Resolution*, 10 (March 1966), 61-64.

——. "Toward a Theory of Political Development." *Midwest Journal of Political Science*, 11 (May 1967), 145-172.

Tanter, Raymond and Manus Midlarsky. "A Theory of Revolution." *The Journal of Conflict Resolution*, 11 (September 1967), 264-280.

Taruc, Luis. *Born of the People*. International Publishers, New York, 1953.

——. *He Who Rides the Tiger*. Frederick A. Praeger, New York, 1967.

Task Force on Urban Development Joint Project of the National Economic Council and the USAID/Philippines. *Profile Reports on the Cities of: Bacolod, Baguio, Cagayan de Oro, Iligan, Legaspi, and Zamboanga*. USAID/Philippines, Manila, 1968.

Taylor, George E. *The Philippines and the United States: Problems of Partnership*. Frederick A. Praeger, New York, 1964.

Tiaoqui, R. V. "The National Budget System of the Philippines." *The Philippine Economic Journal*, 2, no. 1 (1963), 21-31.

de Tocqueville, A. *The Old Regime and the French Revolution*, trans. John Bonner. Harper & Bros., New York, 1856.

Toro-Vizcarrondo, Carlos and T. D. Wallace. "A Test of the Mean Square Error Criterion for Restrictions in Linear Regression." *Journal of the American Statistical Association,* 63 (June 1968), 558-572.

Treadgold, M. and R. Hooley. "Decontrol and the Redirection of Income Flows." *The Philippine Economic Journal,* 6 (1967), 109.

Trinidad, Ruben. "An Inquiry into the Sources and Methods of National Income Accounting in the Philippines." M.A. thesis, University of the Philippines, Quezon City, August 1958.

————. "Some Proposed Improvements in the Estimation of Capital Formation in the Philippines." *The Statistical Reporter,* 4 (April 1960), 28-40.

Tryon, Joseph L. *Internal and External Terms of Trade in Post-War Philippines.* Field Work Report No. 14, Center for Development Planning, National Planning Association, Washington, D.C., April 1967.

Ullman, Edward L. "Trade Centers and Tributary Areas of the Philippines." *Geographical Review,* 50 (April 1960), 203-263.

United Nations. *Demographic Yearbook.* New York, 1966.

USAID Mission to the Philippines. *Survey of Philippine Law Enforcement.* Manila, 1968.

Usher, Daniel. *The Price Mechanism and the Meaning of National Income Statistics.* Clarendon Press, Oxford, 1968.

Van der Kroef, Justers. "Patterns of Cultural Conflict in Philippine Life." *Pacific Affairs,* 39 (Fall-Winter 1966-1967), 326-338.

Vellut, J. L. "Japanese Reparations to the Philippines." *Asian Survey,* 3 (October 1963), 496-506.

Vidallon-Carino, Ledivina. *The Politics and Administration of the Pork Barrel.* Local Government Center, School of Public Administration, University of the Philippines, Manila, 1966.

Waterston, Albert. *Development Planning: Lessons of Experience.* The Johns Hopkins Press, Baltimore, 1965.

Wernstedt, F. L. and J. E. Spencer. *The Philippine Island World: A Physical, Cultural and Regional Geography.* University of California Press, Berkeley, 1967.

Whitaker, Arthur. "The Pathology of Democracy in Latin America." *American Political Science Review,* 44 (1950), 101-118.

Wilcox, Clair. *The Planning and Execution of Economic Development in Southeast Asia.* Occasional Papers in International Affairs No. 10, Harvard University Center for International Affairs, Cambridge, January 1965.

Wilensky, Harold J. *Organizational Intelligence.* Basic Books, Inc., New York, 1967.

Wolf, Charles, Jr. *The Present Value of the Past.* The Rand Corporation, P-4067, April 1969.

Wolfgang, Marvin E. *Patterns in Criminal Homicide*, Science Edition. John Wiley & Sons, Inc., New York, 1958.

———. "A Sociological Analysis of Criminal Homicide." *Federal Probation*, 25 (March 1961), 48-55.

———, Leonard Savits, and Norman Johnston, eds. *The Sociology of Crime and Delinquency*. John Wiley & Sons, Inc., New York, 1962.

Wood, Arthur. "Crime and Aggression in Changing Ceylon." In *Translations of the American Philosophical Society*, 51, pt. 8 (December 1961), 5-126.

Zeitlin, Maurice. "Economic Insecurity and the Political Attitudes of Cuban Workers." *American Sociological Review*, 31 (February 1966), 35-51.

Index

Abraham, William I., 184-185

Age and voting behavior, 67, 67n

Agricultural prices, 14, 17

Agriculture
  data for factor analysis, 174-175
  dependence on, 174
  structure of, 14
  value added ratios in national
    accounts, 201

Agriculture, Department of, 111

Albay, 17

Almond, G.A., 26n, 29, 30n, 34, 35, 36n

Angeles, HMB control in, 148, 148n, 149

Asia Research Organization of Manila,
  155

Balance of payments crises, 6, 95, 108
  and elections, 109
  and political system, 151

Bantegui, Bernardo G., 81, 190, 191

Barber, Clarence L., 186

Barrios
  and HMB control, 138n, 139-146
    passim, 149
  in Pegasus sampling procedure, 156

Bataan growth rate, 17

BCS. *See* Bureau of the Census and
  Statistics

Bhapkar's statistic, 160n

Bicol voting behavior and pork barrel,
  58

Board of Investments, 96, 111

Bohol politics, 19

Budget Commission, 43n, 99

Budget policy
  bureaucrats' role in, 42, 45, 46
  and fiscal data, 99
  legislators' role in, 42, 45, 46

Bulacan
  manufacturing employment in, 91
  modernization, 89

Bureau of Agriculture Economics Crop
  and Livestock Surveys, 197

Bureau of the Census and Statistics

on economic performance, 110
  financial data controversy, 81
  and national accounting procedures
    controversy, 186, 189-195
  surveys, 71
  UP-BCS findings on GNP, 189-195

Bureaucracy
  attitude toward public, 26
  and economic problems, 111
  information system and handicaps, 113
  perceptions of political system, 43-45

Business Day on financial data, 81-82

Camarines Norte
  growth rate, 17, 22
  modernization in, 13n

Capital outflows, 108

Capital-output ratios NEC data
  criticized, 187

Cardenas, Ramon Bello, 200

Cavite robbery and theft rates, 119

Caviteño, Commander, 148

Cebu, 17
  politics in, 19

Cebuanos
  Macapagal supported by, 61
  and politics, 19

Censuses. *See* Economic Census;
  Population Census

Central Bank
  credit loosening, 108
  economic data, 84, 99, 102, 111
  and fiscal cycle, 102
  fiscal policy evaluation, 102-106
  on foreign exchange losses, 108
  and government spending programs,
    96-98
  and import restrictions, 108
  national income estimates, 184, 185

Central Bank Department of Economic
  Research, 184-185

Central Bank Indexes of Real Wage
  Rates in Manila, 111n

Chinese influence on HMB, 147

INDEX

Christian Social Movement, 67n
Cities
    crime in, 124, 126, 127, 128
    in Pegasus sampling procedures, 156
Clark, HMB control near, 148, 148n, 149
Coconut industry
    crime in areas of, 19
    during depression, 17
    in factor analysis, 17, 175
    unrest in areas of, 17
Cole, David, 186
Commission on Elections (COMELEC),
    48n
Communality defined, 12
Communications in factor analysis, 175
Communism
    HMB Maoist and Moscow factions,
        147
    in Pampanga, 138n
    of Sumulong, 149
Composite factor analysis, 14-19, 25,
    176-180
Congressional appropriations, 99
Congressional Economic Planning
    Office, 70
Congressional Questionnaire, 181-183
Congressmen. See Legislators
Constabulary
    crime data, reporting system, 118n,
        119
    and HMB, 132-134, 136, 146, 150
    data on HMB terror and control,
        139, 141
Consumer price index, 98
Consumption changes in NEC data,
    and GNP estimates, 192
Consumption function, criticism of
    NEC data on, 187
Copra prices, 17, 19n
Corruption in government public views
    on, 31, 32, 36, 44, 138
Cost of living, 98
Cotabato
    median family income, 58n
    Muslims in, 56n
    and pork barrel, 58

226

Court system, public views of, 32
Craft occupations, 76, 77n, 85
Credit
    for business investment, tightening, 98
    liberalizing, results of, 107
Crime, 114-130, 151
    in cities, 124, 126, 127
    data on, 117-120
    and ethnicity, 14, 115, 121, 130
    modern labor force opinion of, 94
    overstatement of problem, 115n, 120,
        130
    related to politics, 115
against property, 14
    provincial variation in level of, 120
    public concern about, 115-116
    opinion of the unemployed about, 78n
Crime rates
    relation to arrest rate, 120-121
    cities, variations between, 124, 126
    in coconut areas, 19
    relation to economic policy, 130
    in factor analysis, 175
    relation to migration rates, 176
    NBI data understated, 118
    and population growth, 121
    and socioeconomic factors, 130n
Crop and Livestock Surveys, 197
Crop prices. See Agricultural prices
CRUSAC (Crusade against Crime), 119

Data analysis, 152
Data reporting systems, 4-7, 117. See
    also Economic data; Crime;
    Unemployment
Davao growth rate, 22
Depreciation
    of farm capital, 199
    figures, in GNP estimates, 195, 199
Depression, 17
Devaluation, 19, 108
Dissidence, 131-150
    distribution of, 14
    modern labor force concern about, 94
    and political constraints, 132
    reason for, 138

homicide rate, 123, 126
view of politicians, 32-33, 37
attitude toward violence, 117, 129
violence of, 121, 123
voting behavior, 50, 50n, 56, 58, 61, 65

Nacionalista Party, 47-51
and pork barrel, 52, 53
National accounts, 81, 83, 111. *See also*
National income accounting
National Bureau of Investigation,
117-118, 118n
National Economic Council
on economic performance, 110
financial data inaccurate, 81
GNP data low, 82
national income accounting procedures
and controversy, 186-194, 197
office of Statistical Coordination and
Standards, 111
split exchange rate, treatment of, 201
National income accounting, 111, 184-201
input-output tables controversy,
189-192
Negros, 17
Net Domestic Product, 197, 198
Nueva Ecija, 56n

Office of Statistical Coordination and
Standards, 111, 190-192
Olongapo City, robberies in, 119
Osmeña, Sergio, 47
Osmeña, Sergio, Jr., 48

Pampanga
dissidence in, 14
attitude toward government officials,
33
opinion of HMB in, 136
and HMB control, 138n, 139, 141n,
144, 149
and Marxism, 138n
violence not a concern of people in,
117
voting behavior, 50, 50n, 56, 58n
Pangasinans

concern about crime, 116, 117
voting behavior, 58
Pegasus (Philippine ethnic group
attitude surveys), 26n
on crime, 78n, 115-116
data processing, 159-161
on economic problem, 109
on government's influence, 28
on views of government, 62
interview areas, 157
interview structure and procedures,
155-156, 158-159
on minority group treatment, 78n
on modern labor force opinions, 93,
93n, 94
purpose of, 155
Questionnaire, 161-173
sampling procedures, 156-158
and unemployment, 78
on violence, 129
on voting behavior, 53-54, 58, 66
Philippine Constabulary. *See*
Constabulary
Philippine National Bank, 99
Police
attitude toward, in HMB areas, 136
per capita, and crime rate, 121
public's view of, 32
Police Commission, reporting system
for crime data, 118n, 119
Policymaking
analysis capabilities need
improvement, 70, 113
legislators uninvolved in issues of, 42
regional nature of, 152
Political parties as voting criteria, 67
See also Elections; Nacionalista Party;
Liberal Party
Politicians
bureaucrats responsive to, 45, 46
on economic problems, 111
farmers' attitude toward, 63
in HMB areas, public opinion of, 138
HMB protected by, 132
information system handicaps, 113
modern labor force attitude toward, 94
attitude toward public, 26, 38-43

SELECTED RAND BOOKS

Baum, Warren C. *The French Economy and the State*. Princeton: Princeton University Press, 1958.

Becker, Abraham S. *Soviet National Income 1958-1964. National Accounts of The USSR in the Seven Year Plan Period*. Berkeley and Los Angeles: University of California Press, 1969.

Bergson, Abram. *The Real National Income of Soviet Russia Since 1928*. Cambridge: Harvard University Press, 1961.

Chapman, Janet G. *Real Wages in Soviet Russia Since 1928*. Cambridge: Harvard University Press, 1963.

Dole, Stephen and Isaac Asimov. *Plants for Man*. New York: Random House, 1964.

Dorfman, Robert, Paul A. Samuelson, and Robert M. Solow. *Linear Programming and Economic Analysis*. New York: McGraw-Hill Book Company, Inc., 1958.

Downs, Anthony. *Inside Bureaucracy*. Boston: Little, Brown and Company, 1967.

Fisher, Gene H. *Cost Considerations in Systems Analysis*. New York: American Elsevier Publishing Company, 1971.

Halpern, Manfred. *The Politics of Social Change in the Middle East and North Africa*. Princeton: Princeton University Press, 1963.

Hirshleifer, Jack, James C. DeHaven, and Jerome W. Milliman. *Water Supply: Economics, Technology, and Policy*. Chicago: The University of Chicago Press, 1960.

Hitch, Charles J. and Roland N. McKean. *The Economics of Defense in the Nuclear Age*. Cambridge: Harvard University Press, 1960.

Hsieh, Alice L. *Communist China's Strategy in the Nuclear Era*. Englewood Cliffs, N.J.: Prentice-Hall, Inc., 1962.

Johnson, John J. (ed.). *The Role of the Military in Underdeveloped Countries*. Princeton: Princeton University Press, 1962.

Johnson, William A. *The Steel Industry of India*. Cambridge: Harvard University Press, 1966.

Johnstone, William C. *Burma's Foreign Policy: A Study in Neutralism*. Cambridge: Harvard University Press, 1963.

Liu, Ta-Chung and Kung-Chia Yeh. *The Economy of the Chinese Mainland: National Income and Economic Development, 1933-1959*. Princeton: Princeton University Press, 1965.

Lubell, Harold. *Middle East Oil Crises and Western Europe's Energy Supplies*. Baltimore: The Johns Hopkins Press, 1963.

McKean, Roland N. *Efficiency in Government Through Systems Analysis: With Emphasis on Water Resource Development*. New York: John Wiley & Sons, Inc., 1958.

Meyer, J. R., J. F. Kain, and M. Wohl. *The Urban Transportation Problem*. Cambridge: Harvard University Press, 1965.

Moorsteen, Richard. *Prices and Production of Machinery in the Soviet Union, 1928-1958*. Cambridge: Harvard University Press, 1962.

Nelson, Richard, T. Paul Schultz, and Robert L. Slighton. *Structural Change in a Developing Economy: Colombia's Problems and Prospects*. Princeton: Princeton University Press, 1971.

Novick, David (ed.). *Program Budgeting: Program Analysis and the Federal Budget*. Cambridge: Harvard University Press, 1965.

Pascal, Anthony H. *Thinking About Cities*. Belmont, California: Dickenson Publishing Co., 1970.

Pincus, John A. *Economic Aid and International Cost Sharing*. Baltimore: The Johns Hopkins Press, 1965.

Quade, E. S. (ed.). *Analysis for Military Decisions*. Chicago: Rand McNally & Company; Amsterdam, North-Holland Publishing Company, 1964.

Speier, Hans. *Divided Berlin: The Anatomy of Soviet Political Blackmail*. New York: Praeger, 1961.

Trager, Frank N. (ed.). *Marxism in Southeast Asia: A Study of Four Countries*. Stanford: Stanford University Press, 1959.

Williams, J. D. *The Compleat Strategyst: Being a Primer on the Theory of Games of Strategy*. New York: McGraw-Hill Book Company, Inc., 1954.

Wolf, Charles, Jr. *Foreign Aid: Theory and Practice in Southern Asia*. Princeton: Princeton University Press, 1960.

——— and Nathan Leites. *Rebellion and Authority: An Analytic Essay on Insurgent Conflicts*. Chicago: Markham Publishing Co., 1970.